Hamburg

* The Cradle Of British Rock

D1477814

Design: David Houghton
Printed by: Unwin Brothers Limited

Published by: Sanctuary Publishing Limited, The Colonnades, 82
Bishops Bridge Road, London W2 6BB

Photographs: courtesy of the Alan Clayson Archives, Redferns
International, Rick Hardy, Frank Allen, Horst Fascher, Astrid
Kirchherr, Siegfried Lock, Bob Vincent, Dave Humphreys, Dieter
Radtke, K&K, P. Neimeier, Michael Ochs, David Redfern and Jurgen
Vollmer

ISBN:1-86074-221-1

Hamburg*

* The Cradle Of British Rock

Alan Clayson

Also available from Sanctuary by Alan Clayson

THE QUIET ONE: A Life Of George Harrison

RINGO STARR: Straight Man Or Joker?

DEATH DISCS: An Account Of Fatality In The Popular Song

JACQUES BREL: The Biography

Available 1998

SERGE GAINSBOURG: View From The Exterior

BACKBEAT: Stuart Sutcliffe: The Lost Beatle (with Pauline Sutcliffe)

CALL UP THE GROUPS: The Golden Age Of British Beat 1962-7

About The Author

Born in Dover, England in 1951, the author lives near Henley-on-Thames with his wife Inese and sons, Jack and Harry. Described by the *Western Morning News* as the "AJP Taylor of the pop world", Alan Clayson has written many books on music – including the best-selling *Backbeat*, subject of a major film – as well as for journals as disparate as *The Independent*, *Record Collector*, *Medieval World*, *Folk Roots*, *The Times*, *Discoveries*, *The Beat Goes On* and, as a teenager, the notorious *Schoolkids' Oz*. He has been engaged to broadcast on national TV and radio, and lecture on both sides of the Atlantic.

Before he become better known as a pop historian, he led the legendary Clayson And The Argonauts in the late 1970s, and was thrust to "a premier position on rock's Lunatic Fringe" (*Melody Maker*). The 1985 album, *What A Difference A Decade Made*, is the most representative example of the group's recorded output.

As shown by the formation of a US fan club in 1992, Alan Clayson's following has continued to grow as well as demand for his production talents in the studio, and the number of versions of his compositions by such diverse acts as Dave Berry – in whose Cruisers he played keyboards in the mid-1980s – and (via a collaboration with ex-Yardbird Jim McCarty) New Age outfit, Stairway. He has worked too with the Portsmouth Sinfonia, Wreckless Eric, Twinkle and Screaming Lord Sutch among others.

Alan Clayson is presently spearheading a trend towards an English form of *chanson*, and feedback from both Britain and North America suggests that he is becoming more than a cult celebrity. Moreover, *Soirée*, a new album released in autumn 1997 on Havic Records, may stand as Alan Clayson's artistic apotheosis if it were not for the promise of surprises yet to come.

"The focus on Hamburg as a music centre was that it was one of those constellations of the right time, the right people, the right situation. The nearest German word for it is *Zufall* – which means literally 'to fall into one'. We don't have a precise word for it, but that's how it happened as far as I'm concerned: the pieces fell into place"

Tony Sheridan

To everyone who was ever in The Argonauts

CONTENTS

PROLOGUE

What'd I Say

**"Some of these stories are like: 'next door's got a push-bike'.
By the time it gets to the end of the road, it's a Rolls-Royce"**
Trevor "Dozy" Davies (Dave Dee And The Bostons)

A combination of drudgery in a grammar school C-stream and a middle-class upbringing centred on the Church awoke in my adolescent self a wish to have been born five years earlier with a destiny as a 1960s pop star. Diversifying into other artistic realms, I would arrive at the gateway of the next century with all of my hair still on my head, more money than sense, and loaded with all manner of honours that I'd accepted with a becoming modesty. My pain-free lifestyle and good works would be sustained into old age as much by income and acclaim for my latest ground-breaking masterpiece as the repackagings of classics I'd recorded decades earlier.

Naturally, tales would still be told of my period of romantic bohemianism working the clubs in Hamburg's notorious St Pauli, a red-light district that, according to legend, was the cradle of British rock. There, I'd surfaced as the darling of the ladies, respected by the gangsters and admired by the other visiting British musicians.

Well, the nearest I got to that episode of my teenage dream was during a tour of Holland with Clayson And The Argonauts in 1976. The itinerary included dates in a club – that I now suspect was part-brothel – in the heart of Amsterdam. Among cherished memories of one of those nights is a slight and inadvertent mispronunciation of a Dutch word turning my opening greeting to the audience into a mortal insult.

That was Clayson And The Argonauts' "Hamburg", a strenuous incubation in a European vice area from which we were supposed to have emerged as a world-beating force in pop. Well, we didn't – but, even in the 1960s, there were British groups that did who hadn't had much of a Hamburg either; among them Cliff Richard And The Shadows, The Dave Clark Five, Georgie Fame And The Blue Flames, The Kinks, The Rolling Stones, The Who, The Yardbirds, The Zombies and Status Quo.

Of course, you had to have been there, but how do you quantify the respective atmospherics of *Five Live Yardbirds* from London's Marquee, The Big Three's *At The Cavern, Live From The Kingside, Stockholm* from The Dee-Jays*, Georgie Fame's *Rhythm And Blues At The Flamingo*, *The Beatles Live At The Star-Club In Hamburg*; *1962*, *A Nite At Great Newport Stree*t by The Downliners Sect and any number of other in-concert releases, legal or otherwise, from the early 1960s?

There were, you see, other Hamburgs, some of them closer to home than you'd think. With coat torn off and shirt hanging out, Eric Burdon's orange-peel complexion had poured sweat as a savage Alan Price Combo (later, The Animals) drove him through all-nighters at Newcastle's Downbeat, a dingy club well-named as it was balanced above a semi-derelict warehouse near the docks. At the plusher Tottenham Royal Ballroom, "you had to work your arse off to play to the same audience three hours a night, four nights a week," said The Dave Clark Five's drummer-leader. "You had to change your repertoire and your songs to keep the thing interesting."

Yet three Hamburg venues surfaced as more prominent Valhallas in 1960s youth culture than the likes of the Downbeat, the Kingside, the Tottenham Royal and the Flamingo. Ian "Tich" Amey of Dave Dee's Bostons would theorise that "in a way, the clubs were more famous than the people who played there", but the Kaiserkeller, the Top Ten and the Star-Club each remain on a par with the Cavern as places where The Beatles cut their teeth before

---

* A Cambridge unit featuring singer Clive Sands, brother of 1961 chart-topper Eden Kane. While they didn't make much headway in their own land, The Dee-Jays were big in Sweden in the 1960s

the myth took hold.

How badly do you want to continue believing that myth in preference to dull truth? Would it shatter too many illusions to learn that Dave Dee And The Bostons (later, Dave Dee Dozy, Beaky, Mick And Tich) were more adored in Hamburg (and then all over Germany) than The Beatles – or that a Scottish rock 'n' roller called Johnnie Law, who came over in 1965 and never left, is as well-known in the city today as Tony Sheridan?

Just as the Mona Lisa is the only painting a certain type of tourist in Paris wants to see when visiting the Louvre, so a certain type of pop fan's sole interest in Tony Sheridan is 'My Bonnie', the single he made in Hamburg with The Beatles – whose impact during their seasons there has been fictionalised in tomes ranging from their first biography in 1964 to *Fatherland*, the 1993 best-seller by Robert Harris, which mentions "a piece by a music critic attacking the 'pernicious Negroid wailings' of a group of young Englishmen from Liverpool, playing to packed audiences of German youth in Hamburg".

In the light of new and rediscovered information about the scene from the late 1950s compared to what is left of it today, the deeds and personalities of some of the more obscure acts turned out to be just as much the embodiment or prototype of some facet of British pop in Germany as those of The Beatles, Searchers *et al* who became popular on a global scale.

Mention of these and other UK groups in Germany during the early to mid 1960s still brings out strange stories of what folk claim they saw and heard. Did a member of a now-renowned combo really defecate loudly and abundantly one evening on a club stage somewhere in Baden-Württemberg in 1966? Perhaps all he did was belch into a microphone, but "burp" may have become a mischievous "fart" in an early retelling of this music industry equivalent of a fisherman's tall tale.

Conversely, many ex-beat group musicians who are today's solid heads of families, tend to gloss over the escapades of youth – especially those to do with sex – like a promiscuous schoolgirl playing virgin. As well as avoiding an upset with wives who might be lacking in moral generosity, such evasions may be motivated by sobering knowledge that enough of the racketeers who controlled night spots in the Fatherland in times past are still alive and dangerous.

I became aware of this too during investigations that were further complicated by interviewees contradicting each other, and leaving me to unravel whether, for instance, one prominent German entrepreneur could speak perfect English or needed an interpreter. More pointedly, did amphetamines disappear down throats as carelessly as beer – or was it the case that, as Ricky Richards of The Jets contended, "you didn't need drugs in Hamburg. The whole place was a buzz"?

While anecdotes and observations concerning events that took place up to forty years ago became collectively – and predictably – more nebulous and ambiguous, it became more constructive to define as widely as possible more general social, cultural, economic, environmental and other wider undercurrents that have prejudiced and polarised what hitherto has been understood about Hamburg. Pop historians have tended to shy away from these areas – even though they form a more tangible basis for investigation than treating a subject's flippant remarks as gospel or, on the false assumption that those who happen to be in the same profession are intimately acquainted, squeezing a few paragraphs from an encounter between, say, Dave Berry and Gerry Marsden in a Southsea hotel bar in 1988 when a puzzled Berry was embraced by a Gerry buoyant with rose-tinted nostalgia for the Swinging Sixties. Dave hardly knew Gerry then.

Overall, I opted for unadorned expressionism rather than trainspotter baroque. Sections are devoted to such as the food the musicians ate, the clothes they wore, the stimulants (physical and chemical) they sampled, the violence they faced, the hairstyles they adopted and, above all, the music they played, but you will not be embarrassed with too much detail (if any) about, say, the gauge of guitar string used by Ritchie Blackmore in 1965 when he was with The Three Musketeers in the Bochum Star-Club or who replaced drummer Mike Sloan in The Georgians when he left in October 1964.

If such data is of value to you, Pete Frame's *Rock Family Trees* series is recommended unconditionally. Spencer Leigh and Pete

Frame's *Let's All Go Down The Cavern* (Vermilion, 1984) proved useful too during the researching of this book. Further works of reference included my own previous books, chiefly *Call Up The Groups!*, *Backbeat* (with Pauline Sutcliffe) and *Beat Merchants*, as well as relevant back issues of *Record Collector*, *The Beat Goes On*, *Mojo*, *Melody Maker*, *Discoveries*, *Zabadak!*, *Bravo* and other journals.

Particular debts of gratitude are owed to Ian Amey, Trevor Davies, Bruce Brand, Billy Childish, Ian Drummond, Rick Hardy (Ricky Richards), John Latimer Law, Sandy Newman, Crispian St Peters, Tony Sheridan, Dick Taylor and Chris Warman for their co-operation, trust, candour and imparting of privileged information.

Let's have a big hand too for Penny Braybrooke, Jeffrey Hudson, Michelle Knight, Eddy Leviten and the rest of the team at Sanctuary.

Whether they were aware of providing assistance or not, thanks are also due in varying degrees to Hans Alehag, Frank Allen, Wally Allen, Pete Barton, Cliff Bennett, Dave Berry, Stuart Booth, Carol Boyer, Eva Maria Brunner, Harry Clayson, Inese Clayson, Jack Clayson, Don Craine, Ron Cooper, Tony Dangerfield, Spencer Davis, Dave Dee, Denis D'Ell, Kevin Delaney, Peter Doggett, Mark Ellen, Tim Fagan, Wayne Fontana, Pete Frame, Freddie Garrity, Steve Gibbons, Chris Gore, Eric Goulden, Helen Gummer, Bill Harry, Mike Hart, Michael Heatley, Susan Hill, Dave Humphreys, Tony Jackson, Garry Jones, Chris Kefford, Denny Laine, Brian Leafe, Spencer Leigh, Jon Lewin, Phil May, Jim McCarty, Colin Miles, Steve Morris, Mike and Christine Neal, Julia New, Russell Newmark, Mike Ober, Mike Pender, Ray Phillips, Chris Phipps, Laine and Jule Rawlinson, Mike Robinson, Simon Robinson, Jacqueline Ryan, Mark St John, Dave Sampson, Jim Simpson, Lord David Sutch, Pauline Sutcliffe, Vic Thomas, John Tobler, John Townsend, Paul Tucker, Twinkle, Marthy Van Lopik, Jurgen Vollmer, Bob Wilson, Lennart Wrigholm and Pete York.

It may be obvious to the reader that I have received help from sources that prefer not to be mentioned. Nevertheless, I wish to express my appreciation of what they did.

I shall close this prologue with a suggestion that constipation can be cured most effectively by editing an important manuscript on an old-style Amstrad word-processor in the evening of its life. A few flashes of "Drive is not ready" or just one of "Unexpected end of file" will have your bowels dissolving in no time.

Alan Clayson, July 1997

CHAPTER ONE

Trink Trink Bruderlein Trink

"I can't bear to see the city dying. She is dying and will never be saved"

William Joyce ("Lord Haw-Haw")

It began with mediaeval pirates – spiritual and probably genealogical descendants of the Vikings – working much mischief among the Baltic fishing fleets and trading vessels. Inland traffic was harried too by the toll-exacting rulers of fiefdoms bordering the long, level plain of the Elbe, lifestream of the Old Saxon seaboard where fishing villages had grown into key trading centres of northern Europe. Once a marshy if potentially fertile wasteland, the duchy of Niedersachsen (Lower Saxony) had become a hard-won land of thriving tillage and prosperous, self-protecting towns.

For mutual defence, there evolved in the mid thirteenth century a union between the rival but troubled merchants of Hamburg and Lubeck where the neck of Denmark's windy peninsula connects with the shoulders of Germany. By slow degrees, this "Hanseatic League" – from *hansa* meaning "band of men" – widened to embrace every vital settlement from Flanders to the Gulf of Finland. Thus was reached a zenith of political and commercial control of the Baltic Sea. Its decline was caused by a combination of internal competition in business, the defection of the crucial herring shoals to the British coast and, ultimately, loyalty to each community's territorial sovereign. Yet after the League's wind-up meeting in 1669, Hamburg was still the "Free and Hanseatic City", nominally acknowledging its past just as Birmingham would by naming its police force and other civic institutions after Mercia, the Anglo-Saxon kingdom that had cradled the hamlet England's "Second City" once was.

With its stock exchange, open tidal harbour and the biggest market hall in Europe, Hamburg continued to fight the battle fought by every municipal republic in Europe; the battle for exports, the battle for money as its boundaries expanded, swallowing surrounding villages in its wake as incomers came from the Netherlands, Spain, Portugal and Germany itself. These included numerous wealthy Jewish families like the Mendelssohns who were to spawn both a prominent banker in Abraham, and a famous composer in his son Felix.

After the Industrial Revolution, Hamburg had become to Germany as landlocked Birmingham to England and lakeside Chicago in North America: a confluence and terminus of road, rail and river connections from which were shunted myriad manufactured goods; from that crane-buckling consignment from the country's premier ball-bearing works in Altona to this coil of rope from the chandlers along the cobbled Reeperbahn – "Rope Street" – main thoroughfare in the dockland suburb of St Pauli. Though sixty miles from the sea, Hamburg – twenty-five miles wide with a state boundary well over one hundred miles in length – had surfaced also as the third largest port in the world and thus the Reich's *Tor zur Weit* (Gateway to the World).

From the Landungbrucken – floating landing stages – in St Pauli, both merchant clippers and commuter ferries chugged along a shoreline of wharves, refineries, metal works, clerking offices and warehouses as well as moorings to which dray horses dragged cargoes to be loaded onto either domestic barges on the Alster and the Bille – the Elbe's principal tributaries – or ships soon to be a smudge on the Baltic horizon.

Thanks to the investment of old money into the Victorian shipping boom, it was the labyrinthine waterfront that dominated working class employment, whether as a boiler-maker or, like the young Johannes Brahms, a provider of background music in a seamen's tavern. However indirectly, their diverse sweat and strain paid for the luxuries visible around *nouveau riche* business folk and those noble houses that their forefathers had once served across the counter. Yet conservatism and long residence in Hamburg remained prerequisites of entry into polite society.

City culture benefited as much as its industry from high finance and aristocratic patronage. Catering for the recreational whims of various such paymasters, Handel premiered his operas in the Deutsche Opernhaus – the first permanent opera house in Europe – while Telemann and his successor CPE Bach dwelt in Hamburg too as musical directors of its five principal churches. However, following the Great Fire of 1842, their works were more likely to be heard in the neo-baroque Musikhalle, built through a bequest in the will of a local shipowner, though other such buildings came from what amounted to a subscription scheme via the auspices of Patriotische Gesellschaft – the Patriotic Society – founded in 1765 "to foster arts and useful crafts".

To this end too, the ivy-clung Hanseatic University was founded immediately after the Great War to engulf in its academic shadow several other colleges of higher education, new and old, as well as numerous museums and libraries.

More overtly entertaining recreation than public lectures on Etruscan vases or the inner waterways of Latvia was available within the walls of a retinue of cabaret cellars, showboats, music halls and similar establishments that orbited round thirty more capacious auditoriums such as the Deutsche Schauspielhaus (State Playhouse), the Hanss – more variety than drama – and the St Pauli Theatre.

The moralising first century apostle after whom this quarter was named might have merely turned in his grave had he known that it contained a playhouse, but, even as you read this sentence, he might be revolving unstoppably in it, having realised that St Pauli is better-known for a red-light area that had developed since the pillaging French destroyed its church in 1814.

By the time it was rebuilt in neo-classical fashion, Hans Albers Platz, a forlorn sideroad off the Reeperbahn, had been nicknamed Kleiner Kiez ("little red-light district") for its alehouses, gaming rooms, and palais where roistering customers – mostly sailors – could be as dissolute as they pleased, rounding off the evening with "the celebrated rites of Venus" as the more nicely-spoken tearsheets would have it in those days.

Gradually, the action fountained from Hans Albers Platz into the half-kilometre of the Reeperbahn itself and up a street opposite that divided St Pauli and Altona. With attractions like casinos, bars, massage parlours, cinemas and tattooists supplementing sex, sex, sex, tourists could be forgiven for misconstruing the meaning of *Die Grosse Freiheit* – because its translation as "The Great Freedom" refers to the religious and commercial independence it had enjoyed when Altona had been a borough discernably removed from Hamburg in atlases printed between the wars when Germany was still rooted in its ancient patchwork of independent states.

The difference between Hamburg before and immediately after World War II was akin to that of a person before and after going senile. Traces of the old personality peeped out, but otherwise the victim was lost in dementia. Just as the brain was so pulped, so the Allies destroyed Hamburg in 1943's hot summer. Alarm bells and sirens executed a discordant threnody as, during this maiming of an important connection to Berlin and the east – as well as half of the Reich's heavy industry – houses and theatres, shops and cinemas, public buildings and blocks of flats crumbled in a haze of smoke and powdered plaster or else were blown more cleanly out of existence by direct hits throughout round-the-clock aerial bombardment of ton upon booming ton of death and destruction.

Ancient trees that had sprung from saplings in suburban calm snapped like twigs, and the surface of the slip-slapping Elbe shone with the brightness of flames that gushed like a swollen river along the streets, consuming any obstacles in their path. Tarmac was reduced to bubbling pitch until the dousing water veins of the city were slashed. "Horror reveals itself in the howling and raging of the fires," wrote Hamburg's chief of police, "in the hellish din of explosions and in the cries of the tormented people. Words fail before the extent of the terror which shook the population for ten days and ten nights."

Beneath the storm, civilians huddled on stone-flagged subway floors below grubby posters exhorting Strength Through Joy. When the hostile shadows vanished from the sky, the lull allowed these human moles to emerge and find broken crockery from their cupboards, burnt mattresses from their beds, and splinters from their furniture scattered across the streets, and the crunch of grit, brick-dust and shards of glass under their feet.

After Berlin fell in 1945, Lord Haw-Haw, the English traitor, roaring drunk at the microphone, relayed his last "Jairmany cawling, Jairmany cawling, Jairmany cawling..." script on what was left of the Reichsrundfunk radio network from a Hamburg soon to be aswarm with refugees – and enemy detachments whose officers requisitioned the best hotels where the taps were running, and the view across the Alster looked surprisingly normal.

There seemed to be little animosity between vanquished and victors and, though few lights showed along the Reeperbahn, it was jammed with parked army vehicles. Traffic up and down stairs was as heavy in both those hushed parlours where you'd be scrutinised through a spy-hole and refused access if you were less than a lieutenant, and in the noise and crush of the lowest dives where lower ranks whooped it up and conducted negotiations via their own abominations of bad German, and smatterings of English connected with their profession by straggly-haired, half-naked prostitutes, chewed upon and spat out by the war.

All this might be soundtracked by the oompah of a lederhosen-clad band with flushed, happy faces beneath feathered Tyrolean hats. In the hullabaloo, someone would catch the melody propelled by the accordion, and his beer-choked mouth would trigger unison singalongs, tankards swinging, to the pounding rhythms that pervaded everything from filthy barrack-room ditties to sentimental ballads about roses and stardust. 'Night And Day', 'Bye Bye Blackbird', 'Sonny Boy', even insensitive requests for the likes of 'The White Cliffs Of Dover', you name it, the musicians inserted it into a repertoire of 'Trink Trink Bruderlein Trink', 'Madel Ruck-Ruck-Ruck', 'Muss I Denn Zum Stadtele Naus' and further examples of earthy drinking music from time immemorial – though it was thought prudent to drop disturbingly stirring selections from a more recent past such as 'Horst Wessel Lied', 'Heil Hitler Dir' and like Nazi exultancies.

You'd have some search to find any German who proclaimed himself a Nazi throughout the creepy year that followed the Führer's suicide and unlikely sightings of him, alive and well. A favourite saying of the time was that when the occupation sectors were shared out, the Soviets were given the agriculture, and the rest got the ruins. There was some truth in this as the western territory included the worst bombed cities like Kiel, Hamburg and the wrong end of Berlin.

Yet, in their partition at least, the western powers would not be guilty of the mistake made at the end of the previous conflict by squeezing the losers until the pips squeaked. Instead of creating a breeding ground for another latter-day Attila by making matters worse, those guarding and monitoring West Germany chose to assist with the mending of its industry and environment – and the decade finished with the defeated nation in a better situation than certain others that had, supposedly, won the war.

Magnanimous in victory, the man-in-the-street in New York, London and Paris stopped thinking twice about stroking dachshunds; exchanged civil words with Aryan-looking holidaymakers, and took to admiring German craftsmanship from cars to musical instruments – though an inevitable element of assembly-line machine-tooling had assumed a more pronounced role with increased demand. Indeed, "Bechstein" became the name most likely to trip off Average Joe's tongue during discussions about acoustic pianos. The opinion of Richard Strauss that this Berlin firm's keyboards were "the most beautiful and refined in the world" was to be echoed in the 1950s by such disparate musicians as Leonard Bernstein, jazzman Dave Brubeck – and flamboyant rock 'n' roller Little Richard who would serve as living testament to the Bechstein's structural sturdiness when he beat hell out of one in the 1956 movie, *The Girl Can't Help It*.

Regardless of who was present in middle-class (*Mittelstand*) living-rooms where geometrically-patterned linoleum was the sole hint of frivolity, a parent would often switch off a wireless set if it was broadcasting jazz, pop and whatever else had been derisively lumped together as "swing" – because it represented the depraved cacophony that was the distinguishing feature of the modern music that was subverting all that was good and true. Yes, the Führer had had his faults, but pouring active scorn on this rubbish whilst succouring the Fatherland's classical heritage hadn't been among them.

However, deprived of pop for the duration of the war, many Germans were no longer bothering with an observed exhibition of reverence when Wagner was on the wireless. Some forsook him altogether to become avid listeners to the British Forces Network (BFN) whose opening transmission in 1946 coincided with the inauguration of the BBC Light Programme. Ploughing a light entertainment furrow too, BFN broadcasted from the Musikhalle, one of the few public buildings in Hamburg left standing, and also from the Friedrich Ebert Halle – which doubled as a school assembly hall – in Harburg, once as separate from Hamburg as Altona.

BFN staff included such future denizens of BBC Broadcasting House as Brian Matthew, Cliff Michelmore – and Alexis Korner, later recognised as "the father of British blues", who moonlighted as presenter with the Nordwestdeutsche Rundfunk (closed down in 1955), and was recalled by Michelmore for his expeditions "in search of jazz along the Reeperbahn".

Most continental jazz bands were inclined to absorb their music second-hand from British sources, owing more to traditional jazz revivalists like Ken Colyer and Chris Barber than originators such as Bunk Johnson and Louis Armstrong. This was exemplified by The Dutch Swing College Band and The Old Merrytale Jazz Band, each regarded respectively as pre-eminent among Holland and Germany's emissaries of "trad". If nothing else, their performances were so polished and cleverly arranged that renowned British and US musicians would proudly "sit in" on mutually familiar set-works like 'Sweet Georgia Brown', 'Ain't She Sweet', Hoagy Carmichael's 'Up A Lazy River' or 'When The Saints Go Marching In', a ragtime warhorse that a diehard "trad dad" would hear no more than a mariner hears the sea at the Frankfurt Jazz Festival or the International Hot Jazz Meeting in Hamburg

A stronghold of teutonic jazz, Hamburg's smoky Cotton Club – as well as less intimate sessions in the Markthalle and elsewhere on Sunday lunchtimes – sucked in earnest enthusiasts who sometimes knew more about the music's history than the players. Sometimes, the "jazz" content in the numbers attempted was negligible because, if trombonist Barber, his clarinettist Monty Sunshine or trumpeter Humphrey Lyttelton had recorded a particularly definitive solo, it was thought politic to learn it note for note for regurgitated display of an artistic inferiority complex at every performance. Into the bargain, a front-line horn player doubling on vocals would think that a hoarse monotone was all you needed to sing like Louis Armstrong. It was not unknown either for purists to boo if a trad band included a saxophonist, ditched banjo for guitar or deviated in any other way from precedents created on genre classics like the Barber band's *New*

Orleans Joys LP in 1954.

The odds seemed to be stacked against other forms of German jazz too. Horst Jankowski, a most accomplished mainstream pianist, calculated that he could get richer by mining an easy-listening seam akin to that of US bandleaders Lawrence Welk and Ray Conniff than by arranging for Oscar Peterson, Ella Fitzgerald, Benny Goodman and Miles Davis amongst others. Rather than a follower in Theolonius Monk's footsteps, Jankowski was to be remembered chiefly as a precursor of sorts to fellow German and keyboard player James Last, then awaiting his destiny as a European middle-of-the-road colossus. Similarly, Udo Lindenberg was a teenage drummer in a Cologne modern jazz combo who improvised round cabaret themes like 'The Shadow Of Your Smile' – which would find a place in his vocal canon after he too switched to pop and got ready to rake in the Deutschmarks.

CHAPTER TWO

Que Sera Sera

"The Germans were just coming to the end of their jazz era, and the American rock 'n' roll thing had really taken off. For the Germans to bring in all these stars from America would have cost a fortune, and there they had, just across the channel, these English blokes that were copying the Americans and doing it very well. There were very, very few places for young bands to play in Britain. So it was easy to bring them in for twenty quid a week and work them to death"

Dave Dee (Dave Dee And The Bostons)

Among the first – and one of the most significant – of these English blokes would be a certain Anthony Esmond O'Sheridan McGinnity who, at the age of eighteen in 1958, was to hack off a hated surname to metamorphose into singing guitarist Tony Sheridan. His had been an unhappy childhood. He and his younger brother were the issue of an espousal that had ended when a Liverpool-Irish father deserted their Jewish mother. She remarried – to a Mr Guymer – and the family moved from London to Norwich around the time that she embraced Christianity.

All the eagerly-absorbed doctrines of the late convert were thrust upon her sons, obliged as they were to attend divine service regularly, even after the elder boy at least had had his fill of mouthing the holy sounds that were novel and unintelligible at seven, over-familiar and rote-learnt at thirteen. Exasperated attempts to elicit his mother's understanding of this only brought to the fore how little she ever considered not only how different his values might be to hers, but whether he had even formed any of his own.

"There wasn't much communication between us," admitted Tony. "When Norwich was bombed, I was evacuated to a children's home in Macclesfield – which really messed me up, deprived me of my mother's love at an early age. She blamed the Germans for anything that was not Christian."

Nevertheless, like her *Mittelstand* counterpart in Hamburg, Mrs Guymer regarded jazz, rock 'n' roll *et al* as ephemeral and lowbrow – and, for the sake of domestic harmony, Tony may have supposed she was right. Fuelling her mitherings was the received information that it was unwise to see popular music as a viable career. It was a facile life anyway, a vocational blind alley.

No purveyor of teenage pop lasted very long unless he either reconstructed himself as an "all-round entertainer" like Tommy Steele – who was pushed initially as Britain's Elvis Presley – or went for "quality" material *à la* Frank Sinatra or Tony Bennett, whose flop singles were excused as being "too good" for the newly-established *New Musical Express* record and sheet music sales charts. Better still, you could get your voice trained to European *bel canto* standards with the concomitant vowel purity, plummy eloquence and nicety of intonation. This process was to be epitomised in Germany by a teen idol, Drafi Deutscher, who was to drop pop and begin a new chapter by enrolling at the Berlin High School of Music as a would-be opera singer.

Mrs Guymer would have welcomed such an ambition in her Anthony who, as she had ensured, "was involved in classical and sacred music only, nothing else. I played violin in all sorts of youth orchestras as well as singing in madrigal societies, choirs, anything my mother permitted, for ten years. Pop music on radio and then TV was taboo. Yet when Bill Haley and Elvis happened, and then The Everly Brothers and, especially, Buddy Holly, I was hearing guitars coming from a juke-box when going past the pub in Prince of Wales Road, where the US servicemen were hanging out. I was about sixteen and still at the City of Norwich Boys' Grammar School, and just the sound of these strings turned me on – but it was Lonnie Donegan doing skiffle in Chris Barber's Jazz Band, Dickie Bishop,

Johnny Duncan, that got me started, infected me, whatever – and it was hearing Buddy Holly that made me realise that it was possible to be a singer and a guitarist at the same time – and that was what I wanted to be.

"My next move was to get myself a guitar – so I turned criminal. In the school music room, there were all kinds of instruments lying about, so I decided that the one needed the least was an old clarinet – which I nicked to exchange for a beaten-up guitar in a second-hand store in the city centre.

"The CID came to the school a week later, and we had to parade through a room for the guy from the shop to pick me out. However, the headmaster was very kind in that he did nothing about it except to tell my parents that they ought to buy me a guitar. Apart from anything, I was needed in the school orchestra."

Once the guitar had been associated mainly with flamenco heel-clattering, but now it was what Lonnie Donegan played. Closer to home than Elvis Presley, Donegan had left Chris Barber, and was dominating the skiffle craze throughout its 1957 prime. He can be seen now as more credible than Tommy Steele as a British "answer" to Elvis in his vivacious processing of a vigorous alien idiom derived from blues, gospel, hillbilly and further ingredients in North America's musical melting pot.

His impact was to ripple across the decades, but the most immediate effect was the emergence of hundreds of – mostly amateur – skiffle outfits in every shire. Founded on primaeval rowdiness, makeshift instrumentation and a "Bert can play washboard" attitude, each was fronted generally by an aspirant Lonnie whose innate bossiness had him stage-centre, singing through his nose and thrashing that E-chord on a digit-lacerating six-string for all he was worth.

Such a group usually had an embarrassment of superfluous acoustic guitarists within a nebulous line-up. Most never got beyond strumming a few chords. Tony Sheridan was exceptional in that he took the time to learn properly, labouring over his fretboard late into the evening to the detriment of even that modicom of homework necessary to avoid the cane or a detention. As his fingertips hardened with constant practice, he thought ahead to the acquisition of an electric model that would compare to his present instrument as a fountain pen to a stub of pencil.

With Kenny Packwood, another local guitarist, he formed his first group, The Saints – after 'When The Saints Go Marching In'. As well as this signature tune, the unit's very name was also duplicated throughout the kingdom by other ensembles – including one led by Spencer Davis, then a Customs and Excise clerk in London. Outside office hours, Spencer's Saints busked for pennies while on the lookout for prowling policemen at various West End tube stations.

Davis also mixed with youths who had yet to adopt stage names like Marty Wilde, Cliff Richard, Hank B Marvin and Adam Faith in Soho coffee bars-cum-skiffle clubs like the Gyre and Gimble, the Safari, the Freight Train, the 2I's and, later, the Top Ten. On these stages, some would be noticed by svengalis like Larry Parnes, Jack Good – or Reg Calvert who was to be notorious for his nurturing of human xeroxes of Cliff Richard, Wee Willie Harris, Cuddly Dudley and other teen heroes, short-term or otherwise.

While Calvert was responsible for the most overt culprits, "everyone was copying," noticed Tony Sheridan, by then an art student. "Two guys called The Bachelors* wanted to be The Everly Brothers. Cliff was being Elvis and so was Marty Wilde; Joe Brown was doing a Chuck Berry. Hank Marvin in his glasses identified himself with Buddy Holly." In an enormous bow-tie and hair dyed shocking-pink, Wee Willie Harris was bruited by his manager as London's very own Jerry Lee Lewis, while another singing pianist, Roy Young from Oxford, was attempting to corner the Little Richard market – "easily the hardest to carry off," judged his pal, Adam Faith, "if you didn't happen to be Little Richard."

Yet copying US pop stars was how you gave yourself the best possible chance of being elevated – like the stock chorus girl to sudden Hollywood stardom – from the dusty boards of a skiffle club to small-fry billing on round-Britain "scream circuit" package tours and a slot on *Oh Boy!*, Jack Good's ITV pop spectacular on which a parade of mainly solo turns, usually accompanied by either Lord Rockingham's XI or The John Barry Seven, followed each other so quickly that the screeching studio audience scarcely had pause to draw breath. "Jack Good used to come into the 2I's," reminisced

---

* Nothing to do with the Irish trio of the same name who had hits during the 1960s

Tony Sheridan, "and say, 'You, you and you are on the telly next week. Come to rehearsals and you'll get five or six quid for doing it.' We were overjoyed to do it."

A certain Alex Harvey had hitch-hiked all the way from Glasgow to audition there, having gained wider celebrity in 1956 when he won a *Daily Record* competition to find the "Tommy Steele of Scotland" – "though anyone less like Tommy Steele I couldn't imagine," said Bill Patrick, saxophonist in Harvey's skiffle-and-trad group. "Alex was a screaming blues singer where Tommy was polite, but they were photographed shaking hands as a publicity stunt."

That Harvey had undertaken such a long journey to the 2I's was indicative of the venue's supremacy among all other such shop-windows for nascent pop talent in the same square mile, bordered by the bustling consumer's paradises of Regent Street, Bond Street, Park Lane and Oxford Street. By the 1950s, however, it had slid into seediness. The back-alleys that spread from Soho Square now proliferated with striptease joints, illicit gambling hells and clandestine brothels. In dimly-lit basements, even those clubs with nothing to hide had a dank sordidness about them that was part of a perverse attraction for "tired" businessmen who coughed up wads of notes to indulge their fantasies with no fear of identification.

On the surface, however, "Soho was quite exotic to a lad from Norwich," said Tony Sheridan. "The smells of cigars, coffee and Greek and Italian restaurants; very cosmopolitan. It was a stepping stone towards Hamburg. Of course, it all meant a newly-found freedom, partly expressed through music."

Tony had surfaced at the 2I's as a sensational lead guitarist and, to those in the know, one of few native rock 'n' rollers regarded with anything approaching awe – though a search for anything more exciting in continental Europe was a virtual waste of time beyond, say, a holidaying Jack Good spotting Italy's Little Tony and his Brothers, and, despite profound language difficulties, importing them to wow giddy British females briefly with their Latinate charms.

The most fascinating aliens, you see, had to come from the States. Freddie Bell, his role model Bill Haley, Jerry Lee Lewis and Gene Vincent had already made quasi-regal progressions through the realm, though Jerry Lee had left under a cloud over his alleged cradle-snatching and bigamy. Yet the scandal helped to touch up the Lewis legend and cause other incoming executants of classic rock to command something akin to submissive admiration mingled with a touch of scepticism – as if they weren't quite real.

A parallel may be drawn, perhaps, between the entrancing "over-paid, over-sexed and over-here" American GIs during the war and the common-or-garden Aldershot-drilled squaddie with his dung-coloured regimentals, peanut wages and in-built sense of defeat. Yet the typical UK pop entertainer accepted his second-class and, arguably, counterfeit status in better spirits, glad to breathe the air round those that he'd been used to worshipping from afar, those who'd outfitted him with vestments of artistic personality.

Onstage and sometimes off, fat drawls replaced Geordie, Welsh and Home Counties accents as musicians trained themselves to insert "man" into sentences where "mate" had once been. They also got used to a "guy" – not a geezer – "shafting" a "chick" instead of a bird, even if only a "cheap" girl didn't "save herself" for her future husband. She might be as keenly inquisitive about sex as the pimpled fumbler of her bra-strap, but a true daughter of 1950s Britain would have none of it whilst still unwed – not even from a Yank.

Because he'd actually lived in California in early youth, a Vince Taylor from Hounslow had had greater licence to at least talk to chicks than most other fellows who'd paid half-a-crown to shuffle about in the gloom past the burning footlights in the dance halls. He gave himself even readier access to female flesh after he appeared on *Oh Boy! en route* to 'Jet Black Machine', his only British chart entry. Some (including the youth who was to be Screaming Lord Sutch) reckoned that Taylor had had everything it took – except the voice – to be not only a second Gene Vincent but a contender for Presley's crown. Tony Sheridan's assessment, however, was that "Vince was a great performer, and he should have given us the value of the American experience, but he was a poor vocalist and we budding idealistic musicians didn't have much respect for his attempts at singing".

Vince had been the main attraction at the Top Ten in Berwick Street after an abrupt decline of the 2I's as the place to be. "It was starting to go downhill," noticed Richard Hardy, a *norf* London rock 'n' roller then known professionally as "Ricky Richards". "One night in 1959, I was singing down the 2I's. The next night, I was resident in the Top Ten. From then on, all the action was in Berwick Street."

How could Ricky have known to what extent his life was to interweave with that of Tony Sheridan, fully professional now, who had moved up, initially as a backing guitarist to Johnny Gentle, Marty Wilde, Vince Eager and other young men groomed by Larry Parnes? Garbed in a sports jacket, Tony had made an *Oh Boy!* debut as a lead vocalist on 18 February 1959. He'd been greeted by familiar faces at the Hackney Empire where the programme was rehearsed before "live" transmission: "Kenny Packwood had joined Lord Rockingham's XI. Roy Young was around too, and my recording career got under way backing people like Cherry Wainer and Vince Taylor with whom I'd played on *Oh Boy!* 'live' sessions. I did seven editions of *Oh Boy!* before I got sacked for not turning up in Hackney at eight o'clock in the morning, not bringing my guitar and being a general nuisance."

You wonder how Sheridan might have fared in Britain had his momentary flowering on national television not been nipped in the bud by his own inner nature and desires. "I've never be one to look for that acceptance that means Making It, topping the charts," he explained. "There had been a possibility of me joining The Shadows [Cliff Richard's celebrated backing quartet] as lead guitarist, but there was never any definite talk. Hank Marvin and I knew each other very well, and if he hadn't done it, I probably would have, but he was more into accompanying other people – which I wasn't."

Most home-reared pop acts that record moguls signed after the demise of skiffle were those who fitted the sumptuously orchestrated mould of the post-classic rock doldrums; obeyed the condescending voice calling them to order via the control-room intercom, and were still amenable to aping the Americans. Even those rare signs of resistance to US sway were manifested usually in domestic covers – such as Sam Cooke's 'Only Sixteen' by Craig Douglas or Gene McDaniels' 'Tower Of Strength' by Frankie Vaughan – that achieved higher positions in the charts than the originals through being played more often by xenophobically-inclined Light Programme disc-jockeys. Thus another go at 'Tower Of Strength' was also a "turntable hit" for a certain Paul Raven – formerly Paul Russell, leader of The Rebels, toast of Hillingdon Youth Club.

The only pop phenomenon peculiar to Britain then was a jazz era more distinct than that which was drawing to a close in Germany. During the hiatus between sixth-form and university, many ex-skifflers had denoted their Presley and Donegan "kids' stuff" to jumble sales, and transferred their allegiance to trad – which, when it permeated beyond the intellectual fringe and "Ban The Bomb" marches, boiled down to the toot-tooting of Mr Acker Bilk, a chin-bearded Somerset clarinettist. He, Chris Barber and other leading "dads" breached the Top Thirty, and *Trad Tavern* would occupy the spot once filled by *Oh Boy!*. Furthermore, most "with it" youth club do-gooders and the impresarios that counted applauded the new trend that confirmed their bias towards parochial outfits with blandly plinking banjos, a confusion of front-line horns, and matching Roman togas, barrister wigs or some other ridiculous variation on the striped waistcoats and bowler hats worn by Bilk and his Paramount Jazz Band.

With their younger siblings now in paroxysms of ecstasy over Acker, Chris and Humphrey, disgruntled collegiate partisans began dropping buzz-words like "Monk" and "Brubeck" into conversations; exuding further "cool" by strewing the associated modern jazz LPs artlessly about their "pads", and displaying the pensive, slump-shouldered surliness inherent in the fading "kitchen sink" realism that had articulated the post-war mood of the Angry Young Men. Vigour not subtlety had been the name of the game in the movement's aggressive books, plays and films – *Billy Liar*, *Look Back In Anger*, *Room At The Top et al* – all containing liberal use of the word "bloody", then the vilest oath censorship would allow.

Yet the rougher diamond of rock 'n' roll hadn't been smoothed by the pressures of fashion or officialdom – merely suppressed. Most of the old wild men were either dead like Buddy Holly, jailed (Chuck Berry), disgraced (Jerry Lee Lewis) or otherwise obsolete. The Everly Brothers were about to enlist as marines when Elvis was demobbed. He would survive by catching the flow of an era ruled by insipidly handsome boys-next-door like Bobby Vee, Bobby Vinton and Bobby Rydell with their twee ballads and "blues-chasers" – period record reviewer jargon for any piffle with a lightweight tune and bouncy rhythm.

In this desert, there were scattered but revitalising oases. Without compromising their rhythm and blues determination, Ray Charles and Fats Domino were still Top Thirty challengers while Barrett Strong's 'Money (That's What I Want)' and 'Please Mr Postman' by The Marvelettes were among the first fistful of US entries for Tamla Motown, a promising black label from Detroit, in what compilers had just stopped styling the "sepia" charts.

Such discs and others from untold North American independent companies wended across the Atlantic to Alex Harvey by means as mysterious as a particular brand of footware had to St Kilda, the most far-flung Hebridean island, barely a year after its appearance in chic Victorian London. Chicago blues from the likes of Muddy Waters and Bo Diddley – obscure even in the States – filtered through Harvey's Scottish vocal cords as early as 1958 with the formation of his Soul Band – also the first UK outfit to work the word "soul" into its name. Too early to have been inspired by Tamla Motown, it had come from a feature in *Crescendo*, a US magazine, that wrote of "Soul Jazz" in reference to pianist Horace Silver.

Augmenting the Harvey band's textural complexity was a conga player – and Jimmy Grimes, player of the first Fender Jazz bass in Glasgow. After Freddie Bell and his Bellboys had appeared at the Liverpool Empire with one in 1957, the acquisition of a Framus model – huge and played in an upright position like a bull fiddle – enabled Crosby's James Boys to metamorphose from skiffle group to Kingsize Taylor And The Dominoes, full-blown rock 'n' rollers – while Clay Nicholls And The Blue Flames' Pete Wharton sent frissons through nervous systems when throbbing his new Fender for the first time at a holiday camp ballroom in Filey.

Soon all units not wishing to be anachronisms would be stampeding the member on bass – "the sort of thing people got lumbered with," groaned Scouse skiffler, Paul McCartney – into buying an electric instrument to go with the solid-body electric guitars and the orthodox dance band kit as road-tested by the first rock 'n' roll drummers. Their hire-purchase debts for these demonstrated that such musicians meant business, even if the bookings that helped pay the installments could be unsatisfying in substance now that pop was at its most harmless and ephemeral.

Unless specifically requested, most groups scarcely bothered with hits by British stars as only a handful were up to US specifications. Among these were Cliff Richard's 'Move It', 'Apache' from his Shadows, Billy Fury's entire *The Sound Of Fury* LP, 'Crazy Man Crazy' by Don Charles, Vince Taylor's 'Brand New Cadillac' and climactic 'Shakin' All Over' from Johnny Kidd And The Pirates – and the forty-fives among these had all been earmarked initially as B-sides. You wonder how some artists might have turned out had they not submitted to additional executive advice to follow the path trodden by all those Bobbies and now poor, deluded Elvis with his post-army movies: semi-musicals of cheery unreality, even worse than those into which Cliff Richard, reading the signals, was sinking.

There'd been a fleeting instant when Dave Sampson had been on a par with Richard when both had operated in the same Cheshunt-Potter's Bar-Walthamstow triangle of engagements, but Dave would blame an inability to sustain the momentum of his only chart entry, self-composed 'Sweet Dreams', on being forced to record Bobby-esque non-originals that bore small relation to his own inclinations.

It was much the same for Neil Christian, another singer who could have given Cliff pause for thought too: "We always had to record something that was foisted on us by the record company," he said. "If only we'd been allowed our own choice, I'm sure the story would have been very different."

Wan emasculations of classic rock weren't that far removed from the more up-tempo items played by provincial palais orchestras in braided costumery and neat coiffure. These conformed to the tastes of those for whom the extremes of palatable modern pop were still represented by 'How Much Is That Doggie In The Window', 'Que Sera Sera' and Frankie Laine's quasi-religious 'I Believe'; all epitomes of a belief in the permanency of "decent music" to accompany each night's veletas, cha-cha-chas, square tangos, hokey-cokeys and bluebell polkas plus a degree of *salvo pudore* in-song comedy. Seated on the bandstand, "featured vocalists" ranging from, say, a baby-voiced female – with yards of tulle petticoat – and a neo-operatic tenor, would wait their turn to commandeer the central microphone for numbers peculiar to themselves. There was usually a heavily masculine sort too, who specialised in check-shirted country-and-western and its Tin Pan Alley crossovers, whether maudlin "sincerity" or clippety-clop propulsion, from the likes of Laine, Tennessee Ernie Ford and Guy Mitchell.

As the 1950s drew to its close, Jim Reeves had become a name that abided above all these in the repertoire of the "showband", an eclectic entertainment institution peculiar to Ireland and cells of Irishness in other regions, just as Scotland cradled legion country dance outfits in artistic debt to the olde tyme medley style of bandleader Jimmy Shand, and counties west of Wiltshire did to mock-yokel outfits like The Wurzels, led by former Acker Bilk road manager, Adge Cutler.

Changeless and changed after rock 'n' roll, the old bands continued delivering a mixture of across-the-board favourites, but internally they had polarised into those musicians who wanted to stick to the tried-and-trusted guidelines, and younger ones that aspired to be highly proficient, non-stop copyists of whatever North American pop commotions were stirring up the nation. A spirit of appeasement might permit maybe two current smashes and one dip into classic rock per session after it became as customary for smart alecs to request them as others would 'The Anniversary Waltz', 'You Are My Sunshine' or 'La Paloma', a tango favourite whose correct title hardly anyone knew.

Homogenous local rock 'n' roll groups had long banned themselves from such functions on which they might have depended for nearly all their bookings had they played "decent music". Doing their bit to cast out the pestilence, staider parochial showmen would bar Teddy Boys – and "coloureds" – from their venues, and adult dancers would savour specific evenings with, as some posters stressed, "No Jiving! No Rock And Roll! No Teenagers!". In a prudish Britain Gloucester city burghers would bar The Sapphires from ever defiling its guild hall again because the lead vocalist's trousers were "crude" round the thighs and crotch.

As if this kind of carry-on wasn't enough, what wasn't reported in local journals was how often these guitar combos either didn't turn up altogether or came with only half their equipment, a player short or slovenly onstage attire. According to The Outlaws' guitarist, Ritchie Blackmore, "We had been ostracised by the business and couldn't get work anymore. We were regarded as criminals and got banned all over the place. Our humour wasn't appreciated."

Many of these infamous groups had got off the runway by begging elderly promoters for intermission spots to the palais bands from which many of their senior members had sprung. Bern Elliott And The Fenmen, fresh out of school, managed it at Dartford's Scala Ballroom where their future manager, Ronnie Vaughan, was resident crooner. If so allowed, the youngsters usually played between nine o'clock and just after the pubs closed. Then the rock 'n' roll temperature was lowered for the influx of grown-ups and an interrelated return of the orchestra to bring the evening to an end in squarely "professional" manner.

Both the newly-arrived revellers and the older musicians fancied that the Elvis-inspired rubbish to which their children had been cavorting earlier would fade and die so that "nice" entertainment could reign once more – even if the loudest applause was earned for the big band's sanitised "rock and roll" sequence. This afforded quiet pride for the gifted teenage saxophonist who'd fought for it – but when the orchestra had flushed it out of its system, it was back to smoochy slop-ballads, suave patter and strict-tempo. Glowering from the bandstand as he honked into the tedium, he wondered if this was all he'd ever do.

Somehow it was all too pat, too dovetailed, too sensible, this eager-to-please sham of being happy with the situation because all the other players seemed to be. Though it was infinitely more glamorous than a "proper" job, he was so nauseated by this different type of drudgery, that just the remotest hint of a less stifling alternative would be sufficient excuse to up and quit this roundabout of "decent music" which had given him a livelihood only to be rewarded with his mockery.

Heart-searching arithmetic bade him stay where he was. The usual turnover for a palais bandsman was slightly over ten pounds a week – about the same wage as a fledgling business executive in those days – and you got nowhere near that in a semi-professional pop group. Few of these worked often enough anyway for the cash to stay the chill of workaday reality with its school-like sub-flavours of apprenticeships and night-school courses, even when, say, Bern Elliott and his Fenmen swiftly became as renowned in the Medway towns as Cliff Richard And The Shadows were in the hit parade. In a similar circumstance were Wayne Fontana And The Jets in Oldham, the blush-making Sapphires in Evesham, Dave Berry And The Cruisers in Sheffield, The Gamblers in Newcastle, Dave Dee And The Bostons in Salisbury, Kingsize Taylor and his Dominoes in Liverpool – and Glasgow's MI5 fronted by various lead vocalists, each of whom adopted the *nom de theatre* "Johnnie Law".

The last and most illustrious of these, John Latimer, was to loom large in the Hamburg saga – as would The Alex Harvey Soul Band, The Ricky Barnes All-Stars and The Bobby Patrick Big Six, also scrimmaging for position as Strathclyde's and then Scotland's boss group. Such a game of musical chairs characterised other regions too. Furthermore, they involved leading groups that were often mutable in state, drawing their various personnels from the same pool of hometown faces.

Territorial defences would be assailed when a particularly electrifying and committed unit escaped a local orbit – though this wouldn't necessarily improve financial prospects. After weeks of inactivity, a telephone call would banish recreational sloth and, within the hour, a group would be shoulder-to-shoulder in its van again, driving, driving, driving to strange towns, strange venues and strange beds for a fee that an overcharging alternator, a snapped-off wing mirror or a stolen microphone might turn into a minus amount. In 1959, Dave Dee And The Bostons' first cache of professional engagements included one in Ayrshire and on to another far north in Thurso, zig-zagging across the misty Highlands with the dull watchfulness that ensued whenever the van in which they huddled stopped at lonely petrol stations.

When Britain's only motorway terminated at Birmingham, such odysseys were truly hellish: amplifiers on laps, washing in streams, shaving in public convenience hand-basins – and trying to enjoy as comfortable a night's repose as was possible in the front passenger seat after nothing better had come of the customary "Do you know anywhere we can sleep tonight?" enquiry of hangers-on in frowsy dressing rooms. This was showbusiness. It was also staring fascinated across a wayside eaterie's formica table as the drummer makes short work of a greasy but obviously gratifying fry-up while you pick at your dish with less enthusiasm in a transport cafe in Perth that, calculated chips-with-everything connoisseur Johnnie Law, "served the worst food in the world".

"I spent God knows how many years slopping up and down the country in a van," sighed Neil Christian, who was thus able to compare notes with other dependable draws breaking free of provincial fetters like Cliff Bennett And The Rebel Rousers, Tony Dangerfield And The Thrills – both from Middlesex – The Outlaws, Kent's Sounds Incorporated, The Barron Knights from Leighton Buzzard, the foremost Scottish groups – and Johnny Kidd And The Pirates who, unlike the others, had made a record that had actually got into the Top Thirty, and were shortly to experience their period of optimum impact, circa 1960.

"The best English R&B band was Johnny Kidd And The Pirates," estimated a discerning Sidcup art student, Phil May. "I remember going to Blackheath purely to see them." Kidd, like Vince Taylor after he'd emigrated to France, would always have plenty of work assured with or without Top Thirty action, thanks also to a stage act enhanced with *Treasure Island* garb, galleon backdrop and blood-and-thunder taped overture. With a sparse crew of bass, drums and *one* guitar, Kidd was as fervent and devoted a stage performer as Wee Willie Harris, Roy Young and other contemporaries who likewise didn't go Bobby-smooth.

With his Horde Of Savages, David "Screaming Lord" Sutch couldn't even if he'd so desired. His decision to become the antithesis of the Elvis lookalikes vying for public attention captured the imagination of Sunday newspapers and a BBC documentary team that remarked mostly on his pre-Rolling Stones long hair – briefly dyed green – before touching on the leopard-skin loin cloth, the monster feet, the woad, the bull horns, a collapsible cage, a caveman's club, the inevitable coffin and whatever else he'd laid his hands on in a persistent campaign for career-sustaining publicity. Sutch's horror spoofs verged on the slapstick in an "operation" on a

Savage that entailed the wrenching out of heart and liver (bought from the butcher's that afternoon) – and, during 'Jack The Ripper', the simulated murder and mutilation of a "prostitute", ie another Savage in wig and padded bra. At venues filled to overflowing, cases of fainting and hysteria were not unknown.

For all that, Screaming Lord Sutch was to be the most famous English pop star who never had a hit. More so than Johnny Kidd, all Sutch's disc releases were secondary to criss-crossing Britain and then Europe in draughty, overloaded vans. Membership of The Savages passed as an incubation shed for many future stars, among them Paul Nicholas – mid 1960s leader of Paul Dean And The Thoughts and then 1970s actor and chart entrant – who was to aver that "with David Sutch being more theatrical, I was learning another aspect of the business". Ritchie Blackmore, Tony Dangerfield, temporary Rolling Stone Carlo Little and future guitar icon Jimmy Page were Savages too.

All were also hirelings of Neil Christian – thus justifying the questionable citing of this merely competent singer as, it says here, "a pivotal figure in the development of British music". However, like Sutch – and Kidd – before him, Christian's successful pursuit of an EMI contract was advantaged by his living near the heart of the country's pop industry, which then as now was in London. It was more convenient for artists-and-repertoire representatives to cut across the metropolis to catch Neil in his natural habitat than to check out one more dodgy group who'd mailed a demo tape over the edge of the world from Penzance, Cardiff, Aberdeen or anywhere else where the distance from the capital could be measured in years as much as miles. Even if an A&R man was benighted in Manchester, he'd take the trouble but rarely to sound out what was within metaphorical earshot, let alone negotiate the forty-odd miles east or west to do likewise in Sheffield and Liverpool or any of the working men's clubs, welfare institutes and village halls in between.

Records deals were, therefore, a far-fetched afterthought for nearly all groups everywhere. Most couldn't even immortalise themselves on anything other than a domestic reel-to-reel tape recorder as there were scant *bona fide* studios outside London other than customised barns, garages and living rooms. A package containing a demo and clippings of local publicity is mailed by registered post to each of London's four major record companies in turn. When each gives a thumbs-down, it goes out to the producer of the Light Programme's *Saturday Club* and then, even more dog-eared, to someone with the ear of Mecca, Top Rank, Jaycee or a smaller leisure corporation controlling a ballroom circuit. Relentless pestering lands an audition with Mecca in the Lyceum along the Strand. The group endures another terrible journey from Dullsville to London where they spend the night before The Big Day in sleeping-bags, side-by-side in the bass guitarist's married sister's front room.

Yet a lot of outfits – particularly in the north – weren't that concerned about national fame. "It's not so bad when you've established yourself in Liverpool or Manchester," moaned Bern Elliott, "because up there they book you for a week at a time. In the South, you're pretty lucky to get booked for more than two days at the most unless you go on a tour."

Another possibility was a season in a Butlin's holiday camp where a group's duties would include accompanying competitors in the "pop singing" and jiving contests as well as delivering the music every night in the ballroom. Ricky Richards found himself at the Filey camp in 1959 with Clay Nicholls And The Blue Flames, sharing vocals with Nicholls and Pete Wharton. The lead guitarist was Joe Brown who, like Tony Sheridan, aspired to sing too. "We never thought much of his voice," said Ricky, but others did – because Joe had been "discovered" by Larry Parnes. Because co-related appearances on a new Jack Good TV venture, *Boy Meets Girls*, were pending, Joe was available for only the first half of the summer, and had to be replaced by Tony Harvey from a post backing a subsequently displeased Vince Taylor.

Brown was also hired by Good for a six month "Rock And Trad" package tour with sixteen other singers including Dave Sampson, Duffy Power, Georgie Fame and bill-topping Billy Fury – who were all to march through the audience to the opening 'Let The Good Times Roll', sung by Dave, and backed by The Vernons Girls and the all-purpose New Orleans Rockers. The presentation, see, amalgamated salient points of a Mardi Gras and *Oh Boy!*. "I want the show to be fast-moving," agreed Jack, "but with a pronounced Dixieland theme – though don't get the idea that we are abandoning rock altogether." Not knowing what to think, Power's latest single had been a revival of 'Ain't She Sweet' in which he planted feet in both the trad and pop camps.

Acker Bilk's image flickering from *Trad Tavern* exacerbated the frustration of musicians rungs below even Power as the field continued to narrow for those keeping the faith. Every week, another venue that paid a group more than a round of fizzy drinks "went trad", designating what should and shouldn't be played within its walls. Deductions from fees would ensue for any digressions, thus curtailing any deceitful opportunism from lowbrow rock 'n' rollers in disguise.

Those back-of-beyond outfits that couldn't or wouldn't make the switch had to be content or otherwise with recurrent Saturday nights in musty suburban halls, pub function rooms and, especially, youth clubs where soft drinks, swingin' vicars, a solitary light-bulb as *son-et-lumière*, and a wholesome, self-improving reek were the norm. Sport, purposeful hobbies, charity work and the open-air was just the ticket to take your mind off nature's baser urges and any other distractions from loftier ideals.

Skiffle had been a passing fad, but an unobjectionable one as long as it hadn't interfered with school – and God could be relied upon to cast out this plague of electrical guitars too. A prim mother threatens to die of shame if a previously tractable son appears on stage with a pop group, and a strait-laced father forces a guitarist's resignation from such an ensemble because, during a rehearsal, another member was heard to utter "bloody". The drummer goes to dental college where he thrusts aside adolescent follies. Similarly, the careless lead vocalist puts the stifling responsibility of impending fatherhood before rock 'n' roll after a wedding ceremony falsely portrayed by the baby's grandparents as a sudden love-match between their daughter and the dashing young plumber who used to sing with a band as a hobby.

Despite a rapid turnover of personnel, the group stays afloat. Engagements are few and far between but they build up piecemeal a strong reputation as their playing transcends a minimum technical standard that guarantees applause if listeners know the song, regardless of interpretation. After touching a ceiling of local impact, boredom sets in, and daylight hours drag by, loafing round coffee bars and amusement arcades. Finally, the new vocalist's parents disown him after the group is named in an exposé in the local rag about the aftershock of teenage dances at the village institute. It had been reported that gardens adjacent were being used as receptacles for cigarette butts – and, worse, Mr Anderson, the sexton, had once come upon what looked like a used rubber contraceptive in the long grass round the churchyard!

CHAPTER THREE

Memories Are Made Of This

"German rock 'n' roll is based on English rock 'n' roll as German jazz is based on English jazz. When I was in the Zoom club in Frankfurt in 1970, there was a top German rock band on stage, and one of them shouted, 'Ricky!' and ran off stage to tell me that he wouldn't have started playing rock 'n' roll if it hadn't been for The Jets"

Ricky Richards (The Jets)

Following Hitler's downfall, Germany evolved quickly into a crowded and partitioned nation that embraced two distinct cultures and political agendas. The division was most piquant in Berlin with the battered flamboyance of the western Federal Republic contrasting like the Earth to the Moon with the grey Communist utilitarianism beyond the "Checkpoint Charlie" border post. Put simply, the Allies thought the Soviets were robots, and the Soviets thought the Allies were degenerates. In 1961, the Berlin Wall was erected to stop anyone swapping sides.

Whatever the zone, every city had become a realm of queues for employment and items of food and clothing. Belying a setting evocative of her night-club scene in *The Blue Angel* eighteen years earlier, prevalent desperate conditions in post-war Germany were summarised in part via Marlene Dietrich's appositely spivvy 'Black Market' from the soundtrack of the 1948 film *A Foreign Affair*. How wise Marlene was to remain in Hollywood while the German film industry and all sizes and manner of other enterprises fought for recovery in over-populated conurbations .

By fair means and foul, gangs of youths in the poorer quarters had acquired garb in which only gum-chewing American GIs on passes would be seen dead: snazzy check jackets, hip-hugging slacks, bowling shoes and hand-painted ties with Red Indians or baseball players on them. Like France's *yé-yé* and Britain's Teddy Boys, they had modelled their corporate personalities and gait on sullen, narcissistic anti-heroes like Marlon Brando and James Dean on celluloid and then Elvis Presley on vinyl.

As it was in Britain, the United States seemed the very wellspring of everything glamorous from Coca-Cola to electric guitars to off-duty occupation servicemen who would burst upon the fun palaces of Berlin or Hamburg, acknowledging with waves of fat cigars the bemused stares from both the citizens and British soldiers stationed on the Rhine. Yet when the rock 'n' roll epidemic spread from the States, older GIs were just as aghast as European adults at its noise, gibberish and loutish excesses; the mingling of C&W and R&B provoking mutterings from "redneck" contingents about "nigger music".

German approval of the French government's efforts to ban this latest *yé-yé* subversion was less tacit after Bill Haley And The Comets performed in Stuttgart, Essen, Berlin and Hamburg in autumn 1958. Described by *Melody Maker* as looking like a "genial butcher", Haley had begged pardon of the British press for the knockabout stage routines of his paunchy dance combo, who were neither the most enduring nor suitable ambassadors of rock 'n' roll – but they were the first to visit West Germany, and the fans went as crazy as fans could go. At West Berlin Sportspalast, seven thousand of them were the *dramatis personnae* of what was described in one national newspaper as the most dangerous riot in pop history, and condemned by Lord Mayor Willy Brandt as "a disgraceful result of youthful boredom". "It was the worst thing I have ever seen," agreed Haley. "Worse than anything in the States."

Beyond jiving in the aisles, the secretive slitting of cinema upholstery and like stylised delinquency patented by their transatlantic and British cousins, Berlin's over-excited and goaded teenagers armed themselves with bits of broken chairs and, with blank bullets cracking above the ear-stinging pandemonium, charged *en bloc* the *Polizei* riot squad lining a stage that Bill and his petrified Comets had just fled. It was left a shambles of up-ended grand piano, smithereens of footlights, and fragments of drum kit, guitar amplifiers and Armed Services Network recording equipment. This damage was but a fraction of the final assessment after fire hoses drove the crowds outside where, with hormones raging and wondering what to do until bedtime, they let off steam in a two-hour orgy of brawling and vandalism in the teeth of tear gas and rubber truncheons.

When news of a score of arrests and as many injuries – including a policeman blinded in one eye – came to the ears of city councillors, further pop (and jazz) concerts were banned at the Sportspalast, and Haley denounced in a front page editorial in *Neues Deutschland*, a Soviet sector journal, for "turning the youth of the land of Bach and Beethoven into raging beasts".

The next show at Hamburg's Ernst Merck Halle had a similar outcome. *Der Abend* noted that the recital was relatively calm until a nervous Haley hurried off after running through his biggest hits and wonderful-to-be-here vapourings as quickly as possible. The Essen bash was brought to a close with dogs and water cannon at the first sign of trouble – though Stuttgart was peaceful, even though Staff Sergeant EA Presley was known to be backstage on a fraternal visit.

The Fatherland did not find its first encounter with gen-u-ine US rock 'n' roll easy to forget. It might have appalled the old and square, but all but the most serious-minded of their children had been entranced by the trash. Lost in dreams and half-formed ambition, some decided to try rock 'n' roll themselves, and thus submit themselves to an infinity of incomprehension, deprivation, domestic uproar and derision – especially derision because the results, particularly vocal, were generally nothing like. The spirit was willing, but a German rocker tended to be raucous not passionate if he even got as far as shedding enough of his inhibitions to cut up rough.

On the radio, these mechanical reproductions did not sound virtually identical to the US prototypes as they might have done at the tender mercies of British artists. The problem was mostly the clipped solemnity born of someone singing in a language not his own over accompaniment riven with complacent exactitude and often a quasi-martial beat. While I must add the raw information that when the American Constitution was being drafted in 1787, German had come within one vote of being adopted as the Union's official tongue, rock 'n' roll had developed into an English-language music, and would remain so for all time.

In all areas of mainstream pop, West Germany had nurtured few who became known to a wider world. As it was with the BBC, programme planners would foist on the electric media what the public ought to want. This had meant that the first stirrings of rock 'n' roll had been brushed under the carpet as another transient craze before a return to the eternal verities of "decent music" by singers who, in that bilious journalistic cliché, Grew Old With Their Audience under the batons of Hans Busch, Berthold Kaempfert, Horst Wende and other middle-aged middle-of-the-road orchestra leaders who had first refusal of virtually all record dates in German studios throughout the 1950s. It was as if domestic pop couldn't be done in any other way or with any other players than those bound by the rigidity of radio-imposed conservatism.

Teenagers, therefore, had to put up with the same music that their elders and younger siblings liked – with no middle ground between nursery rhymes and Horst Jankowski unless you could be bothered to search out static-ridden bursts from the American Forces Network, Radio Luxembourg – or the Light Programme for its weekly pop series *Saturday Club* and even *Two-Way Family Favourites*. This Sunday lunch-time array of record requests was mostly for the benefit of UK occupation forces in Germany where the link was Chris Howland, an English disc-jockey whose German was so fluent that he became a television quizmaster on Norddeutscher Rundfunk (NDR), the second largest regional broadcasting undertaking in the Federal Republic.

Transmitted from Hamburg from 1955, it addressed itself to the over-thirties like most other German stations who'd understood that, while there was not yet – or ever likely to be – any *bona fide* domestic "answer" to Elvis or even Cliff Richard, there were plenty of schmaltzy Ronnie Hiltons, Harry Secombes and David Whitfields built to last until well into the 1960s.

Chief among these was Freddy Quinn, a bass-baritone unknown internationally but selling records by the ton on his own patch for

Polydor, Deutsche Grammophon's pop subsidiary. A former merchant navy deckhand, Quinn thrived on a picaresque charm that might have satisfied the requirements of a Mills and Boon man-who-has-known-sorrow. His breakthrough was with German versions of Dean Martin's 'Memories Are Made Of This' and Tennessee Ernie Ford's 'Sixteen Tons' in 1956. This set a pattern of at least one smash per year for over a decade; some of them recorded under the supervision of Horst Wende and, later, Bert Kaempfert who, when not fronting his orchestra, was a freelance power on Polydor. One with Kaempfert's stamp on it was 'Die Guitarre Und Das Meer', one of several tie-in singles to movie vehicles starring Quinn – now so popular that the single word "FREDDY!" plus the place, date and time on a poster was sufficient to fill the biggest German theatre or cinema.

Film roles also came the way of another Teutonic hitmaker, Udo Jurgens, whose commercial penetration into adjacent territories caused him to be omnipresent at every mid European song festival on the calendar. Nevertheless, Freddy's closest rival was saturnine Fred Bertelmann, called *Der Lachend Vagabund* ("The Laughing Vagabond") after he struck luckiest with a 1958 million-seller of the same title, warbled in a light tenor similar to that of Britain's Donald Peers, 'The Cavalier Of Song'. As engaging as Quinn before TV cameras, he was honoured by a Reeperbahn night spot naming itself after his alias.

Like Quinn and Jurgens, Bertelmann was the proverbial "pop singer who can really sing", and this and his choice of material put him in a different rather than higher league to the likes of Ralf Bendix, Peter Kraus, Tommy Kent, Drafi Deutscher, Ted Herold and Fats And The Cats who gave the German consumer their idea of rock 'n' roll. Of them all, the most successful was Bendix whose translation of Buzz Clifford's 'Babysittin' Boogie' sold more than the original throughout the continent. Yet Deutscher was the more experienced rock 'n' roller, having fronted various combos – notably Charlie And The Timebombs, and The Magics – before a watershed performance at an outdoor event in Berlin and its upshot of a full and lucrative date schedule that took him all over the country.

Why should impresarios waste time trying to get Elvis to tour when German boys were already doing the job? The answer was that teenagers were so dismayed by most indigenous pop that the coin-operated sounds of Elvis, Gene, Cliff *et al* were preferable to such an act if it was booked for a local club. It rather than the juke-box was the intermission, an opportunity to go to the toilet, talk to friends, buy a drink. If anyone bothered listening, it was for the wrong reasons as the perpetrators in struggling to scale the heights of their aspirations, afforded glimpses of high comedy to their audience.

"There was no really good German rock 'n' roll," Ricky Richards would notice. "They only had dance bands that played three numbers, and took a five minute break, played three more in a different tempo, took another break and so on." Looking for a solution, some German club owners thought big. Making tentative enquiries, the more out-of-touch were astounded at the astronomical costs of engaging this Elvis *schmuck* that everyone's talking about. What was the difficulty? Wasn't he near Frankfurt just then, in the middle of his stint as a soldier in the US Third Armoured (Spearhead) Division?

At his manager's insistence, Presley wouldn't even strut his stuff within the confines of the US bases whose entertainment officers were settling instead for contrasting and cheaper fare from Britain such as Liverpool's Royal Caribbean Steel Band and the sixteen-piece Ivy Benson All-Girl Orchestra with a petite, red-headed leader in a see-through blouse, whose bangle-festooned forearms did not cramp her skilled manipulation of the alto saxophone. The Orchestra's trek round Germany in early 1960 had been beset with the expected occupational hazards from predatory males, and was culminating in a long residency at the Lido Dance Hall above Hamburg's Kaiserkeller, a *Tanzpalast der Jugend* owned by a disabled ex-circus clown, fire-eater and acrobat named Bruno Koschmider.

"At the time, Germans liked the idea of 'foreign'," observed Chris Warman, a Hampshire drummer soon to be working in Frankfurt. "That is, British groups that gave them the comfort of being an 'original' item."

The new policy would be most rampant in Hamburg where, like everywhere else, time was measured by "before", "during" and "since" the war. Rebuilt and reconstituted, its new landscapes of glass office blocks, churches like dental surgeries and overspill estates of raw red brick symptomised many but not all shifts in the order of things. A Burgermeister remained first among equals on the city council, and

Herren in leather breeches carried on quaffing huge steins of lager in open-air beer gardens.

Down in St Pauli, life's losers still spent nights in the cells of Davidswache police station – which continued to be featured regularly in film and television thrillers – and, after a night's work on the Grosse Freiheit, Roman Catholic whores in terror of eternal punishment for sin were careful to turn in the direction of the façade of bombed St Joseph's Church, and make the sign of the cross before retiring to bed to actually sleep.

"The mentality struck me as being still pre-war," was to be Tony Sheridan's initial impression of the red-light district. "It was very much a seamen's place. It was composed of all sorts of nationalities. We were just another bunch of incoming foreigners. There was nothing Nazi or even much German about it – unlike Munich, Hanover or somewhere more typical. St Pauli isn't German, never was, never will be."

On stumbling across embarrassed mention of St Pauli-Reeperbahn in official guide books, tourists, sightseers and voyeurs might ogle, gloat and disapprove during daylight hours, but many would return as more active pleasure-seekers to the tempting evening streets where wanton perfume laced the air, and the more forward pimps beckoned from brilliantly-lit doorways of bawdy houses and striptease palaces. Clothes might be shed to the records of Bertelmann, Bendix and Quinn in surroundings that might have an apt nautical theme – like the Kaiserkeller with its puffer-fish lamps; replica lifeboats as dining alcoves, and a ceiling decked with fishermen's nets in which were caught fake crabs, lobsters, turtles and dolphins.

Business was always briskest on the Reeperbahn itself, and competition was hot for premises there. Many entrepreneurs had to accept second-best in neighbouring streets and alleys. These ventures were seldom very successful after the fleeting spell of popularity enjoyed everywhere by any well-publicised new venture with the paint still tacky on opening night.

In every city in West Germany, promoters were voracious for fresh angles, new faces and the latest adult toys to exploit and discard for a fickle public. Some novelties came and went, but bowling alleys, one-armed bandits and, hanging the expense, pool tables stayed for keeps, many of them obtained via US Forces officers' messes.

Britain, however, was a principal source of flesh-and-blood amusements. In 1959, Mr Acker Bilk and his Paramount Jazz Band had been well-primed to capitalise on the imminent trad boom through an offer from Dusseldorf's New Orleans Beer-Bar to work seven hours a night, every night for six weeks for "the highest money he'd ever earned in his life", according to Bilk's biographer, Gordon Williams. "We were all celebrating," laughed Acker, "drinking pints on the money we were going to get in Germany."

His account of the band's season in Dusseldorf was an encapsulation of much that UK musicians brought to Germany later would also experience. Take, for example, the Beer-Bar's proprietor, Herr Vortmann. "One of these big Germans, he frightened me," Bilk was to say from the safety of Somerset. "Though that was just his looks. Really he was a decent bloke, and all he wanted to do was keep us on because we were doing such good business for him. The thing was that he held our passports, and I was beginning to think we'd never get them back. I was just being worried about nothing. When he saw we really wanted to get back home, he sent us off in style.

"Pity there ain't more places like that in this country to give some of the young bands a chance to practise their music in a swinging atmosphere. Man, he really gave us a chance to blow our hearts out. You just blew and blew and blew, and had twenty minutes off for a drink, and then you were back blowing again."

Just blowing, blowing, blowing...Within months, however, trad was old hat and from the New Orleans Beer-Bar to Cologne's Storyville to Kiel's Starpalast, bastions of teutonic jazz closed to reopen with new directives whereby pop and trad groups shared the same bills for a while before all-pop nights became the rule.

Yet it was not to be anywhere in Dusseldorf, Cologne or Kiel but Hamburg's St Pauli, once the musical fount of little else beyond a few jazz clubs, that was about to become as vibrant a pop capital in its way as Soho – from whence would be found the transforming element.

By 1960, Tony Sheridan had become "the best rock guitarist in Britain" in the opinion of Ricky Richards. "When Conway Twitty and people like that came over to England, they'd insist that Tony was the one hired to play for them." Sheridan was, however, less interested in skulking beyond the main spotlight than striking out on his own as central figure in a trio with Brian Locking on bass and – also foreordained to join The Shadows – drummer Brian Bennett. With unusual flair, he chose not to duplicate recorded arrangements of classic rock, preferring, as he put it, "to take a song and ravish it so that it came out in a slightly different fashion. It was how a song happened at a given moment." When he too trod the boards with Sheridan, Ricky Richards was to cope likewise with Tony "restructuring the numbers because he'd never play three chords when ten would do".

The exhilaration of the impromptu on the boards did not reconcile easily with the precision expected in the more sterile surroundings of the studio – and without a record deal, how was any advancement possible? Yet, within the industry, Sheridan's talent wasn't unrecognised: "I'd nearly been the first guy to record for Top Rank in 1959. 'Only Sixteen' was to be my first single. That sort of stuff wasn't my style at all. There was a big fuss in the music papers – in which they made out falsely that I was only seventeen – but Top Rank took Craig Douglas instead – probably a wise move."

"Tony was a very complex character," surmised Ricky Richards. "He had a lot of insecurities, but haven't we all?" Sheridan's self-destructive streak was consigning him to an obscurity largely of his own making. Depressingly familiar was the cancellation of his spot on *Boy Meets Girls*, headlined by Gene Vincent, when, in his own publicist's words, Tony "went haywire [failing to be on time, arriving without his guitar etc]".

Television was, therefore, closed to him, but Larry Parnes permitted The Tony Sheridan Trio ten minutes on the all-British supporting cast of the legendary Gene Vincent-Eddie Cochran tour of 1960 that ended with Cochran's death in a road accident on 17 April. "Eddie was everything I wanted to be," confessed Sheridan. "When he was killed and Gene badly injured after the last night in Bristol, I'd been very glad that there'd been no place in the taxi for me. Instead, I was stranded alone in the dressing room when everybody else had gone. For the first and last time in my life, I'd bought myself a bottle of whisky and was trying to vent my frustration at being an inferior British musician by getting sloshed. In the end, I smashed the bottle against the wall – but the next day, I was still alive and well."

Throughout the expedition, Sheridan had displayed both an

impetuous exuberance as a performer, and a wanton dedication to pleasing himself rather than the customers. "Tony used to sing with his eyes closed," observed Ricky Richards. "It didn't go out to the crowd. He wasn't expansive, he didn't project but he'd be under tremendous emotional strain – which is why he got stomach cramps on stage." Nevertheless, bound up in himself as he was, Sheridan could be mesmeric, creating true hand-biting excitement as he took on and resolved risky extemporisations in the same manner as Lonnie Donegan and Jimi Hendrix, respectively before and after him.

This might seem a silly analogy, but, on paper, Tony Sheridan had everything it took to be, perhaps, The Rolling Stones to Cliff Richard's Beatles. "Yet I've never been one to look for that acceptance that means Making It, topping the charts," he'd reflect with the candour of middle age. "All my artistic desires – as a stage performer anyway – were satisfied very early on in Hamburg."

Within weeks of the Vincent-Cochran expedition, Tony was among a ragbag of other London-based rock 'n' rollers at a loose end, who were taken on by the first Hamburg impresario to put action over debate apropos *Englander* rock 'n' roll. With an ingrained passion for taking pains, Bruno Koschmider had set off for London and the Soho coffee bar that seamen visiting the Kaiserkeller had assured him was still the shrine of British pop.

At the 2I's, he was introduced to Iain Hines, a keyboard player whose curriculum vitae included spells backing Vince Eager, Ricky Valance, Tommy Bruce and, when still living in his native Glasgow, Alex Harvey.* He was invaluable in assisting Bruno's quest for musicians to be transported across the North Sea for reassembly as "The Jets" – after the gang in *West Side Story* – to work six nights a week on the rickety stage of the Kaiserkeller for an exploratory period.

"I'd returned to the 2I's to play for a couple of evenings," recalled Tony Sheridan, "and was approached to work in Hamburg for two months. My motives for going were deep-seated. When I was twelve, I'd spent a week in the Rhineland on an educational visit with the school. We had a good time, but my mother was always rattling on about half the family – including her own father in 1917 – being dead because of the Hun and blah, blah, blah. Unconsciously, I suppose, part of the reason I got into rock 'n' roll and went to Germany was to spite

---

* Iain was also the brother of television actor Fraser Hines, notable for roles in BBC's *Doctor Who* (as "Jamie McCrimmon") and, later, in ITV's rural soap opera, *Emmerdale Farm* – which also starred Clive Hornby, former drummer with Liverpool beat group, The Dennisons

my mother – who'd wanted me to be either a priest or Yehudi Menuhin!"

Yet Ricky Richards proffered "only one reason why Tony came to Hamburg: running away from the police over a guitar – a Martin Super-Dreadnought D28 with twin pick-ups from Boosey and Hawkes." Although an admirable young man in many ways, Sheridan had a lackadaisical attitude towards the accumulation of debt. The London booking agent Tito Burns had discovered this when, after lending the twenty-year-old – technically a minor in those days – the down-payment for another guitar and assenting to act as guarantor, demands arrived for unpaid hire-purchase installments.

Down-to-earth Ricky, however, was not beset with any psychological or financial motivations: "I'd tried to go abroad in the army, but, because I was downgraded, I'd spent all my National Service in England. Up until Hamburg, I'd never been out of the country, and I desperately wanted to go." At twenty-six, Ricky was to be the oldest member of The Jets. Though primarily a singer, his guitar chords were to cement Tony's lead solos and obligatos. If no Sheridan, Richards' fretboard style was held in high enough regard for him to have been invited to play on an album by Miki and Griff, Britain's first well-known "sweetcorn" C&W specialists.

Nevertheless, despite playing alongside Ricky in Clay Nicholls And The Blue Flames too, another recruit, Pete Wharton, was, in his colleague's view, "still a learner", having not got far past the twelve-bar blues and other cyclical clichés that recurred *ad nauseum* in rock 'n' roll. Functional rather than virtuoso too were Colin Milander (*né* Crawley) an extra rhythm guitarist, enlisted because, explained Ricky, "Bruno couldn't imagine a dance band with less than six people." Making up numbers in every sense of the phrase too was James Macken, an Irish youth who'd called himself Jimmy Ward before settling on Del Ward, possibly a genuflection towards Del Wood, a female honky-tonk pianist from Nashville, much admired by Jerry Lee Lewis.

It was Ward who was to mind the tickets and documentation, and, on Koschmider's contract, be designated The Jets' *de jure* "band leader" whose instructions "have to be obeyed by all members of the band". Iain Hines was more hardened a UK pop shellback than Ward –

and possibly even Sheridan or Richards – but any question of conflict over *de facto* leadership of The Jets was academic as Hines neglected to show up on the morning of 4 June at Liverpool Street station for departure for Hamburg.

There was comparatively little equipment of any description for The Jets to transfer from train to cross-channel ferry to train in an era when it wasn't laughable for a professional group to travel without a road manager. Who needed one when a school satchel could serve as case for an amplifier "with a ten-watt punch", soldered together from a kit advertised in *Melody Maker*?

Midnight had long thickened when The Jets climbed down with their hand-held luggage amid the gusting engine steam and belching smoke in Altona, a few stops from the main terminus, Hamburg-Hauptbahnhof. Red-eyed and unshaven, they were bundled into a car ordered by Koschmider. "We got to the Reeperbahn on 5 June at about two o'clock in the morning," recalled Ricky Richards. "At that hour in London in 1960, it'd be like a ghost town, even in the West End, apart from a few discreet night clubs like the Embassy and the Cafe de Paris. You could walk down Charing Cross Road and Shaftesbury Avenue and not see one car either in motion or parked. They made films like *The League Of Gentlemen* on location in London by shooting them early on a Sunday morning at first light in the summer.

"We couldn't believe the Reeperbahn! It was like Piccadilly Circus at nine o'clock in the evening: flashing lights, plenty of people about, all the clubs open – though the Kaiserkeller was pretty empty when we arrived."

Taking delivery of the human freight in his office, Bruno pondered aloud to his assistant, Ollie Limpinski, about whether he'd been sent short weight. Where was Iain Hines? Moreover, as The Jets were also lacking a more obligatory prerequisite – a drummer – the customers might consider that there was a bit missing from the music too. "Well?" demanded their new employer. Thinking fast, the Bert-can-play-washboard skiffle veterans' eyes fell on an antiquated Trixon dance band kit that stood behind him. Any fool can bash drums. They'd take turns on the Trixon – if Bruno didn't mind them using it.

Almost as broad as he was long, Herr Koschmider was reminiscent of one of Wagner's subterranean Nibelungen. No neck, a button nose, bushy eyebrows and lavishly whorled hair punctuated a countenance like a bag of marshmallow. At least it drew attention away from a manifest limp that indicated that Bruno's journey to middle life hadn't been peaceful. The injury had been received during war service, but its exact nature was not clear. In any event, while day to day administration of *Bruno Koschmider Betriebe* (Bruno Koschmider Management) was delegated to Ollie Limpinski, Koschmider was still able to run the Kaiserkeller with remarkable facility. "Bruno was a man with a little class," granted Tony Sheridan, "or he had had when he was younger. He was quite an intelligent chap, but he'd obviously seen better days and had ended up in St Pauli trying to make money out of dance halls, juke-boxes and teenagers."

If Koschmider's manner seemed stern at first, he did not seem ill-disposed towards the British entertainers. It wasn't in his interests to be – unless the customers didn't like them. Making amends perhaps for the slight flare-up over the absence of Iain Hines and a drummer, Bruno was amenable to suggestions about presentation that were counter to his own and every other clubman's perception of pop music in St Pauli. "He wanted us to play three numbers, then sit down for five minutes and do three more," said Ricky Richards. "We told him we'd lose our audience if we did that. We'd do an hour, take a half-hour break, then play non-stop for another hour and so forth."

As aware as Bruno of the chasm into which they might plunge, The Jets steeled themselves to face facts in front of a foreign audience – if there was going to be any audience at all – that would have no qualms about letting them know just what it thought about them. Nevertheless, as showtime at seven pm the following night approached, the overall mood was one of quiet confidence. "We didn't need to rehearse," attested Ricky Richards. "We knew each other's numbers. Sheridan had backed me hundreds of times down the 2I's."

Guiding each other by count-ins, nods and eye contact, The Jets in their matching open-necked shirts had a walkover. "The audience went berserk," gasped Ricky, "because we weren't amateurs, and we were belting out rock 'n' roll like the clappers. What with Sheridan and his guitar too, they'd never heard anything like it. They wondered where we got such flat-out energy from."

An instant and howling success with a clientele for whom the personality of every previous house band had been secondary to boozing, punch-ups and the pursuit of romance, the impetus was sustained for every working evening that followed: five hours during weekdays, seven at weekends. "We had a Midas touch," said Tony Sheridan. "There was no question of failure. It was nothing like we'd ever experienced in England."

Koschmider could not bring himself to be extravagant with praise, but he was secretly delighted as the sustained cheering and scattered screams for The Jets rang in his ears – and, more, with the sharp upward turn of his profit graph that resulted. "The place was packed from the word go," confirmed Ricky Richards. "Ollie Limpinski used to insist that it was always like that, but the gangsters I asked later said that the place used to be half-empty before we came. Everyone who was anybody was there on that first night. The Old Merrytale Jazz Band and some of the Ivy Benson girls turned up – and the word got around that there was this amazing English rock 'n' roll group playing at the Kaiserkeller. It was fun. I can't recall a single bad night."

Naturally, the contract was renewed, and Bruno was quite happy to overlook infringements of clauses that forbade or frowned upon "conversation with the public by use of the microphone"; eating or smoking on stage, and bad language. "If you're a young rock 'n' roll band, are you going to take notice of any of that?" sneered Ricky Richards. "We'd make jokes, swear like troopers because they couldn't understand us. We'd sing 'Sloop John B' with our own rude words. For Christ's sake, the club was full to suffocation. It was doing fantastic business like it had never done before. He wasn't going to stop us cussing, smoking or drinking beer on stage. You don't kill the goose that lays the golden eggs."

Bruno was far less minatory than he could have been too, concerning the stipulations about "the available two rooms at the establishment...used for lodgings under the provision that this place shall be kept extremely clean by the members of the band. NO WOMEN ARE ALLOWED IN THESE ROOMS." He was on thin ice here in any case – because The Jets may have had many complaints themselves about the ostensibly cheerless underground accommodation. "Without the lights on, it was like a photographic dark room," sniffed Ricky Richards. "It was a bit unsavoury in there sometimes."

In the grey of every morning of the week except Monday, The Jets would flop into bed after hours spent on stage, seizing songs by the scruff of the neck and wringing the life out of them. According to Tony Sheridan, "Our repertoire was about fifty per cent rocked-up skiffle, fifty per cent rock 'n' roll." This embraced a wide spectrum from Miki and Griff-esque weepies like 'Nobody's Child' through the "hard" C&W of Hank Williams to window-rattling 2I's showstoppers from Ricky Richards like 'C'mon Everybody' and 'I Go Ape' – and torrid work-outs of Ray Charles' 'What'd I Say' that once finished with Tony Sheridan's collapse after over thirty minutes of trading its "heys" and "yeahs" with a responsive mob left wanting more. "We were putting new numbers in all the time, and they'd run for different lengths," said Ricky. "We didn't know what we were going to play next."

This was just as well because, like Lonnie Donegan, Sheridan was given to launching impetuously into items unfamiliar to the other musicians as he built up a perspiring intensity not known in pop *sur le continent* before 1960. His boys on the Vincent-Cochran tour and now The Jets could keep effortless pace, but many a pick-up outfit in the decades ahead was to panic behind him as such a piece degenerated to mere degrees short of open chaos.

Yet they and other later visitors to Hamburg would feel honoured to be on the same stage, learning the tricks of the trade from one nicknamed "The Teacher". "He was excellent," concurred Chris Warman, "tight on stage and demanding the best you could give. He was a nice guy too. I still have a signed photograph from him, given to me afterwards." However, Screaming Lord Sutch likened Sheridan's attitude towards his transient accompanists to "a sergeant-major. He was really snappy towards them."

Tony's has become the name that trips most readily off the tongue whenever British pop musicians in Hamburg are discussed by lay persons. This metamorphosis began during that first season when the original group swiftly became known – informally anyway – as Tony Sheridan And The Jets. "I was an ingredient in the pudding," Tony would concede in 1997, attractive in his phlegmatic modesty. "I don't think that I was any more important than anyone else – except that I was a bit more experienced. That was my plus point."

A more unsung hero was Del Ward, who ministered more

unobtrusively to overall effect, having emerged as The Jets' most adroit sticksman, despite hardly ever sitting behind a kit before. What kind of group nowadays would take such a chance? With extraordinary application, he developed his hand-and-foot co-ordination, accurate time-keeping and even the beginnings of a personal style by public trial-and-error on the old-fashioned kit. When required, Ward would also pound the club's yellow-keyed upright piano, amplified by simply shoving a microphone through a rip in its backcloth, and with more and more surreptitious wires snipped from it to replace broken bass guitar strings as the seasons of The Jets and the acts that followed them went by.

After a fortnight, The Jets and their growing multitudes of fans had become accustomed to both a pianist doubling on drums and Tony – "The Elvis of the Reeperbahn" – hogging most of the lead guitar and vocal spotlight – when Iain Hines appeared at the Kaiserkeller without warning, expecting to mount the platform that evening beside the other five. The thrifty Koschmider was happy with the group as it was, and made it clear that, if Hines was to stay, The Jets themselves could pay for his services from their thirty marks a night. "But we didn't need him," decided Sheridan.

Why should The Jets take on a passenger now that their parochial fame was spreading like ink on blotting paper? Indeed, rivals were casting covetous eyes over Koschmider's hot property to the degree that The Jets had been approached already to administer their rock elixir elsewhere. At the front of the queue was Peter Eckhorn, soon to open a plusher night spot, the Top Ten, on the Reeperbahn itself – unlike the Kaiserkeller which was, said Tony Sheridan, "in a little dingy street, but the Top Ten was on the main drag – which was a bit more respectable in that parents didn't mind their children going there".

The Top Ten was to rise like a phoenix from Der Hippodrom, an indoor arena spacious enough to contain a circus and stables in the cellars for its horses. Since the war, it had hit times so hard that only the uncomplicated *bierkeller* nights with cheery community singing to the usual bombastic oompah band could be relied upon to even cover costs. Such was the state of affairs when Peter Eckhorn returned from a spell at sea. "He had been sent away by his father to learn the ins and outs of running the business," recounted Tony Sheridan, "and part of it was to work on a liner going to America."

As his brow furrowed over the grim balance sheets, it was put to Eckhorn *fils* by twenty-four-year-old Horst Fascher, one of The Jets' most sincerely keen aficionados – and as much of a catalyst in the Hamburg saga after his insidious fashion as Sheridan – that it could only be more profitable to put on rock 'n' roll at the Hippodrom. Despite an improved grasp of modern commerce, Eckhorn's hands were tied while his sire was yet in charge, and seemingly opposed to dragging the business into the 1960s. "Peter was a rotten sod," growled Ricky Richards. "He used to say, 'Soon my father *vill* be dead, and I *vill* be able to run this place as I like.'"

Still very much alive, however, old Herr Eckhorn agreed to differ with his son, allowing that there was nothing to lose in trying out this notion of readjusting to a teenage market. First of all, Peter procured The Jets after he and Fascher, a compound Hercules, "reasoned" with an exasperated but powerless Bruno during negotiations that concluded with the Kaiserkeller releasing the group from the newly-signed contract. As well as higher wages, the outwardly affable Eckhorn also offered sleeping quarters situated two floors above the club. With a balcony facing the church opposite, this skylit, L-shaped dormitory contained a creaky table surrounded by a sink and six ex-army camp beds with hard mattresses and lumpy-looking pillows – but, if plain, it was palatial compared to the dungeons of Koschmider.

After The Jets' finale at the Kaiserkeller on 6 July, they assisted in the decoration of a Hippodrom they'd been permitted to rename the Top Ten after Vince Taylor's venue in Berwick Street. "All of us helped to clean up the place," said Tony Sheridan. "It was a filthy hole, but we threw the rubbish into the backyard and built a makeshift stage in two or three days." After Eckhorn pushed a paint brush into his hand, Sheridan's training as an artist proved useful in the energetic creation of murals depicting individual likenesses of The Jets down the long entrance hall into the auditorium, and a post-impressionist Parisian night scene as the backdrop to their performances.

When The Jets opened the Top Ten the following Saturday, it was as if the old pleasures of the Hippodrom, closed a mere three days earlier, had never been. The Kaiserkeller was forgotten too, particularly as it had reverted – albeit temporarily – to lumbering strippers attracting few onlookers.

Exacerbating Koschmider's misery were the clusters of boys and girls in suede and leather, chattering excitedly as they spilled out onto the pavements after a sweatbath with The Jets at the Top Ten. "We took all the kids away from Bruno," said Tony Sheridan, "and it mushroomed again. It was the only place in town where anything was happening." Rather than racketeers, sailors and tearaways, the Top Ten tended to lure a *nouvelle vague* of not so much "youths" as "young people" whose liberal-minded parents might drop them off in estate cars. Most of them would be collected in between ten and eleven, owing to the curfew regulations that prohibited those under eighteen from frequenting Reeperbahn clubs any later than that.

Tony Sheridan saw "a different class of people: students, arty types – and businessmen and their molls, the music industry, press etc. The waiters were told not to beat up anyone like that." Yet a rougher element had followed The Jets from the Kaiserkeller. These were principally of a type recognised as "Rockers". Some of the females dressed like their boyfriends in an approximate uniform of jeans, motorbike boots, T-shirts and leather windcheaters, but more frequently it was flared skirts with wide belts, tight jumpers, stilettos, ruby-red lips and beehive hairdos. In their imaginations at least, they were as elfin as Audrey Hepburn in *Roman Holiday*. Had they been British, their men's brilliantined ducktails would have had them classified as Teddy Boys; if French, as *yé-yé* – as would their musical preferences and gormless hostility towards interlopers into their corner of the Kaiserkeller or Top Ten.

Narrow-eyed bouncers-cum-waiters had been hired by Koschmider and then Eckhorn to keep order. The most formidable of them all had been Horst Fascher, quickly elevated to such high office that all Kaiserkeller bar staff had been answerable to him. Despite his diminutive stature, Fascher could reduce with a glance a hulking Rocker's most brutish *braggadocio* to low mutterings. His reputation had preceded him for there was no mistaking the crouched force of a former featherweight boxer so talented that he might have represented West Germany in the international ring had not his career been marred by a prominent role in a street brawl in which a seaman had been killed.

Yet the frightening Horst was capable of surprising gentleness and sensitivity. As a paying customer, The Jets' inaugural show at the Kaiserkeller had transfixed him, and he'd been lost in wonder at the glorious onslaught of pulsating bass, spluttering guitars, crashing drums and ranted vocals. He stayed for the next Jets session, and when they stumbled off after exacting their customary tribute from whoever hadn't wanted to like them, what else could Horst do but struggle through the crowd to congratulate them?

A highlight of each succeeding evening – especially after he entered Koschmider's employ – came to be the opportunity to chat with proud familiarity to Del, Tony, Pete, Ricky and Colin. This would be prolonged when Horst was made welcome on the next bar stool as an English-speaking confidante who'd never be so beglamoured by musicians that he couldn't offer constructive criticism. Moreover, because his family had sheltered Jews from the Gestapo, Fascher was justifiably touchy if anyone poked fun at him about Nazis. Sometimes, he'd lash out physically as he would when he punched the lead guitarist of one famous British group. Another member who'd teased him likewise was hauled into a club toilet and soaked in urine.

Thus was imprinted the importance of Horst's loyalty to those musicians he befriended. This did not extend to clubs as Koschmider had discovered after Fascher defected to the Top Ten where his responsibilities grew after Eckhorn discontinued the juke-box in favour of continuous "live" music. This was achieved by adding a minimum number of auxiliary musicians to create two separate acts from The Jets to play in split shifts. "Tony wanted total control of the guitar," said Ricky Richards, "to do it all himself." Therefore, another Tony Sheridan Trio made sense – with its leader calling the shots to Pete Wharton and Ingo Thomas, spotted drumming with Fats And The Cats in a St Pauli bar. With his heart in jazz, Thomas was soon superseded by the more suitable "Nigger Tony" Kavenagh, a black GI who had gladly manned the Trixon kit at the Kaiserkeller on those occasions when Del Ward, unused to the unremitting rhythmic effort, needed to rest his limbs.

A new Jets – with Colin Milander transferred to bass – would be supplemented with players from London – and to this end, Ricky Richards and Horst Fascher set off by road on 6 August, resolving to bring back Iain Hines and Chas Beaumont, once lead guitarist with The

Worried Men, a skiffle outfit that had been a springboard for Adam Faith's eventual celebrity. Though approaching thirty, Chas was game – as was Iain, albeit still weary from a one-nighter in Scotland with Vince Taylor.

What had been a smooth-running operation was scuppered mere miles from Hamburg when the party's Volkswagen skidded onto the hard shoulder of the autobahn near Luneberg Heath, a moorland Nature Reserve, and crumped into a stationary lorry. Asleep in the front passenger seat, Richards was the most serious casualty after being propelled through the windscreen. For several weeks, he'd lie on a hospital bed fuzzy with painkillers, and his head swathed in bandages. He'd carry the scars to the grave – though none were disfiguring. Nevertheless, they were still raw enough for him to mask with onstage sunglasses when he reunited with The Jets.

It never rains but it pours, and the matter of the Martin Super-Dreadnought D28 was soon to pelt down on Tony Sheridan: "I'd forged Reg Calvert's name on the HP agreement because I didn't like him – but I fully intended to keep up the payments. However, the gig in Hamburg went on a lot longer than first imagined. The German police had visited me to suggest that I go back and settle up. At Dover, two plain-clothes guys picked me up, and it was decided to make an example of me. I got stuck in Brixton prison for ten days on remand, and it put me off 'crime' forever. In the end, they let me off."

That both The Jets and the Sheridan splinter group were in disarray one way or another was not the soundest foundation for an extension of the Top Ten season. When the contract expired in December, the retinue scattered like rats disturbed in a granary with only Colin and Tony opting to continue taking their chances on *la vie boheme* in Hamburg.

CHAPTER FOUR

Travellin' Light

"Years later when The Electric Light Orchestra were selling millions, Bev Bevan said that being with The Vikings in Germany were the happiest days of his life, living on cornflakes and wondering how we were going to get home"
Ace Kefford (Carl Wayne And The Vikings)

Other British groups were to work Jets-like miracles all over Western Europe. Of the same late 1950s vintage, Doug Fowlkes And The Airdales were to Parisian *yé-yé* hangout, Le Club Drouot, what Sheridan, Richards *et al* were to the Top Ten. France's US air bases also provided rich pickings for many outfits like Liverpool's Faron's Flamingos whose prize exhibit, Bill "Faron" Russley remembers as "pretty hectic, but we loved it, playing six or seven hours virtually every night of the week. I think we got twenty-five pounds a week each – which was great money then. We never went to Hamburg but we toured France like mad."

From Birmingham, the less boisterous Carl Wayne And The Vikings, formed in 1958, fell upon Germany, having touched the ceiling of Second City impact with "up to twenty bookings a week, doubles and trebles", according to bass guitarist Chris "Ace" Kefford. "We were getting forty or fifty pounds each when my old man was on twelve as a plasterer. I wasn't too happy about the shirts, ties and velvet-collared suits we wore on stage – or the music, mostly Top Twenty and a lot of smoochy ballads like 'My Prayer'. Even when we did Chuck Berry, it was all very polished."

Ace had been the advocate for The Vikings' newest recruit, drummer Bev Bevan, late of Denny Laine And The Diplomats: "I got him into the group. He came in the week before we went to Dusseldorf for a couple of months before moving on to the Storyville in Cologne." Bevan had been promised that "'You'll get thirty quid a week,' Carl says, 'and your first set of dates will be in Germany.' Any hopeful beliefs I might have had that pop could earn me easy money were swept away in those weeks in Germany."

In further flung areas of Britain where Birmingham might have been seen as a halfway house between hobbledehoy obscurity and the Big Time, the broadening of a group's work spectrum usually proved more roundabout. A spreading reputation as a bow-tied, white-socked showband in and around Belfast would bring for The Monarchs an offer from abroad via a Glaswegian vocalist named George Hethrington who was paying an exploratory visit to Ireland in 1962 with a view to finding work there for his own outfit. He sounded out The Monarchs about some kind of exchange trip. This possibility of thereby "going pro" separated the men from the boys in both bands, and the long and short of it was that so many members of each threw in the towel that what amounted essentially to Hethrington and the remnants of The Monarchs – six of them – amalgamated as Georgie And The International Monarchs.

The first nation over which they held sway was Scotland where, as well as covering much the same ground as Hethrington's previous unit, they headlined over a diversity of local turns when warming-up for and then backing Don Charles. Next, they headed for London with more confidence and hope than they could possibly justify. The streets of the capital weren't paved with gold, but along one of them, Georgie And The International Monarchs met Don Charles again, perhaps not really by chance.

He threw down a fraternal line by laying them on with a trowel to an agency that handled bookings for himself and artistes of more chartbusting magnitude like The Temperance Seven. Hethrington and The Monarchs were found a niche providing what archaic posters billed as "swing sessions" in Irish clubs like Birmingham's Hope-and-Shamrock and like oases of draught Guinness, altercations between loyalists and republicans, and the juke-box balm of Jim Reeves. From the same source came a season in West German clubland where their energetic shenanigans were just the ticket for violent bierkellers that made the uglier incidents at the Hope-and-Shamrock seem like tea at the vicar's.

The Monarchs contained a nondescript saxophonist named Van Morrison, an unknowing pop star-in-waiting. His walk with destiny, however, would pale against that of The Beatles who, giddy and stiff, had climbed down from a minibus outside the Kaiserkeller on 17 August 1960 to be conducted to the Indra, another hostelry controlled by Bruno Koschmider, that was about to switch from striptease to pop.

If incensed but unable to prevent (or enact reprisals against) the Top Ten's purloining of The Jets, Bruno had calmed down sufficiently to return to England with a cast-iron contract for a comparable attraction. He came back to where he'd started at the 2I's, but among other contacts was Allan Williams, a Welsh Liverpudlian who, in 1960, had been charged by Larry Parnes with the task of assigning Merseyside groups to back Johnny Gentle, Duffy Power and other of his lesser signings – as The Monarchs would Don Charles – on what were less tours than strings of one-nighters in Scotland.

Three years earlier, Williams, a former plumber, had transformed a watch repair shop in central Liverpool into the Jacaranda, a coffee bar where professional musicians congregated partly because it was near the dole office. Some were also hired for evening sessions on the small dance floor in its basement. The Royal Caribbean Steel Band had been resident there in 1959 until seen by a German sailor. It was through his exhortation that, with Deutschmarks and mention of affectionate fräuleins, the West Indians were poached by a Reeperbahn club manager.

Quite unashamed of their perfidy, letters from them landed on the Jacaranda's doormat, telling of the recreational delights of Hamburg. The opportunist in Williams led him to the Grosse Freiheit too, sampling an evening of music and loose money. Before the night was out, he and Bruno Koschmider, entrepreneur to entrepreneur, had had an investigative talk about the possibility of bringing to the Kaiserkeller some of these Liverpool outfits held in esteem by no less than Larry Parnes. The discourse ended on a sour note when it transpired that a tape of the fabulous groups in question that Allan had threaded proudly onto Koschmider's recorder had been rendered an unlistenable mess through demagnetisation – possibly as it had passed through a customs point.

Back at the Jacaranda, Williams shrugged off this embarrassing episode to concentrate on subcontracting groups to Parnes and also finding them work elsewhere. This may be cited as the origin of one of two equally plausible but opposing accounts of how Allan and Bruno re-entered each other's lives.

A forthcoming 1960 summer season in Blackpool for The Seniors, a combo fronted by a saxophonist named Howie Casey and Derry Wilkie, a pencil-mustachioed black singer, was cancelled by Parnes just as the gentlemen concerned had given up their day jobs and spent a loan on new stage uniforms. Looking for a scapegoat, they marched round to confront one from whom all their woes had emanated. Intimidated, Allan Williams threw a slender lifeline. The next day, he drove The Seniors the long miles down to the 2I's.

To his astonishment, room was made for them to do a turn that very evening through the mediations of Brian Cassar, a Londoner by upbringing but sometime the "Cass" in another Liverpool group, Cass And The Cassanovas. Even more incredible was Williams and the expeditionary Koschmider freezing in mutual recognition across the coffee bar's kidney-shaped tables. Impressed by The Seniors' unbottled exuberance, Koschmider had them on their way across the North Sea within three days.

The other story is that Cassar had met Bruno during the visit that had culminated with the gathering together of The Jets, and had informed the German that, whenever he – Cassar – wasn't in London, it was probable that he could be contacted by telephone at the Jacaranda. It was, however, quick-thinking Allan Williams who answered Bruno's ring. No, Brian and The Cassanovas are north of the border with Johnny Gentle at the moment. Can I help at all?

Whichever tale you choose to believe, The Seniors made the Kaiserkeller thrive again, and Bruno's thoughts turned to his sleazier Indra. He requested another Seniors from his Man in Liverpool who, after dismissing those absent in Scotland, Butlin's or somewhere else, sent over The Beatles, a scruffy five-piece with "arty" pretensions, a novice bass guitarist and a very new drummer. They'd endured a baptism of taunts and slow hand claps, but had become likable for an awry absurdity, derided as "posing" by those whose idea of "being professional" was no-nonsense onstage taciturnity. Most of The Seniors remembered The Beatles as hopeful amateurs, but acceded that they'd improved in the interim between an audition for Parnes in May and their maiden performance at the Indra. "Really this was where we started on the style we use today," John Lennon, The Beatles' leader, would profess. "The idea was to include lots of stamping so the beat could get through above all the other noise in the club."

Both here and in the Kaiserkeller, each resident act's break between sessions caused the respective crowds to thin. Custom was lost, Koschmider presumed, to the hated Top Ten and entrapment by Tony Sheridan And The Jets, together or apart, for the rest of the night. It was a bit unreasonable to expect anyone to rock around the clock without a rest, so, feeling entitled to copy Peter Eckhorn, Bruno unplugged the juke-box, and bridged the gaps with an instrumental act he'd devised on paper by extracting the bass player from The Beatles, the pianist and saxophonist from The Seniors, and Ingo Thomas, once Sheridan's too-jazzy drummer, from another club.

The unit's disparity plus the dissatisfaction of the inconvenienced and depleted Beatles and Seniors combined with complaints about the change of programme at the Indra, but it was the situation's false economy that led harassed Bruno to restore the Indra's gartered exotica – to not a word of moral protest – and move The Beatles uptown to the Kaiserkeller.

Rory Storm And The Hurricanes, an ensemble of like standing in Liverpool, replaced The Seniors who landed a job in another club for a few weeks – but it was mainly the prompt rebirth of the Kaiserkeller as a pop venue that drained the door and bar takes at the Top Ten after its five record-breaking months with Sheridan and Co. At the first perceptible sign of danger, Eckhorn began investigating ways of saving the situation. He had second thoughts about Sheridan, but ultimately The Jets would have to be sacrificed for something fresh – perhaps from this Allan Williams person – to bring the crowds back. Technically, Peter had to keep the chaps on until the contract was up. However, that was no more binding than a necklace of toadspawn. In any case, none of The Jets had a work permit anyway. It had been the responsibility of Eckhorn – and Koschmider – to sort this out, but there were so many loopholes and legal pitfalls that no solicitor the group could afford would be much help beyond making token threats.

The murals of The Jets vanished during the facelift that meant that the Top Ten was still full of builders when Gerry And The Pacemakers were met off the train by Herr Eckhorn at the end of what was to be a familiar and dishevelling trek for many other groups: Liverpool-Hook of Holland-Hamburg. Raised in one of the toughest districts on Merseyside, Gerry Marsden and his drumming elder brother Freddie had seldom been further away than Blackpool, and the outer marches of the group's booking circuit had never extended beyond Manchester. Yet there they were, delivering the goods in a foreign night club, past resistance to circumstances that would make it impossible for Marsden Minor at least to go back to the old life. The Top Ten – his first engagement as a professional entertainer – was to suck Gerry into a vortex of people and places that hadn't belonged even to speculation when, less than a week before, he'd been a delivery boy with British Rail with the prospect of finishing up half a century later as a retired station master with a gold watch.

If no Bobby, Marsden was a showbiz natural of boy-next-door ilk. His grinning vibrancy, strong voice and compelling patter gilded fretboard skills that were to be fine-tuned through paying acute attention to Tony Sheridan as had The Beatles. Both Gerry and John Lennon, for example, were to share the same high-chested guitar stance with Sheridan. Moreover, both groups were, noticed Tony, "very chuffed to meet me because they'd seen me on *Oh Boy!*" – and, according to the more acerbic Ricky Richards, "Before The Beatles heard Tony Sheridan, I don't think they thought that there were more than four chords on the guitar." Like everyone else, The Beatles had also learned to be less concerned with technical accuracy than the generation of a lively all-night-party atmosphere to foster a rapid turnover at the counter, and defuse potential unrest among over-excited customers.

Competition between musicians to outdo one another's stage antics was matched by that for business between the clubs they served. An appetite for live pop, ideally British, put mercantile pressures on further venues, present and future, along and off the Reeperbahn. The

Blue Peter, Menke, the Big Apple, Studio X, Monica Bar, Der Lachend Vagabund, Regina, the Star-Club and, with a Wild West theme, Whiskey-Saloon all procured some sort of in-person musical attraction – even if it was just the Blue Peter's tinkling pianist.

For some, it was a sink-or-swim attempt to recoup losses. When The Beatles too were charmed away to the Top Ten, and Rory Storm And The Hurricanes made it clear that they'd sooner plait toadspawn than continue working for Bruno Koschmider, the Kaiserkeller again saw ruin staring it in the face until it changed its name to the Colibri, and became just what St Pauli needed: another striptease joint.

This backstreet club had always been on the fringe of the rock 'n' roll action anyway, but to Bruno Koschmider, however suspect his conduct, much is due for originating the concept of a unified and robust pop scene in Hamburg. His Kaiserkeller was the Bill Haley to the Star-Club's Elvis – for it was the Star-Club rather than the Top Ten that was to be the most famous landmark in St Pauli.

It was the brainchild of Manfred Weissleder, whose imposing height and clean-cut face beneath golden hair made you think of Hitler's Aryan exemplar. Those of timid temperament were inclined to look away from his friendly smile and appraising eyes – for Weissleder was a "man of respect" from whom fear spread like cigar smoke. He and his retainers ran Der Lachend Vagabund and the majority of St Pauli's strip clubs. They also financed the making of lavish films involving full-frontal nudity of a type generally unavailable in Britain where "the shameful parts" were either airbrushed out or out of camera range.

Many of Manfred's flicks were premiered at Stern Kino, Grosse Freiheit 39 – next door to Monica Bar – until it was commandeered as the location of Hamburg's latest pop club when, in 1961, conversion began with the gutting of the cinema and the fitting of settee-style seating and tables in two saloons and a snack bar. A winding staircase was to lead to a dance floor up in the balcony – while lanterns hung from a suspended trellis ceiling to give a more intimate feeling to the rear area of the club. For the artists, there were dressing rooms with mirrors bordered by light bulbs. Plush curtains fringed a grand stage made grander by a depiction of the Manhattan skyline as it would be from a tenement scene in this backdrop's foreground.

Manfred had also appropriated the most suitable staff for the task ahead. The torn underarm of a drummer's jacket or beer down the front of a saxophonist's trousers, even half an hour prior to showtime, were to be entrusted to Rosa, a sexagenarian maid-of-all-work known affectionately as "Mutti" ("Mama"), and previously *Toiletten-Frau* for Koschmider and then Eckhorn. Another familiar face was that of Horst Fascher, who had graduated from organising the strongarm battalion at the Top Ten to more general management at Weissleder's place – where he was even to venture onstage and sing the odd lead vocal with some of the groups.

Everything was in place by two pm on 13 April 1962, the time fixed for the opening of the Star-Club. It was far more of an occasion than that which had started the Top Ten. During this first season the club had no fewer than four acts a night (including The Beatles and a band led by *Oh Boy!* refugee, Roy Young). Each had to play for only two one-hour stints each between six in the evening and three in the morning, leaving an hour in which to drink up.

A promise of an engagement at the Star-Club was used as bait by agents who wanted Dave Dee And The Bostons to work at the Top Ten, and Johnnie Law And The MI5 to undertake a less prestigious residency in Kiel. "Everyone knew about the Star-Club – and the Top Ten too," said Ian "Tich" Amey of The Bostons. "You'd have played there for nothing – which we virtually did anyway." Fellow musicians at home, however content and prosperous, would wistfully drink in travellers' yarns of Hamburg with an inner ear cocked to the far-off roar of the crowds there that, if such tales were to be credited, were prepared to adore any rock 'n' roller from Great Britain, whether he speak in cockney rhyming slang, like a proper Lord Snooty or with the t'ickest brogue in Ireland.

In this sceptre'd isle, pop was seen principally as musically worthless if exploitable. Even the very record company moguls that oversaw its production regarded it as a lower class novitiate for a life as an "all-round entertainer". After notching up a handful of hit singles, a pop star would "mature". Waving a cheery goodbye during the finale of ventriloquist dummy Lenny the Lion's show on children's television would lead to a prime-time evening duet of some simpering old evergreen with Max Bygraves (prefaced by scripted ad-libbing between cheeky young shaver and jovial voice-of-experience). From a subsequent comedy sketch with Mike and Bernie Winters on ITV's *Blackpool Night Out*, there would unfold a flow chart of pantomime, soft-shoe shuffling, charity football matches, blink-and-you'll-miss-him roles in B-movies and a *vita nuova* as a third-rate Sinatra in northern cabaret for the luckier teen idol who toed a winsome line of acceptable pseudo-rebellious behaviour. Well, we were all a bit wild once upon a time, weren't we?

Yet rock 'n' roll was now being perceived in Germany as less a starting point than the entire purpose, however transient, of a musician's career. There needn't be any higher plateau where standing with a teenage audience had no substance. Its practitioners were a little more likely to be seen as belonging to a romantic tradition, naive art perhaps, no matter how primitive or light their cultural load. Raphael, Mozart, Shelley, Chatterton, you name 'em, they'd each shed the bulk of their artistic cargo during a brief optimum moment too.

This isn't to say that a German child's passion for pop might not bring puffy smiles to the lips of parents. Their blood ran as cold as that of British grown-ups at its loutish excesses. Nevertheless, coupled with a time-honoured Teutonic fondness for heavy-handed rhythm, the directness of rock 'n' roll's repetitious lyrics enabled those adults who couldn't comprehend a word of English to be swept along emotionally, even become superficially aroused, by 'Hound Dog' more readily than their opposite numbers in the UK who dismissed any opus containing the word "ain't" as gibberish, a guttersnipe corruption of the language.

It was, therefore, easier in Germany to be lionised as an Artist full-stop rather than someone who might become Max Bygraves or Freddy Quinn if he lasted the course. More to the point, it spelt, as Paul Raven was to discover, "plenty of women, plenty of booze and, most importantly, plenty of work". A season in a German club also meant that once you were there, "you've got your amps and drums set up," said The Beatles' George Harrison, "and you get used to one sound." Moreover, you didn't have the transport worries you had during one nighters in Britain where jammed starter motors, flat batteries, snapped towropes and long waits for Automobile Association patrolmen were very much part of a day's work.

The offer of the Kiel residency had come after Johnnie Law And The MI5's bass player – uninsured to drive it – had written off the group's expensive new van, and thus triggered a fortnight of profound tactical problems of moving the operation from A to B. Nevertheless, it wasn't unusual for an outfit to walk equipment to nearby venues or rely on public transport and kindly bus conductors who might allow them to stow the gear overnight at the depot whenever the need arose.

You had to be as truly committed as Johnnie Law And The MI5 to go the distance, however. "We thought it would be good to go to Germany," said Johnnie, "playing every night for two months with our new guitarist, get the band really together, and then come home and slaughter everybody." Such musicians would see the crunch coming that would separate the cans from the can'ts, the staid from the untamed, the dedicated from the indifferent. "One of the biggest things that could happen to an unknown group was to be offered work in Germany," said Don Powell, drummer with Wolverhampton's In Betweens, "because that meant going abroad, travelling and even going professional. We were offered a month's work over there, and we jumped at the chance."

Other groups would baulk like gymkhana horses refusing a fence. Guitarist Colin Manley was an executive officer with the National Assistance Board whilst moonlighting with The Remo Four who, if recognised as Merseyside's top instrumental ensemble, were not prepared then to give up their day jobs. In Manchester, Peter Noone, later singer with Herman's Hermits, was similarly cautious: "Most of us didn't take playing in bands too seriously. We listened to our parents who said, 'Put that guitar down and do a job with your hands.'"

While potential opportunities in the Fatherland were to either engender such circumspection or liberate the gypsy in many a soul, a trip to the Reeperbahn by Hemel Hempstead's Barry Edwards And The Semitones was cancelled because the bass player's Jewish mother wouldn't countenance him setting foot on German soil. Under similar constraints, another bass guitarist, John Lodge quit The Krew Kats – who were to mutate into The Moody Blues – in the interests of higher education rather than undergo a different kind of training in the clubs of Hamburg and Hanover. He was, however, to be reinstated later after extricating himself from the clutches of a lass who, according to Denny Laine, "didn't want him to move out of Birmingham".

Chris Warman was "already earning a living from music when asked to do the German jobs", but for most groups, earnings weren't sufficient to jack in school or full-time employment until something like Hamburg came up. Then perhaps the group's leader or manager (if any) might call round to affirm to doubting parents his faith in an immediate future which was like a working holiday. Who could argue with thirty quid a week? What was not said was that, as Tich of The Bostons found out, "The money was okay by English standards but didn't go a long way in Germany."

The supplicants sensed that their man needed only courage to hold out against his mithering mum and dad and chuck the predatory fiancée allied with them and the Youth Employment Centre in prevailing upon him to be sensible. Tipping the balance for many a red-blooded young brute was the *sotto voce* imagery of the saucy, fancy-free "birds" you get in Germany, in an age when a nice British girl would tolerate no more than snogging.

Gallivanting off to Kiel five years into his training as a mechanical engineer, Johnnie Law felt that, "It would have been okay to go to the army and maybe get badly wounded or killed, but leave home to do your own thing was against the grain. We all had steady girlfriends, and them and our parents weren't too pleased – because they all reckoned we'd never come back."

Even if they did, it wouldn't be like it was with National Service whereby their old jobs would be waiting for them after they'd flushed this pop nonsense out of their systems. Nevertheless, if rare, there were those who would support their offsprings' self-motivated activities with a zest that other parents might have thought excessive. Such a son had had to merely ask for a guitar and it had been his. If he chose drums, he'd be bought a kit with skins of calf-hide rather than plastic. Group rehearsals would take place in the living room with mother supplying refreshments and fielding neighbours' complaints about the din. When the group was ready for public consumption, she'd act as their agent, ordering a gross of business cards from the printer's, and picketing for bookings from pub landlords, social secretaries – and agents for club work overseas. Her boy could pack his cases for Hamburg with her full approval.

To those with more elbow-grease values, a decision to throw away a blue-collar apprenticeship or a job-with-a-suit to play rock 'n' roll to

Germans was the icing on a cake of follies that began with the very formation of the group. In days before synthesizers as sixteenth birthday presents and government grants to make pop music, the very idea of a son venturing onto the professional stage in such a context was almost as deplorable as a daughter becoming a stripper.

Furthermore, how some musicians dared not only to go but to spend weeks on end in Germany without inviting the sack from their "proper" jobs astounds me. Some did, of course. Typical of these was Ron MacKay who joined Acker Bilk's Paramount Jazz Band two days before Dusseldorf: "I was getting more keen on the drums, and was playing at night and getting into the office late all the time. One day, the bloke said this wasn't good enough so I said, 'Okay, don't bother. If I'm going to have to choose, I'll chuck in the job.'"

Others had more forbearing supervisors or else obtained release by taking summer holidays that weren't actually in summer, or by means not entirely honest – involving forged sick notes, false bereavements or simply going AWOL. Many were students who cut college. "We were going to the Star-Club every few months," recounted The Searchers' John McNally, "and getting time off to do it. At the time, the Star-Club was paying us fifty pounds a week – so in the end, we decided we'd all turn professional. My father went crazy. There were so many people on the dole at the time. I was enjoying what I was doing so I took the chance."

There had, nevertheless, been enough hesitation from McNally and the group's other guitarist Mike Pender that drummer Chris Curtis and bass player Tony Jackson lined up replacements. "There was Johnny Guitar from Rory Storm's Hurricanes," Tony recalled, "and Howie Casey, sax player with Derry Wilkie And The Seniors, but, virtually at the last minute, Mike and John said they'd come."

Making a decision like this was not as noxious as it might have been if seen through the prism of early 1960s adolescence or by anyone whose concept of self-advancement was decades removed from that of older relatives who'd borne the brunt of the Depression. It was a way out of facing the real world of starting married life in your in-laws' home; the close smell of typewriter correcting fluid; the rhythmic clanking of conveyor belts, and cramped, jolting commuting on the bus with its body pressure and banal chit-chat through testy rush-hour traffic.

There were no handy pegs on which to hang your frustrations when you slammed in to the stench of soiled nappies and over-cooked cabbage. During a weekly grind as humdrum as the classroom and its compounding of mediocrity, you'd already absorbed the habits of idler co-workers; stopping the service lift between floors for a quiet smoke, stealing illicit squints beneath desk-top level at *Record Mirror* or enjoying rounds of darts on a board hung in the basement. Glancing over your shoulder for the nosier members of staff, you'd make use of the office telephone for group business.

After most bookings with the group, you'd get home as the graveyard hours chimed, and grab what rest you could. On the bus to work by seven-thirty am, you'd debate how best to get through the time-serving day on automatic, greeting with a snarl those few lower in rank than yourself who approached your desk or work-bench. Slide rules and ledgers would swim before budgerigar eyes as your double life burnt the candle to the middle.

It was never too late to give up music and try harder for a raise and even promotion, instead of just waiting for Friday to roll around – but who wanted to keep their nose clean and slip into a "cushy" position and henceforth into dull and respectable old age when there remained even the remotest possibility of a more glamorous alternative?

If a group jumped the hurdles of domestic opposition, and obtained passports from Petty France in London – from the emergency department if at short notice – another hiccup before even leaving Britain for those members who hadn't reached their majority (twenty-one until reduced to eighteen in the later 1960s) was having to ask permission from a magistrate to go. Your legal guardian would have to stand the required surety – one hundred pounds by 1965 – and be told to guarantee that you reported to the British consul on arrival in Hamburg for much form-filling. As well as a further obligation to report back to the magistrate within seven days of return, an adolescent musician would be as subject to curfew regulations as any German. Seventeen when first she sang at the Star-Club, Beryl Marsden "had to be out of the club and off the streets by ten-thirty pm. When I was getting up for breakfast, the others would come rolling in from being out all night."

The younger players would also be more prone to scrutiny of work permits and residency visas (as well as passports) by *Der Auslander Polizei* (the Aliens Police). Before you so much as addressed the labels on your luggage, these had to be granted by the German embassy in Amsterdam with all the attendant turgid bureaucracy and unhelpful slowness.

So the Great Adventure began. An expedition like this was sometimes the first occasion that a youth from a back-of-beyond British town ever breathed foreign air. None of Dave Dee And The Bostons had done so when they lugged all their equipment to Salisbury station and onto the train – where it spilt out from their compartment into corridors and toilets. The same type of terrible journey was braved by Faron's Flamingos to get to France: "None of us were old enough to drive, so we went everywhere by train: Liverpool to Euston, across London to Victoria, down to catch the boat, struggling with all the drums, bloody great home-made speaker cabinets, guitar cases, the lot. We were met at the station by a truck sent out from the base."

"We went by train and ferry too," said Chris Warman. "Can you imagine carrying a full Ludwig kit from Southampton to Frankfurt that way? Looking back, I can't believe I did it." Neither perhaps could Ringo Starr who'd elected to travel separately via Paris from the rest of Rory Storm's Hurricanes. During the usual scramble when changing trains, he lost track of his drums. Misunderstood attempts to explain his dilemma in sign language brought *gendarmes* into the picture. Fortunately, one of them understood English, but the kit was not located until the next morning.

A group had no control over situations that occurred on the railway, but it could seem to have some if it went to Germany by road. The difference between getting there by train and getting there by van had similarities to that between going to the launderette and owning a washing machine. After the loss of their vehicle, Johnnie Law And The MI5 grubbed around for the crumpled eighty pounds that paid for a hand-me-down replacement, maybe one oil change from the breaker's yard, and with all the inherent forebodings of calamity. "It broke down in the middle of England," grimaced Johnnie, "so you can imagine that the journey after that was unbelievable."

In worst-case scenarios, Bedfords, Commers and even the new Ford Transits gave up the ghosts somewhere between Zebrugge and

Eindhoven. After, say, cleaning the plugs and then trying the ignition, the more naive groups would be optimistic that the jolly old Belgian AA would breeze in, fiddle about with the engine and send them on their way by the time they'd drunk their coffee in a convenient transport cafe. A rueful but light-hearted mood might persist for the four hours before a surly mechanic came, grunted "eez no good" under the bonnet, and went away again. Like Jack Hawkins in the life-raft in *The Cruel Sea*, someone would bully the others into quizzes, charades and 'Ten Green Bottles' in an attempt to keep spirits up and quell thoughts of hitch-hiking to Zebrugge and throwing themselves on the mercy of the Consulate (if we had one there).

Telephone contact with a perplexed club manager would be established, and he'd see what he could do. Everyone could now descend into stoic cynicism lent piquancy when Cliff Richard's 'Travellin' Light' dribbled from the juke-box. Endless centuries later, a breakdown truck would come to cart the Englishmen and their wretched van twenty kilometres to the nearest large village over the border in Holland. On the move, there'd be a general recharge of wakefulness to be deflated while loafing about the garage as a church clock rang the hours. The grease monkey's diagnosis would be disheartening: no new parts available for two days...lucky you didn't have an accident...three hundred guilders before I even start...should've left it in *Groot Britannie*...Thirty-six sleepless hours with a paranoia of abandonment would come to a head. Summoned into the discussion, a nervous proprietor would know of an outwardly serviceable mini-bus that would make it to Hamburg as long as you didn't push it above forty.

In the event of a breakdown, Nottingham's self-contained Beat Men would have been at least comfortable in their immobility. They'd taken the trouble to customise a double-decker bus with sleeping, washing and cooking facilities just like the one that Cliff Richard and his fellow wonderful-young-people had had to drive to Greece in 1962's *Summer Holiday* teenpic.

However, already European chart contenders when their time came, The Pretty Things deserved nothing less than an aircraft. "The very first time we went to Hamburg," reminisced their Dick Taylor, "it was on a boneshaking, radial-engined American heap of some sort, apparently especially suited for the steep descent and short runway there. Being a plane fanatic when I was a child, I loved it – but I think it instilled a fear of flying and an appetite for aerial alcohol in some of the band."

On the ground, lowlier musicians would be knocking back the duty-free drink on the ferry and, if green-gilled, being seasick. Unless they were contriving to enter the continent illegally – as did one solo guitarist, later a music journalist, as a quasi-stowaway on a navy cadet training ship – they'd next pass through the concrete desolation of the customs area to suffer the first of many instances of an official's bored hostility at their cissy nape-length locks at a time when veterans of both the Somme and the Russian Front still had their hair planed halfway up the side of the skull.

As the kilometres sped by on the wrong-right side of roads a lot straighter than in Britain, homesickness mingled with apprehension about the mess he might now be, but a new recruit might sink into the uneasiest of slumbers. He'd wake with an eye-crossing headache, the road buzzing in his ears, and with a shower of blokes he wasn't sure he even liked, and whose characteristics he'd certainly never had the opportunity to log at such close quarters.

When the poor little lambs stopped at the German border, a guard slung a rifle over his shoulder so as to free his hands to examine the passports. He might give them a perfunctory glance without even looking at the bearers before waving them on, but sometimes just a meek quip from inside the van about spy novels or an "*Englisher schweinhund, you zhink you play games mit der Master Race!*" would have the post resounding with every fibre of red-tape that jack-in-office unpleasantness could gather. However, though a hitch over freshly-unearthed paperwork could go as far as incarceration in a police cell, unbothered string-pulling from Hamburg could free a group within hours.

Relief might burst a dam of non-stop badinage and sing-songs as the van hurtled through the inky firs of Lower Saxony. Getting bolder, the lads would wind down the windows to bang out a beat on the metal roof and bawl insults at passers-by. Nevertheless, the bravado would die down to small-talk and then virtual silence as they nosed into the outskirts of Hamburg.

"The marks left on the face of the town can never be erased," Hamburg's chief of police had written after the blitzkrieg, but hazy impressions of a blackened city of Wagnerian apocalypse with parking lots formed from bomb sites were as undone as any of a flickering, monochrome Hamburg with horse-drawn carriages in a silent movie. The incoming Britons penetrated instead a modern metropolis recovered more fully than equally shell-shocked Coventry, Dover, Newcastle and the like would be for years, thanks to a more forceful urban renewal programme, both helped and hindered by the attentions of the RAF. Yet while the old Musikhalle stood within the shadow of the neo-bruitalist Unilever skyscraper, lingering austerity was epitomised by ersatz coffee, made with acorns and given to non-private hospital patients who complained that it left an aftertaste like liquid smoke.

Nearer to London than Inverness as the crow flies, Hamburg was the most "English" of German ports, not least for its gaunt "City Exchange"-type architecture along the waterfront, and the sprawl of impinging residential hinterland. Small-time light industry, advertising hoardings and tangles of shopping precincts sat between arteries of droning traffic, boat services and a clattering tram network connecting the suburbs with a city centre that bustled with the latest from Hollywood sub-titled in its cinemas; the comings and goings from the vast dome of Hamburg-Hauptbahnhof, and every civilian archetype transported by time machine from operetta and war film: close-cropped Hermans with sausages of fat bulging over their collars; their equally stout wives window shopping ponderously alongside them; *milchcow mädchens* garbed in the twin-sets of secretaries; Prince Rupert of Schleswig-Holstein reincarnated as a navvy; little old watchmakers shouting the headlines of that afternoon's *Hamburger Abendblatt*, and a prisoner-of-war camp commandant at a high multi-national corporation window, sun-blanked spectacle lenses flashing like a heliograph over a watery city that was nowhere as dirty as Liverpool or Glasgow.

This became apparent in microcosm when, from an overloaded van, an unexpectedly large number of grubby human shapes would clamber at a final destination which was not a former skiffle cellar of arched brickwork, sweating with slippery mould, but an auditorium plusher than the most salubrious palais they'd ever played in Britain. They'd struggle with the first armfuls of careworn equipment into a lofty interior that was as splendid for all its cathedral cold, its essence of disinfectant, its echo of tobacco, food and alcohol intake from last night.

Nonetheless, like the foul coffee served behind the grand façades of some German hospitals, the accommodation provided for the group was at odds with the magnificence of the workplace. Everyone was too nonplussed to joke about tunnelling, Stalag 13, Red Cross parcels and forming an escape committee. Well, it would have sickened pigs: cramped, poky rooms still full of the previous tenants' litter and pungent with sock-smelling frowziness; not enough musty camp beds or frayed old sofas to go round; naked light bulbs coated with dust; improvised ash-trays and chamber pots; lumps of brittle plaster falling at a touch from walls so mildewed that it was as if they were covered with black-green wallpaper. *Ist goot, ja? Nein*, not really.

The Beatles could not complain of any shortage of romantic squalor – well, squalor anyway – after they had been conducted to three small, windowless holes adjoining a lavatory in the Bambi-Filmkunsttheater, a picture-house opposite the Indra. "I didn't know what to expect," said Ace Kefford of The Vikings, "but our digs were worse than what The Beatles had in that *Backbeat* film. It was like a squat. It had no roof!" Bev Bevan would add that it was "ankle-deep in rubbish, infested with rats, and there were blood and semen stains on my bed. We spent what little spare time we had cleaning it all up."

The Beat Men preferred their Cliff Richard bus to the Top Ten bunkroom from where, in order to reach the WC two floors below, a musician risked an affray with Asso, Peter Eckhorn's truculent bulldog, nicknamed "the hound from hell" by Ritchie Blackmore. Asso's teeth sank into the ankles of Alex Harvey, Dave Berry and Paul McCartney amongst many others until he died of rage in 1965, attacking another bass guitarist.

There were no such hazards at Frankfurt's Storyville where Gene Anthony And The Lonely Ones were happy enough with "a huge apartment", remembered Chris Warman, "which we shared with another group, a mile from the club." Often, it was no worse than student hostel rooms within a university campus – and frequently better than many outside it. It was an improvement too upon some of the provisions made for pop entertainers criss-crossing Britain in the early 1960s. On reaching the Southampton stop, a 1960 package containing Dave Sampson, Danny Storm, Baby Bubbly, Buddy Britten and their respective backing combos decamped to the house of the promoter, the celebrated Reg Calvert. They favoured his pet rabbits scampering over the floors to the wet – not merely damp – bed linen provided in the ascribed guest house.

Regardless of how long groups stayed at a given German club, there was a temporary bed-and-breakfast frugality about what, in Swinging Sixties parlance, amounted to a "crash pad" where you'd storm in at eight in the morning and leave soon after stirring for mid-afternoon cornflakes. "We had bunk beds and a little kitchen to cook," said Johnnie Law, "in two rooms, each the size of a police cell."

Under the circumstances, it might have cost him much effort to do so, but the group funnyman would reclaim enough of his ebullience to bark "Raus! Raus! Schnell! Schnell!" when, after a couple of hours of rest, the new arrivals left an ill-lit lair to sort out a small but intense cluster of instrument cases, amplification and unassembled drum kit in preparation for its first recital outside the United Kingdom. A *bar-frau* looked on from beyond the dust-specked half-light of footlights still being tested as a squeak of feedback pitched the unknown musicians into a mildly hysterical "warm-up" (later referred to as a "soundcheck"). After the second chorus, the number came to an abrupt finish, only to recommence after a few low mutterings and yet more "one-twos" through the house public address (PA) system.

Too quickly advanced the time for the peacocks to show their feathers. Alert with hunger and beyond sleep, the group take most numbers too fast; transitions from choruses to middle-eights are muddled; arrangements are shot to pieces; up to three instrumentalists abandon unison riffs to take off in simultaneous cacophony, and the guitarist kicks off 'Roll Over Beethoven' a full tone flat in an atmosphere of cigarette smoke, chatter and suffocating heat solidifying by the minute as more and more teenagers arrive to ascertain the difference between this British outfit and the one that was there the previous week.

A combination of bloody-mindedness and knee-knocking terror

render the group's chief show-off unshowy to the point of inertia until an exasperated order from the wings to move himself. He perks up, flickering across the boards when not required to hog the microphone. Putting the off-stage misery of their predicament on hold too, the whole group rallies, quite tickled when anyone cries encouragement to them. From the disasters and consternations of the previous forty-eight hours comes a sudden meshing forged of the customers' gaiety and the group's own fiery-eyed gusto of bum notes, hit-or-miss soloing, sloppy rataplans and, at the forefront of it all, the raucous derangement of a man in the throes of an apparent fit. The mob almost take over – almost but not quite – as the lead singer, now pulling out every attention-grabbing trick in the book, enjoys a stylised mobbing during a reprise of 'Reelin' And Rockin''.

It's the crassest truism, but the first business of any pop artist is simply to be liked – and British groups could not have succeeded in Germany if the natives on the whole hadn't liked them – and often it wasn't immediately obvious whether or not they did. Johnnie Law and his MI5 began in Dortmund on a Tuesday – traditionally a quiet night – and, recalled Law, "After we finished the first spot at eight-fifteen pm, all the people left, and we were wondering what we'd done wrong – but about twenty minutes later, the place was packed because all those who'd been there first had come back with all their friends, having told them that there was a good group on at the Starpalast."

Nevertheless, it wasn't always a pushover. "With Gene Anthony And The Lonely Ones, we got a brilliant response," said Chris Warman, "but there was a slightly slower start when I went over with The Dowland Brothers and The Soundtracks, owing to the nature of their music – not so heavy and driving. Once established, stuff from The Everly Brothers and The Four Seasons was well received."

You could be bigger than Hitler in your home town, but no-one dared make assumptions. Even The Big Three, Liverpool's most likely lads after The Beatles, "arrived full of apprehension," said bass guitarist Johnny Gustafson, "but we went down a storm. I'll never forget the reaction that first evening: all those shouting, cheering, rowdy Germans."

Suddenly the group was home and dry as involved onlookers rushed towards the stage or clambered onto crammed tables, but, as bottle-tops popped and cigarettes were lit after the shift ended, the prevalent feeling was of deliverance. However, during wakeful periods after they had retired, the full horror of the filthy lodgings reared up in the encircling gloom: duffel bags as pillows; coats for inadequate blankets; jerking in and out of a doze before waking up shivering to open-mouthed snores and the drummer breaking wind before rising to shampoo his hair in a sink in the club toilets. After figuring out how much a Deutschmark was worth in sterling, some began squirrelling away emergency funds for the fare home, wishing that they were in hell rather than here.

With martyred nobility, they let themselves be pushed in whatever direction fate and their paymaster ordained – which boiled down to hundreds of hours on stage. "Seven hours a night, ten at weekends" it was for Ace Kefford with The Vikings in Dusseldorf – while when Dave Dee And The Bostons realised their dream of playing the Top Ten, "It was usually a case of an hour on, an hour off," said Tich, "starting at around six in the evening, and sometimes going on until seven the following morning." Gene Anthony And The Lonely Ones had it easy from eight to two-thirty am, six nights a week.

Frequently, groups were required to play twice in one evening at venues up to one hundred miles apart. Exhausting for the musicians but lucrative for Peter Eckhorn, Dave Dee And The Bostons and the Top Ten house band were often embroiled in these "round robin" productions – with many a slip between Hamburg and a newer club in Hanover. *En route*, you'd all be quietly relaxed for several kilometres until a flat tyre or shattered windscreen changed everything. The support act would be valiantly over-running when the main group reeled into the dressing room after a frightening sixty-minute dash. Minutes later, they'd shamble onto the boards to the expected uproarious greeting. Hot and bothered, there'd be collisions with microphone stands, tripping over wires and even falling into the front rows. The dimmer lights would swell on a scene not wholly welcoming. Instead of the galvanising run-down into 'Brand New Cadillac', there'd be thuds, electronic crackles, and savage oaths censored with ear-splitting feedback as the two guitarists searched for their own or somebody else's input.

Afterwards, it would be back to Hamburg, then a second journey to

Hanover before winding up for the night in the place that was your half-home. Yet, as it was with living conditions, things could be as trying in Britain. As Ace Kefford tells it: "I worked in the fruit market for about a year. As I started at five in the morning, I'd often clock-in straight from a gig – particularly if it was something like an all-nighter in Kidderminster – still wearing stage gear, and attracting comments." Phil May of The Pretty Things has yet to let slip from his memory "an eight hour stint at the Royal Academy in 1963. When I came off stage, I had blood coming up from my throat."

The Pretty Things were then fermenting in the security of the Home Counties art school circuit where their girlish tresses, if not *de rigueur*, were not the invitation to be beaten up that they were outside college portals. All outfits with hair longer than a short-back-and-sides were becoming known indiscriminately as "beat groups", and were susceptible to short-term exploitation by the kind of agent who, uninterested in career development, sold their services like tins of beans – with no money back if they tasted funny. Why should such a creature care about mismatching a loud rhythm-and-blues combo with, say, a miners' welfare institute where the norm was C&W and amplifier volume not precluding conversation. The agency commission still got paid, didn't it?

In Germany too, there were promoters who turned a hard-nosed pfennig by regarding pop musicians – who they may have found personally objectionable – as commodities to be hired, consumed and replaced when of no further use to a similarly repulsive teenage following. Yet newer venues tended to be run by younger entrepreneurs like Peter Eckhorn, who were not self-deprecating about their knowledge and love of pop, and were more understanding about awkward talent – or at least appreciated that an antagonised group might take it out on the customers.

Despite his deficit of filial affection, and the fulminations of the dismissed Jets, most British musicians found Eckhorn – like Manfred Weissleder – a fair-minded employer from whom bonuses could be expected on a good night. Other fringe benefits included Swiss-embroidered bowling jackets and personalised cigarette-lighters, each with TOP TEN CLUB HAMBURG embossed on the side. Into the bargain, the place served a better quality of beer than many rival watering-holes.

The Top Ten and other Hamburg clubs were, therefore, firmer turf for beat groups of whatever shape or size. However, though The Swinging Blue Jeans found it prudent to drop their trad repertoire overnight, other acts were living examples of the showbiz adage that the opposite of a prevailing trend is always represented to some degree. The besuited Bachelors, three young married men from Dublin, went in for rehearsed spiels, gentle comedy and close-harmony versions of good old good ones like 'I Believe', 'Charmaine' and, from the 1927 silent film of the same name, 'Ramona'. "The Bachelors were more on the fringe of things," noted Tony Sheridan, "but the audience accepted anything which seemed to be authentic, and The Bachelors were part of the British scene."

There were, nevertheless, wrong-headed presuppositions by some that beat groups had to be exclusively male – but, though all-woman outfits were considered a gimmick throughout the 1960s, some like The Liverbirds were booked time and again at the Top Ten and the Star-Club, having proved to be as capable of filling the floor with dancers as any men.

Now and then, an otherwise male amalgam had to satisfy a contractual stipulation about a "featured singer" with a different set of hormones. She might double as a dance demonstrator and passive supplier of onstage glamour, simply sitting on a strategically-placed stool in the midst of the group, dressed as Alma Cogan or as if she'd come direct from the bandanna-ed set of *Oklahoma!*. She'd keep looking patiently pretty whilst awaiting her turn to display synchronised dance steps, add vocal counterpoint and, yes, sing lead as a breath of fresh air in a sphere dominated by masculine bonding.

Barbara Harrison was to make headway in European cabaret after accompanying Faron's Flamingos to France, but often a female in a group was a mere prop. Obliged to bring a girl vocalist when offered a month at a NATO base in France in December 1963, Birmingham's Dominettes roped in the bass player's wife. "She looked great," remembered singer Steve Gibbons, "and that was all the GIs wanted." Both The Searchers and The Beatles had, on various one nighters in Britain, backed Wallsall's Tanya Day, who had a Polydor forty-five, 'Your Lips Get In The Way', and a linked slot on ITV's *Thank Your Lucky Stars* to her credit. After The Hellions carried out a similar function for her at Lakes Inn on the outskirts of Worcester, Tanya – possibly past her best – agreed to accompany them to Hamburg in order to appease the Star-Club's booker.

"Featured popular vocalists" of both sexes could be brought forward to either specialise in numbers thought inappropriate for the usual singer or to allow him a breather. Able to swoop elegantly from falsetto shriek to bass rumble in the space of a few bars, bespectacled Lou Walters, for instance, was the balladeer in Rory Storm And The Hurricanes while runtish Ringo Starr handled the semi-spoken lope of 'Alley Oop' and like humorous material.

Judging by the size of their name on the Kaiserkeller's wall posters, RORY STORM AND HIS HURRICAN (sic) were a bigger attraction than the small-lettered Beatles. More often than not in that "somebody and the somebodies" era, a token "leader" was singled out on billings. He was either the member with the most visual appeal, the most potent vocalist or, in a perfect world, one who combined both. The Alex Harvey Soul Band had a stylish enough resident crooner for a while, but Harvey himself proved of harder mettle in any power struggles for applause. "Alex had great tonsils," agreed Jimmy Grimes. "He was a powerful singer and he wrecked guitars by twisting and bending them when he played. He could handle a crowd and seemed to know what to say and what the crowd wanted."

If you had that indefinable something else – the "common touch" maybe – possessed by the likes of Harvey, Dave Dee, Beryl Marsden and Rory Storm, you didn't have to be brilliant technically to go down well at the Top Ten, Star-Club *et al*. In context, the dominance of spontaneity over expertise was not unattractive, even charming, as such a focus of all eyes was able, via a wink and a grin diffused to the general populace, to make any watching individual feel – for a split-second anyway – like the only person that mattered to the group in the whole of Hamburg.

Gruelling work schedules on top of accommodation politely described as spartan could also infuse the clumsiest rank-and-file player with impressive self-confidence. No longer exchanging worried glaces behind the excesses of the front man, the charmer unzipped his bashful half-smile, the funnyman's theatrical extravagance unfurled, and the others started coming out of their shells too.

On the pavement outside, the casual music lover is brought up short by the metallic beat of a record from within stabbing the evening air. Obscurely captivated, he listens for a few minutes. It isn't a record after all but a group. Entering, he merges into the shadows before taking a chance on the dance floor after he's got used to the weird accents in the continuity, the engagingly ragged dissimilarity to the contrived splendour of pop stars on German television, and the refreshing lack of scripted Bobby playfulness.

The characters on stage are an unruly bunch, indulging in much bucking and shimmying like composites of every rock 'n' roller he'd ever admired. Now openly fascinated, he finds himself fretting when they flag, cheering when they get their second wind, and glowing when a number comes across particularly well. With coat torn off and tossed aside, and shirt hanging out, the vocalist pours sweat as the group drive him through another crescendo of a song. Between the microphones, the guitarists scuttle back and forth like machine-gunners drunk with bloodlust, mowing down krauts. Covering them are the heavy artillery of the bass player and the rifle cracks of the snare drum.

The set ends with a thunderous hurrah. A few iron-bladdered fans remain near the lip of the stage to better gawk at the group after the break. "On my life, they used to dance to the tuning-up," exclaimed Trevor "Dozy" Davies of Dave Dee's Bostons.

Dee and his boys sugared their performances with varying degrees of deliberate comedy as demonstrated by Dave's maniacal laughter in 'Ahab The Arab', and Dozy flinging down his guitar to jump into the singer's outstretched arms during 'Little Darlin''. Such routines – and those of The Barron Knights and The Rockin' Berries – were refined in Germany. In Hamburg too, other outfits became aware of amusing aspects of their act of which they'd once been all but unconscious. Nowadays, a singer could barely suppress an urge to laugh out loud during the lengthy and emotion-charged recitation in 'Are You Lonesome Tonight'. Riding roughshod over the language barrier, less subtle clowns like Freddie And The Dreamers also tied the loose ends of antics that encompassed trouser-dropping, can-can kicks, slapstick, amateur acrobatics and that element of lip-trembling pathos that some find endearing.

That we had ways of making the Germans laugh capsized the notion that, with no tradition of stand-up comedy, their humour was either candlelit Brechtian satire or over-earnest and laced with moral message *à la* Sigmund Freud with his crafty little pleasantry about two Jews discussing personal hygiene. One says to the other: "I have a bath every week." The second Jew replies: "I bathe once a year whether I need to or not." Thus the second Jew's insistence on his cleanliness only serves to convict him of uncleanliness.

No doubt it was the way Sigmund told 'em. Have you heard the one about the fellow in a *Kaffeehaus* who orders coffee without milk? Half an hour later, the harassed waitress pants up to his table with "I'm very sorry, but I can't bring you coffee without milk. Would you like coffee without cream instead?" It probably loses a lot in translation.

However inadvertently, British groups seized upon a type of German nonsense humour called *Blodelei*. It defies succinct interpretation, but assisted their acceptance by crowds no longer depressed by a war that was a playpen memory at most, and determined to be frivolous even if it killed them.

CHAPTER FIVE

Wonderful Land

"I would have stayed on in Germany had I been a bit more mature at the time. Had I a crystal ball in the 1960s, I would have stayed and cemented myself a nice future there"
Chris Warman (Lonely Ones)

As the early evening mass exodus from the Unilever offices approached, the chaps still slept like the dead. It had been a long night because a fleet was in. Afterwards, they'd been riper for mischief than usual, stayed up later, and it was likely that they'd lie-in until an envoy from the club burst in, jabbing at his watch. Groaning expletives, they'd stir and within the hour be ploughing through another round of stupid songs about fast cars and girls with all their customary verve. As Tich put it: "You got up, had a wash, and it all started again."

For the first time in your life, you were totally independent and self-reliant with no parents, teachers or foremen around – and yet, when you weren't either playing or propping up a bar, you were sleeping through it. "When you got to bed by eight o'clock in the morning," said Ricky Richards, "they'd be waking you up to be on stage in half an hour. It was bloody hard to find time to do other things apart from days off or if you went to bed as soon as you finished – but who did that in Hamburg?"

However, if only to dispel the odour of their hovels from their clothes, the British musicians were generally up and about by mid-afternoon, becoming anonymous wanderers anywhere beyond the immediate vicinity of St Pauli. On the first rest day, they might have walked everywhere, but for the next, they'd be bold enough to buy tickets at the U-bahn – underground train station – or board a tram for outings to, say, the antique shops round the *Gansemarkt* (Goose Market); the museum containing the largest model railway ever constructed, the zoo or the mammoth Dom funfair where Freddy Quinn's vocal version of 'La Palama' seemed to engulf the arena of the dodgems throughout 1961.

If in more cultured mood, there were central Hamburg's art galleries, or, if you were able to catch the gist of the dialogue, its theatres and cinemas. Though less so than in rural regions, some city amusements were also regulated by traditions of carnivals, beer festivals and folk fayres like August's *Hummelfest*.

Sometimes, alien denizens of the Reeperbahn would take pot-luck on whatever entertainment an unknown part of the city might hold. From a bric-a-brac shop in one such suburb, Paul McCartney and John Lennon returned to the Kaiserkeller with jackboots and Afrika Corps *kepis* decorated with swastikas.

Others might turn their backs on city bricks altogether to roam on foot or bicycle the open spaces and nature reserves than were more extensive in and around Hamburg than many other *Lander*. Chief among them were the moorlands of Luneberg Heath – near where Ricky Richards had his accident – the birch woods beside the Elbe estuary, and the water meadows of the Alster with its circling gulls, promenade and lake – where George Harrison had once needed much persuasion to remove his winkle-pickers in order to stabilise a rowing boat.

You couldn't hire such a vessel in winter when the boatshed, the Dom and other amenities were closed too, and frozen pitches cancelled home games by St Pauli football club. Listening to the record-player and like indoor pursuits became more attractive as the seasons changed from gold to marble and the cold from the *Westarweg* – North Sea – struck like a hammer.

Hamburg's weather is as changeable as that in Glasgow, so quickly can a trace of vapour in a bright sky grow to a heaven-darkening thunderstorm of Wagnerian intensity. The aftermath of heavy flooding during 1962's rainy autumn was enormous damage and the drowning of over three hundred citizens. Overall, the winter climate is often bitter enough for ice-floes to clog up the Elbe. More frequent is the coming of *Schmuddelwetter*, that "dirty", windy drizzle that is almost but not quite a gale.

Summers are generally hotter than in Britain: hot enough for those sufficiently foolhardy to take a dip from the mudbanks of an Elbe suffused with a soup of sewage and industrial pollutants from as far away as Dresden. Why risk disease when there were plenty of municipal swimming pools? A lot of the smallest half-timbered communities had them – so it was discovered when the visitors were able to explore the arcadian Germany of yore.

"Mad" King Ludwig II's fairy-tale palaces and mountain greenery in Bavaria were too distant, but a few hours' driving could take in the reaches of the Weser where Snow White took refuge with the Seven Dwarfs two centuries before Walt Disney got in on the act. If you started out early enough, you could cover in a day the valleys near Frankfurt, birthplace of the Brothers Grimm, where the Sleeping Beauty slumbered in her enchanted castle, and sheep now nibbled the grass of ancient battlegrounds with not a leaf stirring, a touch of mist on the sunset horizon and a bird chirruping somewhere. Only the whoosh of an occasional aeroplane need remind you of the Coca-Coca century back on the Grosse Freiheit.

If there was time on hotter days, group members might flee landlocked Hamburg for picnic excursions to the North Sea – grey rather than Elbe-brown, though rougher and cooler than both the English Channel and the Baltic. At a resort like Ostsee, musicians pallid with night life could recharge their batteries, and get their collective nerve back to rock till dawn. If there was no work that evening, they might venture to Timmendorfer Strand – where it was sometimes mild enough for night-long palavers round a camp-fire of driftwood – or even go up the throat of Denmark to breathe the purer air shrouding the North Frisian island of Sylt, linked by causeway to the mainland, and containing nudist beaches.

The most intrepid day-trippers tended to be those with greatest command of the language. As it was – and is – second only to French as the main non-classical foreign tongue taught in British secondary schools, boys from A-streams may have had some German already. The most articulate of all was Spencer Davis who, following the sundering of his Saints, had begun a degree course in German at Birmingham University in 1960. During a required period of study in Berlin, he developed a liking for Pilsner beer and the Dust Bowl ditties of Woody Guthrie – quaffing the first and performing the second in the bisected city's beatnik dives. All work and no play might have rewarded Spencer with first- rather than second-class honours – but he was to put aside recurrent thoughts of teaching German when his Spencer Davis Group went professional in 1964, just prior to a stint at the Star-Club that August.

SDN Davis, BA (Hons) was innumerable cuts above those hoi-polloi whose smatterings of German had been confined to exclamatory expressions like "Schweinhund!", "Dummkopf!", "Wunderbar!", "Donner Und Blitzen!" and "Jawohl, Herr Kommandant!", picked up from the homicidal deeds of kraut-bashing "Captain Hurricane" in *Buster*, and *War Picture Library*, a more chin-up comic publication which differentiated between fanatical Nazis and plucky Britishers.

The natives of Hamburg were inclined to speak better English than the new arrivals spoke German, and phrase books and constant exposure to the language enabled most musicians to make themselves understood, however haltingly, in "Dinglish", a mixture of Deutsche and English. They caught and assimilated a local accent – slightly nasal with a quickish delivery – and the Low German dialect that persisted in common speech in the port area. Just as subtly, living in the Federal Republic could affect the grammar, sentence structure and vocabulary of letters home. Now and then, for example, you might begin a common noun with a capital letter.

During his weeks at the Top Ten in early 1961, Gerry Marsden took commendable pains to learn announcements in German – though these were interrupted in heated moments by English swear words. More calculated was the habit amongst British musicians of warping lyrics so that Ben E King's most evocative ballad began "I picked my nose in Spanish Harlem", as a verse of 'Oh Boy!' from Buddy Holly did "All my life, I've been waiting/tonight there'll be no masturbating". Learning all the time, German singers would be parroting them deadpan, as merrily unaware of any vulgarity in them as the journal that printed Tony Sheridan's transcription of the words of 'Skinny Minnie', riven with added obscenities.

Appalling behaviour of a more physical kind from certain of our rock 'n' roll ambassadors, offstage and on, was symptomatic of that insular arrogance peculiar to certain Britons abroad that would come to a head in the soccer hooliganism of the 1980s. Fantastic boorishness would explode like shrapnel all around the Reeperbahn as, brutalising themselves, an ignoble group from, say, a posh part of Essex came on like rough, untamed cockneys. With faces asking to be punched, they'd unwind after the last session by lunaticking into a more upmarket club, everyone sniggering along with Ted, the arch-loudmouth, as he blows a kiss at the heel-clicking doorman; churlishly dishevels a seated woman's sculpted beehive, and marches up to get the drinks in, with outstretched arm salute and a finger across his upper lip. You know the type: every gentleman is a homosexual, every woman a tart, every German a Nazi – and every minute has to be filled with sixty seconds of offensive twittering. "Are you the bastard that bayoneted my uncle?" would issue from the side of Ted's mouth when simply ordering a lager from a barman. There was no answer to that – not in words anyway.

On the boards, he didn't know when to stop either. The rejoinders he used against hecklers were effective, but he couldn't prevent himself hastening their retreat by flinging after them a verbal stone – or worse, as exemplified by John Lennon, by kicking a drunk in the face from the footlights. Needless to say, he and Ted were at the forefront of their respective groups' cursing, "mooning", mock-Hitlerian speeches, goosestepping, *Sieg Heils*, jibes about the War (like "We won. You came second") to audiences, uncomprehending, disbelieving or shocked into laughter.

Ted had just about been able to say boo to a goose back in Essex where he'd lived a suppressed life with his sermonising monologist of a father, and a mother who was the only one in the house allowed to lose her temper, get neuroses and be unreasonable. Once, gazing at magazines of female lingerie had been the depths of Ted's depravity, and, during the journey to Hamburg, he'd fought to control his features when the other fellows belched and used bad language.

It had happened gradually, but hidden prudity flowed out of him as the liquor – and the Great Freedom – flowed in. Now, from burbling away convivially with others who weren't in the mood for sensible conversation either, Ted's lips moved mechanically and loudly with unfunny toilet-talk about krauts, queers and tit, and every situation was an avenue for grotesque unholier-than-thou exhibitionism by one who had never been a life-and-soul of any party before. Privately, he was reviled not as the most John Bullish, homophobic and bigoted male chauvinist as ever walked the planet but a pathetic fantasist, hardly existing when denied an audience, who tried to smokescreen an encrusted hesitancy with respect to sex.

He was determined that nothing was going to show him up as the virgin boy he was. His voice got louder, jokes coarser, eyes brighter and face redder before he staggered off to vomit. The gridiron of a drain fogging in and out of focus was the final vision to penetrate Ted's brain as he slumped into the velvet-blue oblivion that was the prelude to the first unfake hangover he'd ever nurtured.

If such a fellow's nice auntie heard about him behaving like that, it'd break her heart, but the only way she'd know was if it got into the British papers. Yet the stories filtered homewards, and myths took hold. Many of the antics attributed to UK rock 'n' rollers in Hamburg were improved with age like the one about a puddle of vomit in one group's digs that, cosseted like a rare greenhouse bloom over several weeks, gave life to a monstrous fungus of triffid-like size and properties. "Someone might have been sick in a dressing room once," agreed Tich Amey, "and, when it was there for a couple of days, somebody else might have stuck a flag in it to take the mick out of the cleaners – and then the next day, it'd be gone."

Escapades as nauseating took place under the alibi of a stage act or were the result of embellishments, relocations and retimings of the truth. Either that or they were originated by others. Beatle bass player Stuart Sutcliffe's use of a human hose to try for a direct hit on the seat of a moped parked below his third-storey student flat in Liverpool was the blueprint for the golden rain that squirted from John Lennon's bladder over a Reeperbahn balcony onto the wimples of promenading nuns. Lennon's foul-mouthed "sermons" in English from that same balcony were as nothing in comparison to Kingsize Taylor's dramatic reiteration to the syllable – from the Star-Club stage – of one of the Führer's more incendiary speeches.

To Tony Sheridan, Lennon *et al* "weren't that rough at all". More shocking than a Beatle farting noisily in the Star-Club dressing room in

A teenage Tony Sheridan rockin' at the 21's in 1958

Sin City at its apotheosis. The Star-Club is just below the "TABU" sign

Unlike the Kaiserkeller, the Top Ten was advantaged by its location on the Reeperbahn itself

Johnnie Law And The Tremors in the ruins of the Star-Club

The Star-Club was to be as famous a landmark in Hamburg as the Cavern in Liverpool

The front line of The Jets – (l-r) Pete Wharton, Colin Milander, Tony Sheridan and Ricky Richards – slay 'em at the Top Ten

Street of Windows resident Wilma relaxes at the Blue Peter with (l-r) Del Ward, Colin Milander, Horst Fascher and Ricky Richards

The latter-day Jets: (l-r standing) Ricky Richards, Ian Hines, Chas Beaumont and (seated) Del Ward

Paul Raven, circa 1958/9, who was to
trouble the world later as "Gary Glitter"

Vince Taylor

Rory Storm

Ritchie Blackmore as one of The Three
Musketeers

The Star-Club's galaxy

By 1963, touring US icons were including the Star-Club on their European itineraries

In the 1980s, the Star-Club was reborn away from the heart of the Reeperbahn

Cliff Bennett

(L-r) Johnny Gustafson of The Big
Three and fan Monika Pricken

Joey Dee has pride of place
among various Rebel Rousers
and Starliters

Cliff Bennett And The Rebel
Rousers pose before the Star-
Club backdrop

The Fortunes

The Rattles

Johnny Kidd And The Pirates

The Mojos

BRUNO KOSCHMIDER BETRIEBE

Tanzpalast der Jugend

Kaiserkeller
Kaiserhütte
Hamburg

Sanssouci
Künstlerkeller
Bremerhaven

Hauptanschrift:
Hamburg 4, Gr. Freiheit 36
Tel. 31 07 63

Postscheckkonto:
Hamburg 2353 06

Bankkonto:
Commerzbank A.G.
Hamburg - St. Pauli
Konto Nr. 3382

The Management (BRUNO KOSCHMIDER BETRIEBE) and the musicians/singers formed to the Rock'n'Roll type band THE JETS, consisting of MR JAMES MACKEN (band-leader), MR PETER WHARTON, MR TONY SHERIDAN, MR RICKY RICHARDS and MR COLIN MILANDER, agree to the following contract.

① The above mentioned band is engaged to perform at THE KAISERKELLER from 1st JULY 1960 to 15th JULY 1960 with extention until 31st JULY 1960 which includes a 3 day advance notice of quitting.

② The daily performance will be 5 hours from TUESDAY through FRIDAY, 7 hours on SATURDAY and SUNDAY. MONDAY is off (no performance).

③ Salary for every performance at 30DM per person.

④ A set of drums can be used by the band for reasons of performance at THE KAISERKELLER under the full liability of the band-leader which means that MR JAMES MACKEN has to cover all expenses of repair in case of any damage.

⑤ Each performance has to start EXACTLY on time. The management reserves the right to deduct 5DM per person each time the performance is delayed by fault of members of the band.

⑥ While on stage, the musicians are not allowed to eat or smoke. Their dress should be clean. Good appearance and behaviour of language is required. Conversation with the public by use of the microphone is not desired.

⑦ Lodging is entirely at the expense of the members of the band. However, the management has no objection that the available two rooms at the establishment are used for lodgings under the provision that this place shall be kept extremely clean by the members of the band. NO WOMEN ARE ALLOWED IN THESE ROOMS.

⑧ The members of the band are under no circumstances allowed to perform in any other place but THE KAISERKELLER during the period of this contract.

⑨ All instructions given by the band-leader have to be obeyed by all members of the band.

⑩ This contract may be dismissed immediately if any of the detailed paragraphs are neglected.

KAISERKELLER
Inh. Bruno Koschmider
HAMBURG-ST. PAULI
Große Freiheit 36 - Tel. 31 07 63

Tanzpalast der Jugend

The Jets' Kaiserkeller contract. Note that "NO WOMEN ARE ALLOWED IN THESE ROOMS"!

the presence of Little Richard was a member of The Big Three clad in nothing but a pinafore beneath the Star-Club proscenium; Ozzy Osbourne of Black Sabbath bounding on covered from head to toe in purple emulsion, or one of The Undertakers – or was it one of The Big Three or US singer Davy Jones? – donning a gorilla suit and emptying several Freiheit bars before *Polizei* intervention.

That these incidents, disturbing though they were, are among the most told tales demonstrates the mild nature of skylarking that was no more harmful than that of more extrovert (or inebriated) members of the audience. "Halfway through a set at the Star-Club one night," said Colin Manley, then of The Remo Four, "we heard something behind us. A sailor was relieving himself against a painted doorway on the backdrop, and with his free hand waving, was yelling for us to play some Chuck Berry numbers."

Much as some musicians made themselves out to be frightful desperados, they would cry off at the last fence during authenticated instances of attempts to mug this or that pie-eyed sailor who'd been sufficiently impressed by the show to stand them a meal. Shoplifting sprees, nonetheless, were seen as more the stuff of life's small change – and, in many cases, less a delinquent pastime than a blow struck at poverty when you were down to your last pfennig with no sign of any wages from the club owner: *we haff this week many problem with flow of cash...* "Shoplifting was not for fun but out of necessity," confessed Johnnie Law. "Me and The MI5's bass player would put on the biggest coats we could find and go into supermarkets and steal food. One day, we stole a bottle of champagne and a big duck."

When a group was flush, however, certain St Pauli restaurateurs came to accept the splattered wallpaper, the broken crockery, the mucky carpets and the stained, cigarette-holed table-cloths that resulted from late night chimps' tea-parties with beer sprayed from shaken-up bottles, and airborne bread rolls, legs of chicken, spaghetti, chips and like foodstuffs.

Sometimes. it would slop over into working hours, especially in clubs where musicians could avail themselves of free ale and salad – which could be consumed in installments on stage. Squarer meals could be scrounged from obliging barmaids; by striking up shallow acquaintances with any mug with a pocketful of Deutschmarks, or "by invitation from local people," said Chris Warman, "who, I think, felt sorry for us." Further valuable pointers for light-walleted UK groups in Germany were passed on by old hands. "We found that Davy Jones was a master of survival," said Johnnie Law. "You could go anywhere with him and get everything for nothing. He taught us a lot of tricks. After we finished – anywhere between two and four in the morning – we'd go to a bar with maybe an accordion and drums playing. Davy would be up singing, and we'd be drinking and eating and wondering how we were going to pay, but bosses of these places would be so pleased with Davy that they always waived the bill."

No *bon mots* about "fraternising with the enemy" would ensue if your benefactor was a Yank. Iain Hines and Tony Sheridan were befriended by leathernecks from USS Fiske, a destroyer on a goodwill visit to Germany. Gifts pressed upon them included lighters, packets of king-sized American cigarettes – and a T-shirt each. The fronts of these both bore a silhouette of the vessel, its name and, indicating its class, the unfortunate initials "DDR" – which also stood for Deutsche Democratic Republic, the "red" communist zone. This drew hard looks from the jingoistic passers-by as Tony and Iain wore them back to the Top Ten.

Whilst on board the Fiske, the two had been able to stuff themselves with turkey, mashed potatoes, meatloaf, greens, black-eyed peas, apple pie and cream. Such a rich and enormous meal was a rare treat for a musician obliged to feed himself as cheaply as possible, and acquiring quickly a taste for local fare. "When we first arrived at the Kaiserkeller," remembered Ricky Richards, "we were starving after a long journey. They fixed us up with a couple of these *Bratwursts* – the Hamburg equivalent of fish and chips. They didn't taste too good at first, but they did after a while."

Like "luvvie" guest houses in Britain serving dinner when repertory actors rolled in after curtain-down, St Pauli's eating houses catered too for those for whom day had become night. The Blue Peter, for example, didn't even open until three am. On the menu here – and in Der Flunde, the Mambo Shanke, Harold's Schnellimbiss and the twenty-four-hour Nimitz Bar – were *Deutsch Bifsteak* (hamburger), *Berliner* (jam doughnut), *wurst* sausages, *Kartofelpuffers* (potato pancakes), *Apfel Kuchen* (pancakes with apple purée), *Aalsuppe* (eel soup) and *Labskaus,* favoured by German sailors and consisting of a melange of corned beef, herrings, mashed potato, chopped gherkins, topped with a fried egg. Sounds scrumptious, eh? Germans were to gaze as pointedly at individual British peculiarities such as the Coca-Cola laced with melting ice-cream imbibed by the bass player of The Flintstones, and a one-off sardines-boiled-in-cocoa digested by a musician from Cardiff, but the Fatherland's strange combinations of meat and fish were exotic to British palates coarsened by beans on toast in flyblown wayside cafes.

Fast food was available from hot dog stands and *erfrishung* (buffet) bars, but there was also Chinese and Indian cuisine as well as specialist diners such as Zum Pferdestalle. Had he known then that this translated as "The Horses Stable", it may have been possible for first-time customer Ricky Richards to guess what kind of steak was on his plate: "We didn't know at the time that it was horsemeat, but it was cheap and delicious." At the Fischmarkt in St Pauli every Sunday, a scent of death might whet your appetite after you selected from a huge gurgling tank an anxious fish to be netted, slaughtered and gutted before your very eyes.

Dick Taylor would recall that "Tony Howard – who worked for our manager – brought to our attention how close the fare in the food shops and Schnell Imbiss establishments was to the Jewish food he was used to in the East End of London. I suppose it was a kind of legacy from the pre-Nazi days." Perhaps providing a stronger psychological link with home would be a late "brunch" of cornflakes *mit Milch*, something with chips and tea as dished up in many Freiheit cafes. Of greater solace – not wholly nutritional – was building up an appetite for the same food by strolling to the canteen within the "Seamen's Mission" – the British Sailors Society building along Johannis Bollwerk down in the docks. Also boasting a library, rooms to let and a mess room with ping-pong table and upright piano, this was to become for British beat groups what the Down Under Club in London's Earl's Court – "Kangaroo Valley" – is for *emigré* Australasians.

What if you couldn't afford to eat out? "I was sending money back to London to my wife and child so I didn't have much to live on," sighed Paul Raven. "I decided that eating out was too expensive so I bought one of those small electric cookers plus a kettle, a frying pan and a saucepan, and started to cook my own meals." Most tired musicians, however, couldn't be bothered. "We didn't cook very much," admitted Johnnie Law, "just living on one meal a day and making sandwiches with tea. Our main thing was eggs: fried, boiled, scrambled, omelettes."

As an unvaried diet that approximated home cooking consoled a nostalgic stomach, so more cerebral melancholias were either exorcised or exacerbated through tuning into the BBC Home Service on Sunday at noon for *Two-Way Family Favourites* followed by *The Billy Cotton Band Show* and *The Navy Lark* with their soothing connotations of Yorkshire pudding, Bird's custard and armchaired languor. Neither did some musicians fail to miss *The Clitheroe Kid*, *Round The Horne* and *Hancock's Half Hour*, and irritate others with re-enactions of 'I Was Monty's Treble', 'Bridge Over the River Wye' and further sketches from the lately discontinued *Goon Show*, as popular and off-beat as *Monty Python's Flying Circus* would be when the decade ended.

Goonish humour could pervade all aspects of a group's life from stage act to postal correspondence. As well as running jokes, day-to-day trivia, and requests for parcels of comestibles not immediately available in Germany, letters to family might also embrace ruminations on news read in UK newspapers bought a day late at the Hauptbahnhof (main station) – and assurances of impending ascents to fame and wealth.

Though these were founded mostly in wishful thinking, the Freiheit was to provide training for many future hit parade contenders now that links with Britain had been established, and its pop entertainers were streaming in to wipe their shoes on the thresholds of the clubs. After London and Merseyside, other cities and shires – and even distant realms of the Commonwealth – had been scoured for talent and, by 1961, their sundry dialects were resounding round St Pauli, covering all waterfronts from Dave Lee And The Staggerlees' Cornish burr to the Hibernian trill of The Crescendos. Manchester supplied The Raging Storms, Newcastle The Gamblers, Birmingham The Rockin' Berries, Southampton Ricki And The Hi-Lites and, in May 1963, the stockbroker town of Weybridge in

Surrey surrendered The Nashville Teens, following a radical personnel reshuffle. Tayside's Hi-Four moved from Cologne's Storyville to Hamburg's Top Ten – while Tex Roberg And The Graduates blew in from the Transvaal via London to show the Star-Club that South Africans could rock out as long and as hard as the best of them.

More typical, geographically at least, were a Bournemouth duo, David and Keith Dowland, in artistic debt to The Everly Brothers. With a backing combo that included Chris Warman from The Lonely Ones and guitarist Roy Phillips (later organist with The Peddlers), they were as synonymous with Southampton's Royal Pier as Bern Elliott And The Fenmen were with Crayford Town Hall and the Railway Tavern in Dartford. Much changed from the schoolboys begging for interval spots at the Scala Ballroom, now Bern and his merry men were a Medway town's "answer" to Cliff Richard And The Shadows – or Carl Wayne And The Vikings – but there were redeeming features in them for parochial R&B obsessives like Dick Taylor and Phil May. "We used to go and watch them," recalled Phil, "but we would wait for them to play their two Chuck Berry numbers."

Phil would find more to praise after Elliott And The Fenmen underwent a further change from working the Top Ten and then the Star-Club. A visit to Germany was to have a similarly beneficial effect on Tottenham's Chris Farlowe And The Thunderbirds, especially with the addition of guitarist Albert Lee who, with drummer (and future Nashville Teen) Barry Jenkins, had been in Hamburg with The Nightsounds in 1962.

Like Tony Sheridan before him, Lee was a 2I's veteran, and had backed Larry Parnes' ciphers. He had also replaced Jimmy Page in Neil Christian's Crusaders, and developed a fretboard harshness that proved well-matched to Farlowe's style – all strangled gasps and anguished roars – when the pair joined forces, circa 1964. As we shall see, a cordial encounter on the cross-channel ferry between Wolverhampton's Steve Brett And The Mavericks and another local group, The In Betweens, was to have more pronounced a bearing on the lives of the former's Neville "Noddy" Holder And The In Betweens' Dave Hill and Don Powell.

At destinations throughout Germany, an outgoing act, loading up to leave, would often meet a replacement group, a-twitter with excitement. Some members could do little more than pose on stage with guitars as they'd done before wardrobe mirrors (and imaginary thousands of adoring fans) with tennis racquets. Along for the laugh too, more adept colleagues would cover up for them until the joke was over. Sometimes, it was nipped in the bud before the outfit had even left Britain.

"UK agents did not take just anybody," said Chris Warman. "The offer for Gene Anthony And The Lonely Ones to go came from auditions in London with a guy called Marshall. I remember the auditions as being quite tough. Marshall was ignorant about music, but obviously a good businessman."

Other judges could hear more precisely whatever might have been technically wrong. After returning to Britain to back Gene Vincent – then domiciled in Kent – Iain Hines was entrusted to bring over an all-purpose house band for the Top Ten. With himself on organ, this came to consist of the eight-piece Carl Fenn Combo plus Rikki Barnes and two singers – a Canadian balladeer and, on Reg Calvert's books as an R&B shouter, Baby Bubbly. As well as a salary rather than a wage, Hines had been tantalised with promises of his own flat on the premises, and free drinks and meals in an adjoining steakhouse when courted by Peter Eckhorn to be officially responsible for finding other acts for the club.

From Iain's native Glasgow came The Bobby Patrick Big Six – via a try-out in a functions room of a London pub – and The Alex Harvey Soul Band. He also secured Dave Dee And The Bostons for a first Top Ten residency, and briefer stints (often with alternating shifts of ten days in Hanover) for The Beatmen, The Flintstones, The Blue Diamonds from Worthing, and, of the same kidney as Chris Farlowe And The Thunderbirds, Birmingham's Jimmy Powell and his Five Dimensions. Other hosts to such guests included Lee Curtis and his All-Stars, The Outlaws and The Jaybirds, a Nottingham trio whose high-velocity guitarist Alvin Dean – later Alvin *Lee* of Ten Years After – was, according to a 1964 edition of *Midland Beat*, "considered by many the best in the Midlands".

Almost as important as musicianship then was a sharp corporate persona that suggested that an imminent appearance on *Thank Your*

Lucky Stars was in the works, and that a venue would be silly not to book you. Gerry And The Pacemakers, for instance, sported "GP"-monogrammed royal blue blazers with gold buttons and red handkerchiefs for their three months at the Top Ten in July 1961 – while Rory Storm And The Hurricanes first performed at the Kaiserkeller in matching black-and-white winkle-pickers – gold for Storm – and bright red stage suits (light pink for the lovely Rory). Bespoken by a hometown tailor too, The Alex Harvey Soul Band was a sartorial vision in silver lamé with gold bow-ties and white high-heeled boots. However, looking more like cricketers than pop stars, Johnnie Law and his MI5 favoured a simpler get-up of striped ties, dark coats and white trousers. To the expected denim hosiery, The Swinging Blue Jeans added striped blazers, while The Beatles on acquiring black leather jackets (*sans* lapels) and trousers, became very beetle-like in colour and texture when these garments were combined with their grease-glistening pompadours.

More conventional coiffeur, identical Italian suits and stern demeanour tended to give many a group a resemblance to a Mafia hit squad – though much of the menace was dissipated when onlookers got close enough to notice frayed cuffs, dandruff, grimy collars, patches, cheeks darkening with stubble, and indelible stains born of sweat and spillage: all the wear-and-tear expected of people obliged to use public baths (if open) and improvise laundries from communal cold-water sinks, gas rings and indoor washing lines in the enveloping fug of a sunless, crowded room with a film of dust over everything.

Some groups gave up all pretence of a uniform after individuals accrued accoutrements peculiar to themselves like cowboy boots, medallions, bat-winged blousons, leopard-skin cuffs and stringy bandit beards. Next, a messed-up, deadbeat group would lurch onstage in everyday attire; glamour deferring to comfort (and anticipating the hirsute, motley look of The Rolling Stones, Pretty Things and Downliners Sect) – though nearly all such scruffbags were to revert to varying degrees of costumed smoothness back in Britain to please big-shots prowling England's northern provinces during the Merseybeat craze in 1963.

Over in Hamburg where the backstabbing adherent to UK chart climbing had no meaning, rivalry would dissolve into an informal

;0 0   0 0

sense of solidarity when musicians congregated in the prescribed rendezvous where, on terms of fluctuating equality, they could small-talk, compare notes, spread rumours, betray confidences – and borrow, trade and exchange advice about equipment. Tony Sheridan sold a guitar to, respectively, Alvin Dean and Albert Lee, while Ricky Richards went with John Lennon to the Musikhaushummel shop in Frankfurt to help him choose the instrument that he would still be picking at the height of Beatlemania.

Success, it seemed, was always just around the corner, and every performance a triumph in retrospect as groups bragged about imminent record deals, tours of outlandish countries and a surefire certainty of opening for Gene Vincent when he next came to Europe, continuing to behave as if these were still likely long after the trails went cold.

Johnnie Law And The MI5's propensity for gossip and exaggeration was as profound as the next group's, but "What I loved about Hamburg," said Johnnie, "was that everybody got on great. There was never a hint of competition." There were inevitable personality clashes – especially when charismatic new acquaintances disrupted the intimacy of old friendships – but, unwinding over foaming *biersteins*, a companionable atmosphere bred matey abuse, coded hilarity and reminiscences of what little a guitarist from Penzance had experienced mutually with a Geordie organist.

When they went back to work, sessions were sufficiently flexible for public displays of *esprit de corps*. If Pete Best, The Beatles' drummer, was indisposed, Ringo Starr was only too delighted to deputise. It wasn't unusual either for outstanding showmen of the calibre of Dave Dee to vault onstage for a couple of numbers with The Blue Diamonds. On a flying visit to the Star-Club with his future wife in 1961, Ricky Richards joined The Beatles onstage, borrowing Lennon's new guitar to give 'em his 'I Go Ape' and 'C'mon Everybody' showstoppers.

At the Star-Club too, Lennon and McCartney promised to give Cliff Bennett a leg up by writing him a song if The Beatles got famous before he did. Like many other outfits, Cliff's Rebel Rousers were in a state of constant flux throughout their Hamburg residencies. A guitarist and saxophonist had withdrawn before the group had even left Middlesex. Among those passing through the ranks after the singer finally got to the Star-Club were pianist Nicky Hopkins and guitarist Bernie Watson from Lord Sutch's Savages; Bobbie Thompson who plucked lead with both Kingsize Taylor's Dominoes and The Rockin' Berries, and Roy Young, foreordained to usurp Bennett as leader of the band.

Young, allegedly, preferred his Star-Club wage to an offer to be The Beatles' keyboard player. Why waste a lifetime scrimmaging around in Britain when Hamburg was a far better financial bet? Its more voluminous index of possibilities included prospects in other Star-Clubs as far away as Berlin; the Storyvilles; newer venues like Kiel's Henry VIII; US nuclear bases in Kassel and Frankfurt, and further afield to the Netherlands, France, Italy and Spain.

To paraphrase a saying about service in the Indian Raj during the days of Empire, everyone hated Hamburg for a month and then loved it forever. This was not completely true, but it must have had its merits for Derry And The Seniors who, in spite of wretched conditions at the Kaiserkeller, tarried for a while in a club where their music was less of a draw than the cavortings of stripteasers.

Notorious even in St Pauli for its confluence of prostitutes, the Herbertstrasse was home for Ricky Richards and, until a death in the family took him back, Chas Beaumont. They'd rented a *pied à terre* there while The Jets were still at the Top Ten – and after when, with the realisation that adulation was swift to dwindle, the group were driven to deliver their goods in the Bambina, a small suburban bar.

With The Jets' foreseeable disbandment in the air, Ricky had been awake when a telegram arrived for Chas asking if he'd be interested in replacing a guitarist in a peripatetic concert party covering the US bases round Frankfurt. During the necessary telephone conversation to explain about Beaumont's bereavement, Richards talked his way onto the bill as a C&W singer, but was to end up as its compère via the silver-tongued guile that would keep him in good stead during a subsequent and ongoing career as a comedian.

Meanwhile, Tony Sheridan was back in Hamburg, performing solo at Studio X prior to a hero's return to the Top Ten after his hire-purchase debts had been settled by Peter Eckhorn. Tony remains the best-known of all Britain's rock 'n' rollers who elected to stay on in

Germany. Nevertheless, there were many other wasps round the same jam-jar. Ricky Richards was to reside there until 1970, the same year that Paul Raven reappeared in London after an entrenchment of comparable length. From a disagreeable upper room in a Hamburg club, Paul had endured somewhere similar in Kiel's Starpalast before a transition, via a billet with students from the local university, to an apartment with "the biggest bed I'd ever seen in my life, filling most of the room, which was decorated with very traditional-looking German furniture".

Raven had assumed correctly that his exile was not forever. Yet there were those who favoured virtual foreign citizenship to jousting for stardom in Britain. A sizeable contingent of individual musicians in the Hamburg Raj were Scottish; among them Isobel Bond of The Crescendos, Ricky Barnes, MI5 drummer George Gibb and, still there in 1997, Johnnie Law.

Some burnt their boats by marrying German girls. Tony Sheridan and Colin Milander were two who did; the latter even giving up music briefly to get a "proper" job in a brewery to please his in-laws. Ritchie Blackmore's courtship of his first wife was assisted by both her fluency in English, and an intimacy with British idiosyncrasies gained through previous romances with other of the kingdom's rock 'n' rollers, notably John "Beaky" Dymond of Dave Dee's Bostons.

Similarly, Hamburg photographer Astrid Kirchherr's first husband, drummer Gibson Kemp, was not the first Liverpudlian to be worthy of a second glance from her. The "beautiful sadness" of Astrid and Stuart Sutcliffe's love story has been immortalised in the 1994 bio-pic, *Backbeat*, and the tie-in Sutcliffe biography is recommended for deeper insight into the life and times of the fated youth who was The Beatles' first bass player. For all practical purposes, Stuart had left the group by the time he and Astrid announced their engagement and he recommended his art studies at the city's *Staatliche Hochschule fur bildende Kunste* (State High School for Art Instruction).

Occasionally, he would remount the stage for a blow with The Beatles again – and, later, with other visiting groups he knew. A German outfit that had lost its bass player to Tony Sheridan offered Sutcliffe the vacancy, and for a long dangerous moment the now-dormant rock 'n' roller in him peeped out, and he was tempted.

Gibson Kemp and guitarist Paul Murphy – who'd also been associated with Rory Storm – did not withdraw quite so absolutely from the music business as both were to hold down executive appointments with Polydor. Terry Crow, a vocalist with The Nashville Teens, waved the group out of sight after accepting a behind-the-scenes post at the Star-Club where Adrian Barber had become stage manager on resigning as guitarist with the remarkable Big Three, an outfit that had risen from the ashes of Cass And The Cassanovas.

An electronics boffin, Barber probably earned more by custom-building a sound system and recording facilities for the Star-Club (and, later, for New York's Peppermint Lounge) than he ever did as a musician. Among his successors in The Big Three were Brian Griffiths from The Seniors, and Paddy Chambers whose more indirect route to Hamburg was by way of a jazz trio in Paris and Faron's Flamingos – whose leader was to reunite with Chambers as The Big Three's singing bass player.

While the Three were as Big in their native Liverpool as they were on the Reeperbahn, Neil Christian was able to stroll unrecognised through a department store only a few bus stops away from the London borough where his parents still lived. Nevertheless, in Germany – not just Hamburg – it was to be so different a story that Neil moved to Munich, more convenient for his commuting to an ever-increasing workload that included promotions of his latest hits.

From mere parochial renown on Merseyside, Ian And The Zodiacs were steered likewise into the republic's charts when taken on by the Star-Club after it had stuck tentacles into artist management and records. On scoring a Number One with 'Jack The Ripper' in 1963, who could blame Middlesex's Buddy Britten And The Regents either for taking Germany for every Deutschmark they could get? For much the same reasons, The Liverbirds, Kingsize Taylor with most of his Dominoes, Tony Dangerfield And The Thrills – led by Lord Sutch's once and future bass guitarist – and an otherwise unsung Lancashire outfit called The Georgians were forever over there too.

The Remo Four were to opt for work security in St Pauli after stepping tentatively onto the slippery ice of full-time showbusiness with a trek round air bases in France as accompanists to the late Johnny Sandon. In Hamburg, they discovered that, if club work was scarce, a government department called *Arbeitsamt* – "work service" – would help. "I'd go and see a chap who dealt with films and music," revealed guitarist Colin Manley. "He'd say, 'Ah, Herr Manley. Next week, you like Munich, Saturday, yes, and perhaps Weisbaden, Sunday?' He'd fix me up with gigs with no middlemen and tax deducted at source. Travel expenses and accommodation were paid for. Germany was an amazing place to work – much better than over here."

CHAPTER SIX

You'll Never Walk Alone

"One night, a drunken sailor staggered on stage, and threw ice-cream. The bouncers dragged him out into the street and kicked him senseless"

Tony Jackson (The Searchers)

Injured in a twenty-five vehicle pile-up on an autobahn, Paul Raven was left with a mark above an eyebrow. This was not to be such a disadvantage for an aspiring pop star as might be imagined – for after his own road accident, Ricky Richards had been told by some Top Ten Brunhilda "that people didn't mind scars in Germany. It is the mark of a gentleman." Indeed, it used to be standard practice for young males at university to "drink from the soup-bowl of honour" by entering a fencing match, padded and masked but for the cheeks and lower temples. The specific goal was acquiring superficial *schlager* (sabre) gashes that would then be left open to nurture furrowed and permanent duelling cuts for public admiration.

Gymnasium rules, however, did not apply in St Pauli – nor did those of the Marquis of Queensberry when up to a dozen knuckle-dustered waiters-cum-bouncers would pile into a solitary trouble-maker amidst upturned furniture and shattered tankards. To drunken encouragement and bellowed instruction from bestial faces getting an eyeful of unofficial spectator sport, fists often swung harder than musicians who maintained ghastly grins as they soundtracked someone getting half-killed before their eyes. Yelling in stifled panic as gore cascaded from nose, mouth and elsewhere, he'd collapse onto the floorboards, squirming and trying to shield head and genitalia in a forest of piston-kicking boots.

Club proprietors viewed this kind of punishment as just and wise. Some would lend a hand themselves. At the Kaiserkeller, Tony Sheridan witnessed "a drunken Finnish sailor being pulverised, and Bruno [Koschmider] came out with a rubber truncheon and started beating the crap out of the guy now that there was no danger to himself". *Pour encourager les autres*, the blood-splattered and unresisting victim would next be raised aloft weight-lifter style and chucked out onto the pavement.

Such a person once stumbled from one Hamburg niterie with a marlinspike embedded in his neck. Another – a British seaman – was coshed on the back of the head whilst a gas-pistol was discharged in his face. Another who hadn't paid his bill at the Star-Club got off lightly when he was merely held upside down until his pockets emptied. The inside pocket of many a bouncer's own regulation-issue jacket swathed a firearm for use when goaded beyond endurance. Particularly popular was the "Belgian split", a folding rifle that did not create an unsightly bulge, and could be assembled in seconds.

All this was a trifle unsettling to most British youths. "When we saw what was going on, we wondered what we were doing there," said Dozy Davies after it had become swiftly obvious that Die Grosse Freiheit was an area shunned by nice people, and crawling with human predators. An off-duty musician learnt quickly, therefore, to go nowhere alone, carry only an essential amount of money – preferably in small notes. In any establishment, he was to do the ordering himself – and only from a price list that he was capable of reading – rather than trust a waiter or "hostess" not to fleece him of a fortune for some rotgut liquid falsely labelled "champagne". He had to pay for each glass as it came, even if he intended to have another.

If a club adhered – as was common – to the *Umsatz* (turnover) policy, no-one was permitted to nurse one beer all evening as he listened to the groups – especially if he'd got tanked-up somewhere else where bar profits were less vital. A waiter on commission would weigh up how much booze he could "accidentally" spill as, with hardly a second to himself during peak hours, he dashed from table to table with a tray loaded with tumblers of Cola-Rum and steins of lager. As well as bumping up wages with tips, the thieving "below stairs" mentality of many bar staff meant that a drinker who'd had too much could be robbed blind – or, perhaps, not so blind as they had no qualms about going through his wallet quite openly before patrons who were either pop-eyed with astonishment or too hardened by Reeperbahn life to be anything but indifferent to one of the perks of the job.

As well as duties that extended to exultant brutality whenever a customer abused a club's hospitality, its employees were also expected to issue disconcerting instructions to newly-arrived UK groups to purchase small arms and other weapons for self-preservation. Survival could involve wounding and maybe homicide to judge by the Armoury, a Hamburg store that once displayed a sub-machine gun – a bargain at three-hundred-and-fifty marks – as well as further items that could not be owned legally in Britain: flick-knives, gougers, garotters, coshes, and other more conventional aids to self-defence or keeping the peace. Tich Amey would recall his group furnishing themselves with "knives and these spring coshes, a few inches until you flicked them, and they sprang out full-length with a hard bobble on the end".

It was not unusual either for players to sport shooting irons. Temporarily disabling rather than lethal, gas-pistols (activated by starting-gun cartridges) were purchased as much for amusement as protection. "The gas guns bought by Viv Prince and Pete Watts, our respective drummer and road manager, managed to get both of them into a bit of bother," lamented Dick Taylor. "Pete didn't even get his back into Britain; the Customs knew magically that he had something tucked in by the spare wheel of his Zodiac estate car. Viv managed to get his into the country as we witnessed him incapacitating an aggressive drinking buddy with it in a Scottish car park – but that's another story..."

Another could be told about Gene Vincent by Henry Henroid, his British manager.* One night while the entourage stayed at the Hotel Metropole on the Reeperbahn, Henroid was woken by his client's wife with the worrying news that Gene had been waving a gun around, and threatening to shoot someone – anyone – before the room swam round him and he slumped into liquored unconsciousness. She'd confiscated the weapon that Henry thought was a toy until he fired it

* An ex-boxer from London, Henroid also travelled regularly to Britain to book acts for the Star-Club as Iain Hines did the Top Ten

at the ceiling. It was the gas-pistol with which Vincent would clear the Star-Club the following day during his final session at two am.

Customers might leave a club quietly, having kept their hands to themselves whilst there, but "fights were always taking place in side-alleys etc," noticed Chris Warman in Frankfurt. "Once or twice, violence started inside amongst the American and German males, usually over women. It usually sorted itself out." On the steps of the Storyville in Dusseldorf, a doorman's blow with a truncheon landed a would-be gate-crasher screaming in the gutter until he was carried away by an ambulance summoned by his compassionate assailant.

The Storyvilles were toddlers' nurseries when set against, say, the Hamburg Top Ten where, so Ricky Richards observed, "No man was employed unless he could handle himself." Typical was Walter, a short-fused Goliath capable of smashing the most able seaman insensible inside a minute. He had been appointed by Peter Eckhorn to keep riff-raff out. A grievance he had against Dave Dee abated when, said Dozy, "He came into our room on one of his nights off and picked Dave's bed up with one hand, growled something at him, let the bed drop and strode out."

During working hours, disgruntled onlookers could also make things unpleasant for a stage performer. The provocation could be either catching the eye of some rowdy's girl or not playing enough slow ones (or fast ones) to facilitate the winning of a maiden's heart by unattached swains. If pursuit of romance was either unsuccessful or not the principal objective of the evening's recreation, it could be simple irritation at a vocalist's narcissistic endeavours or a guitarist who took his time between numbers: retuning, slurping his beer, mumbling directives to the others, and acting like he wasn't at all flattered by the more-than-passive interest of the fräuleins near the front.

Beyond sexual jealousy from spiritually ugly people who wanted to make everything else ugly too, there were sometimes feelings that perhaps the music was not so good. If you couldn't play very well anyway, all you could do was either look cool – as if you were meant to be in a different key from everyone else – or scowl defiance at those commenting aloud at the flurries of bum notes hanging in the air.

The baleful nature of the catcalls and barracking was not lightened if you lashed out verbally. Back home, even if a group had done nothing to knowingly merit grief, it would transfer its equipment hurriedly from fire-door to van while a gang of silent, unsmiling ruffians, thumbs hooked in belts, watched like lynxes. However, for like-minded locals itching to start a punch-up in Hamburg, it was a waste of time to lie in immediate wait for a group that dwelt in the building where it worked. What's more, if there was to be some sort of vendetta against any musician, he was more sure of aid from St Pauli impresarios than any from their opposite numbers in Britain who couldn't give a damn about what happened to a pop group after it had quit the building any more than they did about the teenagers who had handed over the admission money.

A St Pauli club manager mightn't care much more about the customers either – and "if any musician wasn't going down well," said Johnnie Law, "he'd be sent home." Yet because a competent group had been booked for weeks rather than just a couple of hours, it was in the best interests of all concerned to ensure that its members stayed sufficiently healthy and contented to deliver each night's show.

The terrifying Walter had left his post immediately to investigate an incident reported to him by Tich Amey who, after walking a girl home between sets, had been pursued by hoodlums until, with throat constricting, skin crawling and heart pounding like a hunted beast – which he was – he rounded on them with cosh and knife. When they backed off, Tich ran like hell along the three streets back to the Top Ten.

From the Star-Club, an Irish showband between shifts had been intimidated into handing over its watches and jewellery when unable to meet a ridiculously inflated bill for two bottles of junk champagne in some clip-joint. However, a telephone call from Manfred Weissleder guaranteed the return within minutes of the property by the proprietor himself: dreadful misunderstanding, Herr Manfred...never forgive myself...When Gene Vincent complained about a difficult taxi driver, Weissleder decided that a degree of correction was required. With a few waiters in attendance, he and Vincent searched out the offending cab – which was ordered to be turned upside down.

"Sometimes, some clever bastards would come into the Top Ten and start taking the piss out of us," sneered Ricky Richards, "so over the microphone, we'd shout, 'Horst! Trouble!' All of a sudden the people taking the piss would notice that they were surrounded by a mob of heavies in white coats – like doctors. Someone would snarl 'Raus!', and they'd look up and realise that nobody could take that mob on. You'd get cut to pieces. I've seen heavy-duty bar stools being smashed over heads, blood all over the place – but it never got anywhere near the band."

When in higher office at the Star-Club, Horst Fascher wasn't above pitching in when necessary. Nevertheless, with his own brothers, Uwe and Freddy as lieutenants, he chose mostly to marshal the others, setting them onto offending parties and calling a halt before anyone actually died. Yet, sharp of wit and dress, he did not seem the type. Where were the bloodshot eyes, the cauliflower ears, the neanderthal forehead and the nose as flat as a door knocker?

At first glance, Fascher seemed ordinary, handsome enough if undersized, but his fathomless glare could cause opponents of twice his size and weight to concede some kind of intangible defeat even before he squared up to them. "He grew up as a small man in a society where small men were frowned upon and pushed around," said Tony Sheridan. "Yet he was a very hard man indeed. He was known to have the hardest punch of anyone who ever lived in Hamburg. Yet he could get very sentimental, almost tearful, over certain songs."

Horst may have been a decent fellow in a savage world, once you got to know him, but many teams of waiter-bouncers were drawn from a locality that, as Tony Sheridan put it, "was a meeting place for nutty ex-boxers, petty criminals, weight-lifters, and body-builders". Thanks to the Star-Club and similar venues, the hardest-bitten bruisers in Hamburg were kept gainfully occupied. For the most part, they enjoyed their work. "They all loved to thump people," said Tony Sheridan. "My mother had told me what sort of people they were."

You could tell from the thrust of some of their cruel and battered faces that when schoolboys, they had been as known for their persecution of the helpless as the football captain had been in his chosen area. With the rise of the sap of puberty, they'd taken to beating other lads up to impress girls. Now, grinning with sheer glee at the pain of others, they didn't always respond instantly if a fight broke out in the club, especially if it was several against one. Only when it stopped being fun – say, someone losing consciousness – would they wade in to even the odds.

Visiting his friend Paul Raven in Hamburg, the late Mike Leander found that "the atmosphere in those clubs was always dark and depressing, very hot, frequently erupting into violence, particularly after midnight – rather like being in Old Compton Street in Soho at four am. There were almost constant scuffles – and the band had to play on, no matter what was happening down in the audience."

"We had no alternative but to play on," added Tony Sheridan, "and that helped our own vicious image as we looked down at some guy getting kicked around like a football. It was grotesque, but that's how it was. I wasn't vicious at all, so I pretended to be. I looked vicious, dressed vicious and said things that made people think twice about getting into an argument with me. We were very disturbed people. Now and then, I used to throw a guitar down and beat the crap out of it with one of those heavy-duty microphone stands to instil fear into people who weren't paying enough attention to the music."

As diverting was the nightly combat on the Star-Club stage between the trombonist and saxophonist in Fats Domino's horn section, but this was nothing to the unorchestrated contretemps that took place behind closed doors – like the time Ricky Richards set about Tony Sheridan with a tin tray or, in the same Top Ten dormitory, Sheridan's row with a girlfriend that ended with broken glass and the tearing of the tendons in his guitar-picking right hand; a wound that, needing stitches, was left unattended beyond immediate first-aid as it did not impair Tony's manipulation of the plectrum.

It wasn't any more peaceful over in the rooms provided by the Star-Club where John Lennon halted a poker game with Gerry Marsden and other Liverpudlians to pour a malicious glass of water over The Graduates' slumbering sticksman whose reciprocation moments later prompted the devil in John to advise that if he swallowed the insult, however aggravated, his tough guy veneer would be cracked forever.

Leaping to his feet, Lennon seized hold of an empty bottle and brought it down on the drummer. Fortunately, the latter's pride smarted more than his cranium, and further blows were not exchanged owing to his misapprehension that the rest of the players at the table were going to swoop unquestioningly to a fellow Scouser's defence. Had he known how sickened they were by John's behaviour, he might not have been so hasty in slinking back to a damp bed with as much dignity as he could muster.

Behind the scenes at the Star-Club too, Paul Raven was to have an altercation over a woman with Gene Vincent, an entertainer regarded by even Henry Henroid as "like a living lunatic asylum. We had to go out of our way to keep Gene from the press. We had to hide the things he did. Gene was the original punk. He made Johnny Rotten look like a schoolboy." True to form, Vincent let loose wild shots with real bullets at Raven at a bedroom door and the wardrobe with which it was wedged shut. Heaved away by his minders, the American quietened down, and his conduct towards Paul the next day was as if nothing had happened.

Reliant on his own mettle rather than any firearm, Kingsize Taylor's strapping build and knockout punch had been reassuring assets in the more unrefined Merseyside engagements where he and The Dominoes had worked before coming to a city where his strengths were tested more thoroughly and not found wanting. With petrified admiration, his musicians would tell of his way with promoters who dithered about handing over agreed fees; his knack of fixedly staring hecklers out of countenance, and of when all of a dozen *Polizei* had to be called upon to subdue Kingsize after he saw fit not to bite back on his annoyance with one markedly intransigent barman.

A tarring with the same brush gilded the images of both sham hard cases from Liverpool like John Lennon and the real thing as exemplified by Johnny Hutchinson, The Big Three's ambidextrous percussive aggressor who wielded reversed sticks so that the heavier ends battered his kit, and who could keep hitting a snare drum off-beat in time with one hand while socking a stage trespasser on the jaw with the other.

The same respect was accorded in Hamburg to men from a city north of the border. "People were generally afraid of Glaswegians," reckoned Tony Sheridan. "Alex Harvey was a very feared man. There was a table that ran from the stage down the length of the hall, and he once charged down it, kicking heads as he went."

When prodding the nerve of how far they could go, certain Britons so invoked the ire of their employers that only extreme measures could answer. You could be roughed-up, even hospitalised; threatened with worse to come if you said anything to *Polizei* suspicious of your lacerations and fractured limbs, and reminded of a contractual clause that forbade your group from working in any other Hamburg club within a given time limit without permission – which was withheld.

Aware that enough palms could be greased to circumvent such legalities, an aggrieved impresario could strike harder still by suggesting that *Der Auslander Polizei* inspect the passports and official identity cards of a group's youngest members, ie those he'd hitherto arranged to be exempted unofficially from the curfew that depleted an audience of its teenagers following the legally-prescribed announcement made over the PA system each evening at ten pm, Monday to Fridays, and half-an-hour later at weekends.

The withdrawal of immunity could secure deportation or even a court summons before a German judge and jury tacitly prejudiced by a rock 'n' roller's nationality and peacock appearance. After The Beatles followed Sheridan to the Top Ten in 1961, George Harrison – months short of his eighteenth birthday – was expelled from West Germany forthwith for his nightly violation of the curfew. This was regrettable but not disastrous to the group until, acting fast, Bruno Koschmider had Pete Best and Paul McCartney handcuffed, bundled into a *Peterwagen* (Black Maria) and, after questioning, ordered out of the Fatherland on a trumped-up charge of arson.

For The Beatles to fulfil a four-month Top Ten season later in the year, both the West German Immigration Office and Herr Knoop, Hamburg's chief of police had needed written assurances of good behaviour and additional convincing that Exhibit A – to wit, a charred rag – was all there was to Herr Koschmider's wailing about McCartney and Best trying to burn down the Bambi Kino.

Koschmider had been a central figure in another well-documented confrontation, this time with Rory Storm And The Hurricanes who had conspired to render – via an excess of stamping and jumping – the Kaiserkeller's unstable stage irreparable so that he would be compelled to get a new one. When it caved in during an over-lively 'Blue Suede Shoes', Storm And The Hurricanes compounded their infamy by vacating the club with extraordinary speed.

Instead of decreeing revenge with fist and cosh against the English wrongdoers, Koschmider felt entitled to reduce the group's collective wage – though the ruined stage was never replaced – and make an example of Rory with a technically illegal dismissal for "breach of contract". Storm had set no Deutschmarks aside for such an unthinkable occurrence and, rather than seek repatriation from the British Consulate, roamed St Pauli aimlessly. As he hadn't the means to continue lodging with his Hurricanes in the rather pricey Seamen's Mission, he was found a berth in the Top Ten until his reinstatement by a calmer Koschmider.

For the sake of professional harmony, hatchets were buried likewise after the unpleasantness at Kiel's Starpalast that climaxed when Paul Raven was worked over by six waiters because he dared to become fractious about money owed and, after three years, ask for a pay rise. The more proprietor Manfred Wotilla wriggled and pleaded with a wan smile that the cash was on its way, the harder and blunter Paul's manner became during flare-ups that increased in frequency. Onlookers were appalled but half-admiring of the Englishman who had taken on an antagonist who was to Kiel what Weissleder was to Hamburg.

A shocked gasp ensued after Raven flung down a final gauntlet with a door-slamming threat to wreck all the club's pinball machines. During the consequent assault, he gave a good account of himself, punching out three of his assailants, before his fist went through a window and his entire body through a glass door. However, it was, allegedly, a head butt from Wotilla himself that would deliver Paul, his skull a bleeding rage of agony, to the casualty duty-doctor at the nearest hospital.

Of the-show-must-go-on stamp, Paul Raven made it onto the stage that night. Muzzy with painkillers, his forehead sewn up and his arm in a sling, he sang in a voice honed to razor-sharp poignancy. That he had been game enough to put up a genial front for the customers swung Manfred round in favour of apparent submission to all Paul's demands after, perhaps, one of these semi-amiable "you silly bugger" kind of discussions. The debt would be settled; he'd receive that bit extra, and be paid, as requested, on a nightly basis, albeit in small change sometimes. Tensions relaxed further when a storeroom was converted into the star's private boudoir. Such a pity that he'd needed a lesson.

Johnnie Law's feelings about Wotilla and the strategies that The MI5 were driven to employ to escape his clutches are worth quoting at length as they are illustrative of the sly machinations and downright thuggery that could blight the more hapless British group's sojourn in Germany: "All he had in mind was to cut everybody's money. We later found out he was called Manfred 'Cut Your Money' Wotilla. People like him were in the minority as I found out later. I don't know anyone who played in Hamburg who never got paid, but nearly everybody who played on Manfred Wotilla's circuit had some problem or other.

"The way it worked when you played in Kiel was that you didn't get the contracted amount of money, but you got more in his other clubs to make up the difference. We thought this was fair enough, and at the end of our first week in Dortmund, we asked the woman boss about our money. She said she'd sent all the money for the entire three weeks we were booked there to Kiel. So I telephoned the guy there, and it was: 'Oh, I forgot to tell you that we had to take it all to cover tax and health insurance' – which, as it turned out, was a complete lie. He stole our money.

"Then he suggested asking the woman in Dortmund for a loan of one thousand DM, and paying it back later. We were in a terrible position, but we still asked her for a loan of a thousand DM. She agreed but we had to give her our passports as a guarantee. You must be thinking how could anyone be so stupid, but we weren't much more than teenagers and, funnily enough, we were having a great time even though we'd been in Germany for two-and-a-half months and been paid next to nothing when you take off the expense of getting there. We'd come on a contract for a little less than fourteen hundred pounds and eventually got paid about three hundred.

"We'd played every night and done a great job, and this was the thanks we got. Brilliant, eh? Manfred thought he could keep us playing for him forever. We worked out a plan after a guy saw us playing in Wotilla's Luneberg club and offered us a month at his own place in Eckerndorfe on the Baltic, about thirty kilometres from Kiel. Well, we saw this as a way of getting away from Manfred, but how do we get our passports back?

"We had two weeks to go in Luneberg, and we were getting one hundred DM – about nine pounds – between us each night with the rest supposedly coming at the end – though we knew that wouldn't happen. The Luneberg manager liked us, but could do nothing because Manfred was his boss – so we asked him for some money to send home, and he advanced us twelve hundred DM without any problems – except that he wanted the passports too. The next day, we bought a ticket for Alan, our organist, to go to Dortmund, pay off the loan there, pick up our passports, and come the next day to Eckerndorfe after we'd got the cleaner to let us in the Luneberg club at ten am so that we could pack all our equipment and clear off.

"That night, the Luneberg guy went crazy, and got on the phone to Manfred who told him not to worry as the passports were in Dortmund. He got a real shock when he found out what we'd done. He sent some real heavy guys over to Eckerndorfe to investigate, but the club owner had got about twenty bodyguards to stand along the front of the stage. As Alan hadn't yet arrived by about four am, we thought he'd been kidnapped or something – so we barricaded ourselves in our rooms until the boss suggested that he drove us in his Aston Martin over to the British Consulate in Hamburg so that we could tell them everything.

"Well, here we were, walking along the cobbled streets of Eckerndorfe, surrounded by about ten guys, with the heavies from Kiel in doorways. We got to the car, and all its tyres had been slashed so we had to go back to our rooms. At six o'clock, the police came and wanted to see our passports – and who walks in about half an hour later but Alan. We asked where the fuck he'd been, and he told us he'd met a girl he knew in Dortmund and spent the night with her. What a world!"

Guest workers or not, a group's well-being – especially in Hamburg – did not depend wholly on the efficiency of the *Polizei*. Counting for at least as much was its standing with the local Capones; many of whom had been wafted upwards from the stench of black market spivvery during the war. Like everyone else, Tony Sheridan became aware that "there was a bit of protection going on, not much", and that, as long as, say, no ambiguous utterance was heard by the wrong person, St Pauli could be as "safe" for anyone who was sensible as London's East End was when the Krays held sway.

"I've been with a lot of heavy people, and know a lot of them well," divulged Johnnie Law. "I've never been treated with cheek or indifference, always nice. Despite the story that one of The Beatles told as if it was the norm, I've never seen or heard of anybody coming up

to the stage with a gun pointing at you and saying, 'Play "What'd I Say"!'
Even when you were walking down the Reeperbahn at night, the guys
outside the striptease clubs never bothered you – because you were
British and a musician."

The weather vane of a gangster's tolerance, if not approval, was,
nevertheless, capable of changing direction with the slightest breeze –
particularly when paranoia was sharpened by stimulants. "When they
were sober, the heavy guys were popular," said Tony Sheridan, "but
when they got drunk or were on pills – especially the older ones –
they'd start hurting people."

Partiality by these gentlemen – and by the wealthier brothel
madames – for certain British musicians was manifested in extra-legal
protection if ever such a combo ran into trouble within such an
admirer's sphere of influence. If, perish the thought, you awoke, bleary
and blood-stained in a police cell with no knowledge of the
circumstances that had brought you there, you might be able to guess
whose fixing would cause you to be free by noon, all charges quashed,
because of the strange silence of every material witness.

If a group was bothered, its most frightening fan would be bothered
too. When The Casuals were turned over in one clip-joint, their self-
appointed protector arranged for men wearing *Polizei* uniforms to
smash its every bottle, mirror and tumbler before boarding it up. "Tony
Sheridan was booked to play a gig in Kiel," recalled Tony Jackson. "The
owner of the club had refused to pay him – so some hitmen drove to
Kiel and destroyed the place with hand-grenades."

Underworld worthies would send up crates of liquor and even
plates of food to succour a chosen group, and as prepayment for
requests relayed by an underling tugging at the vocalist's trousers. The
musicians all knew better than to show less than the fullest
appreciation of these – often very expensive – gifts. They might be
swigging liberally at bottles of vintage wine whilst reprising some
impassively craggy but smoothly-dressed Mack the Knife's favourite
song over and over again. Pat Boone's comic 'Speedy Gonzales' was
played seven times by The Undertakers during a single Star-Club
session in 1962.

From clumping table tops to the rhythm, there was the odd
stagestruck hoodlum, bold with beer and false impressions of personal

talent, who couldn't prevent himself from clambering up onto the boards to demonstrate a tyro's vocal or instrumental skills as the musicians' eyes flickered nervously at one another. 'Rosamunde'? No, I don't think we know that one, *mein herr*. What key's it in? The Perry Como one, and not too fast, *ja*?

Backed by The Jets at the Top Ten, one demi-monde Eddie Calvert's speciality was a rendition of the Lancastrian trumpeter's 1955 hit, 'Cherry Pink And Apple Blossom White', but for every passable amateur, there'd be another who, fancying himself as maybe a Teutonic Sinatra, might provide only tragi-comedy, even for sycophants too scared not to tell sweet lies afterwards about how great he was. The truth would destroy his splendid self-assurance about everything he said and did – and might jeopardise their own positions in the gang's hierarchy.

Yet, however much such an interloper's companions blamed his accompanists for any musical shortcomings, German racketeers in general had a soft spot for the Britisher rock 'n' rollers, recognising in them aspects of their own reprobate elitism. When The Pretty Things arrived at the Star-Club, it was during a period when they were being projected as wilder, fouler and more peculiar than The Rolling Stones – sort of Terry-Thomas to their David Niven. Plugging their latest forty-five on television, Phil May's cascading tresses – the longest male hair in Europe – had outraged middle-aged parents, but the effect was felt as keenly by their short-back-and-sides sons, guiltily transfixed by the group's androgyny, offset only by lead guitarist Dick Taylor's beatnik beard.

Pariahs in decent society, the Things were quite accustomed to the company of criminals by the time they reached Hamburg. "We used to go to Freddie Mills, the Starlite Rooms," said May, "and these rather strange night clubs in London that were patronised by a mixture of leftish stars and gangsters – and CID flying squad, funnily enough. People like the Krays were drawn to us because, if they were Public Enemy Number One, we were Number Two."

They were, therefore, fully prepared for the hammer that St Pauli had taken to further moral certainties.

CHAPTER SEVEN

Don't Throw Your Love Away

"Some fellows of fifty have never seen a quarter of what I saw at seventeen"

Ray Ennis (The Swinging Blue Jeans)

A certain type of reader may have been looking forward to this chapter. Nevertheless, more often than not, scenes in dormitory and dressing room were disappointingly innocuous: a card or board game on a middle table, a guitarist tuning up, the drummer shaving at the wash-basin. Yet time that hung heavy between one night's shift on the boards and the next wasn't spent just eating, sleeping, practising guitar, visiting museums and making brassrubbings in the older local churches.

I'm not sure how many people know this, but connections between pop music and sex are much more distinct than those between pop music and "higher" artistic expression. Indeed, the strongest motive for most red-blooded lads to be in beat groups was the increased opportunities it presented to fraternise with girls.

"Fraternising" went no further generally than blushing *faux pas* and awkward gropings in Britain in the early 1960s. Contrary to popular opinion, a bill-topping star on the "scream circuit" could tempt but seldom even the most ecstatic female in the audience to join him in the romantic seclusion of a backstage broom cupboard. In his autobiography, Adam Faith recalled numerous instances of directing his road manager to bring him a "bird" who'd caught his eye from the stage, but receiving only her relayed message that he could get lost.

What sort of girl did Adam Faith think she was? There was a difference, it seemed, between the distant object of the passion that had enslaved her and the mere mortal who picked his nose just like everybody else.

Furthermore, with Conovid, the oral female contraceptive, months away from UK chemists' counters in 1960, and then only available if a teenager had the nerve to see her disapproving family doctor about a prescription, pre-marital sex was as big a step to take as it would be when AIDS and other ailments of the 1980s put the brake on promiscuity for her children. Buying condoms and hiding them from prying parental eyes was near-impossible. Besides, they could burst, and "pulling out" was even less of a guarantee that you wouldn't have either to "do the decent thing" or procure a back-street abortionist.

Humble voyeurism wasn't easy either. Local striptease clubs were banned by the Watch Committee, and, before the abolition of stage censorship in 1968, the Windmill Theatre was by default the sexiest public place in London – though most of the women there wore slightly more clothing than can be seen nowadays on a warm afternoon in Brighton, and those that were nude had, by order of the Lord Chamberlain, to stand stock-still. In staid old Britain too, practising homosexuals were still liable to prosecution as well as persecution; Penguin Books were in the throes of legal proceedings over their plans to publish *Lady Chatterley's Lover*, and Billy Fury had been obliged to moderate his sub-Elvis gyrations.

Other European counties were, if anything, more ridiculously staitlaced in such matters. The Honeycombs' itinerary in 1964 included a month in a night spot in Rome where, remembered lead vocalist Denis D'Ell, "We got into diabolical trouble. When it got hot, I undid my shirt. This sparked off some screaming which I milked with a James Brown routine. The second night the police were there, holding sheets in front of me so that the audience couldn't see – so I clambered on top of the amplifiers. They closed the place down after the second night for obscenity."

In Italy as in England and other countries, professional sex was in its infancy when compared to West Germany. It tended to be furtive and grubby: shady hotels in Ostend letting rooms by the hour with the body smells of others still lingering in the sheets – or common soldiers picking up whores in a certain backstreet pub in Aldershot, 'Home of the British Army', to be smuggled into the barracks for joyless assignations. A soft "Want business, man" from a doorway's dark interrupts the ambulatory brooding of an accountant on his way to the last train from Birmingham New Street.

Such chill, empty moments were far rarer in brightly-lit Hamburg where the ways and means of indulging both the weirdest and the most straightforward sexual proclivities were contained in known areas where they were celebrated, not submerged. They were better organised too, almost regimented in places. Though some prostitutes were self-employed "kerb-swallows" – some of them students doing holiday work – most were controlled by madames and pimps who shunted them round from strasse to strasse, brothel to brothel, to ensure a continual change of faces and flesh for the regulars. "A female friend of mine who was involved in the British 'leisure industry' found the openness of what was going on in Hamburg quite interesting," said Dick Taylor, "but probably preferred the amount of independence she could have in London."

From the client's perspective, however, Hamburg provided a more efficient and ample service. Though the area round Steindamm in the St Georg quarter on the other side of the Main Station wasn't far behind, St Pauli had the greater reputation as Europe's premier erotic fairground, the neon starting point of innumerable evenings of perfumed temptation. If you liked it plain and simple, sundry orthodox corruptions – strip-tease, street-corner hookers, peep-show arcades, bordellos – were to the Reeperbahn as steel to Sheffield.

However, a few hours in and around the Reeperbahn could also be an eye-opener for anyone who'd assumed that humans could only be sexually gratified without mechanical appliances and only with other humans. A veritable Pandora's box of "kinky" sex would reveal itself as the flow chart of immorality unfolded. "Shops sold coshes like dildos, dildos like coshes," gasped Dick Taylor, "and the sort of pornography only available from the back streets shops of Soho who paid the police off."

Naked before their conquerors, Germans of all sexes would perform all the obscene tableaux illustrated in such magazines and films, frequently inciting others to join in the fun and indulge twisted appetites. Yet bare ladies wrestling in mud or fornicating with donkeys was, said Ricky Richards, "The sort of thing that you see once and don't bother seeing again – unless you're one of these blokes who can't get anything."

The boys from Britain would arrive like John McNally of The Searchers – "an innocent kid, seventeen years of age" – and, like Lewis Collins of The Mojos, "come back an old man, having experienced just about everything that's in the book". Collins – like Tony Sheridan – had still been a virgin at eighteen. Moreover, a few UK musicians, stuck between the sensuality of their new surroundings and their own ingrained compliance to Christian values, would take sheepish communion at the Roman Catholic church next door to the Star-Club. When such a person looked about the pews, a wave of shame would swamp him when he recognised a *bar-frau* whose breasts, now swaddled decently, he had squeezed the night before.

If glad of the business, the more soft-hearted bawds were saddened to see so many fine young men coming to St Pauli for the first time to gorge themselves on the forbidden fruit. Whatever would their mothers say? "Everybody around the district," George Harrison remembered fondly, "were transvestites, pimps and hookers, and I was in the middle of that when I was seventeen." Advisedly, lewd sniggering and shadowy thighs did not leap out of the pages of letters home – though Chris Warman's naval officer father and many other British servicemen had wartime memories of the flesh-pots of Europe, and knew that travellers' tales about them were hard fact – as their sons were thrilled to discover. As guardian of his daughter's innocence, Cilla Black's dad wouldn't hear of her going to Hamburg as featured singer with Rory Storm And The Hurricanes.

When first they came to St Pauli, Storm's group had been guided round the district's diversions by The Beatles, just as all newcomers were by incumbent groups as nonchalantly as they'd been themselves to, say, the Hippo Bar – the one with women grappling in mud – and the Telefon Club where customers could ring hostesses at the tables. *En route*, they would amble, goggle-eyed, past hucksters in navy blue coats with gold braid, extolling the delights of perhaps "gorgeous schoolgirls in a bath of pink champagne! Five marks!". The jewel in the crown, however, was the Herbertstrasse, the shocking "Street of Windows". "You couldn't see into it," said Ricky Richards, "because of great big iron doors either end like the entrance to a concentration camp."

The younger musicians would be ragged about notices forbidding minors from entering the Herbertstrasse. Unofficially, females who weren't on the game were less welcome. "I bought over a girlfriend from England called Susan for her holidays," laughed Ricky Richards, "and I took her through the Herbertstrasse. As she walked through, you should have heard the cat-calls and obscenities! The prostitutes hated seeing other women along there because men were all possible customers; women could only be sight-seers."

They could be unless, of course, they were lesbians, looking the sluts up and down like farmers at a cattle auction. Some establishments, however, catered more precisely for such predilections. As well as homosexual dating bureaux and male brothels – catering for an inordinate number of the sailors supposedly loved by all the nice girls – there were places like St Georg's Pulverass (Powder-Barrel) with its Crazy Boys troupe of male strippers, and, back in St Pauli, the Roxy Bar where transvestites congregated in their sequins and stilettos. "The first time Skip Allen, our drummer, came to Hamburg with us, aged sixteen," smiled Dick Taylor, "we 'forgot' to tell him about the sexual identity of the 'girls' in the Roxy. He found them very glamorous until we told him. They in turn seemed to take to us in a big way. They particularly liked our tour manager Pete Watts' 'mod' hairstyle, and I can remember him sitting there, being preened."

Dick's Pretty Things may have anticipated the red carpet treatment there when, according to Screaming Lord Sutch, "The man-in-the-street in Britain couldn't imagine any of The Pretty Things even being married – except to each other." Sutch himself had had hair of comparable length – and so too had Chris Curtis of The Searchers. While it would have branded Curtis as a "nancy boy" back in Liverpool, and even invited comments on the streets of his Lordship's Soho, men who looked even more like ladies – and vice versa – were but minor aberrations. "I recollect standing next to some local long-haired guys on the street one day," said Dick Taylor, "and being harangued by a shouting old man. When I asked what he was saying, I was told that he was ranting about how in his day we would all have been sent to concentration camps. I must say that this was the only incident of this kind that I ever experienced in Hamburg."

There had always been a degree of cross-dressing on British stages – with "dames" and busty "principal boys" in pantomime; drag kings like Vesta Tilley and – the original "Burlington Bertie from Bow" – Ella Shields ruling the music hall, and female impersonators such as Danny La Rue and Bobbie Kimber continuing to make a socially acceptable living in variety. Through these precedents, a Briton may not have felt as much like a fish out of water as other foreigners did in certain clubs where you'd get stared at if you weren't at least androgynous.

A hulking rock 'n' roller from the Gorbals, now over an initial revulsion, would come to know that no aspersions would be cast on his manhood if he was seen in the Roxy, paying his respects to "The Duchess", an amusing and erudite character whose command of many languages, and encyclopaedic understanding of people and places, interactions and outcomes, provoked such lively and irresistible debate that his-her sexual identity would become a thing of minor importance. "None of us were gay," Tich Amey assured me, "but we used to go there because you could have such a great conversation with the Duchess. She – or he – knew so many things about the world. One of his-her best friends was Johnny Kidd."

The "look' of Johnny and his Pirates had proved almost as critical as their music and, while experiences like the Roxy might not have eradicated or even tempered any of the ferociously heterosexual bluster with the lads down the pub back in Britain, many of Kidd's Hamburg contemporaries became more receptive to a wardrobe that was not aggressively masculine. Bolero jackets, frilly shirts like whipped cream and even mascara (which Gene Vincent was man enough to wear) were not quite so out of the question when a group strode back onto the low local stages from whence it had sprung. Homecoming rock 'n' rollers were now less who-are-you-lookin'-at-pal? defensive after experiments with dye divided mousey hair with a three-inch turquoise stripe. They'd mooch down to the corner shop in a fluffy pullover knitted by a Roxy admirer, and not be embarrassed if caught applying lacto-calomine lotion to pimples. Just as the widest river can be traced to many converging trickles, so a source of the glam-rock movement of the 1970s must lie as much in the Roxy as in the precedents of Vesta Tilley and Danny La Rue.

Adolescent narcissism informed Hamburg photographer Jurgen Vollmer's most abiding memories of the young George Harrison who stuffed the tips of his winkle-pickers with cardboard to stop them curling up like Arabian slippers. Few musicians of his age were able to pass mirrors without stopping to pinch out some more blackheads or whip out a comb for a quick adjustment to a glacier of brilliantine.

Whether or not there was a steady girlfriend in Britain, they seemed perpetually on the look-out for an unsteady one in Hamburg where bartering in sex was more brazen. Back home, he might have fled if accosted by a prostitute, but, with Mum and girlfriend not looking, a teenage Briton from a sheltered background might abruptly lose his virginity in the practised and robust caress of a painted princess twice his age who, in a transparent shift, had openly exhibited her seamy charms along the Street of Windows.

A decision to make an embarrassed if enthusiastic go of sex for sex's sake was often prompted by the ribald teasing of those who, if they were to be believed, had already staggered along the same route, trying to disentangle jeans from ankles when advancing on a gigglingly supine harlot in her haze of cheap perfume. During *Die Premiere*, he had probably ejaculated too quickly, and, though he may have thought himself one heck of a chap before he rolled out of the bed, he'd realised later that her smile of drowsy satisfaction had been fake, mechanical.

If the soppy lyrics he sang on stage – about dream lovers and sweets for my sweet – were anything to go by, he'd been conned out of something. Girls only went all the way if they truly loved you, didn't they? That was how it had been with the earnest damsels he'd pursued when a gawky church youth clubber. They'd looked as if they couldn't wait for a game of chess or ping-pong, followed by a chat about life-after-death or Sabbath Day opening over an orange squash.

Beneath it all, were their whole tweedy beings screaming for sex as much as his still did, however depressed and nauseated his induction had left him? Well, next time – and it'd be very soon – he'd be the one who, with rough and new-found confidence, would lead the unbuttoning, buckle-searching, finger-sliding way, even if the tart concerned telegraphed the most blatant "come on" in St Pauli.

With no awkward "I love you: I *luff* you also" formalities, practice could be made perfect via these most competent tutors – but however nimble the whores of Hamburg were *in situ*, their bodily fluids could bequeath inadvertent souvenirs of a night's pleasure. The more incautious wench would age fast, addled by recurring bouts of social disease with a positive result of a Wassermann test for previously undetected syphilis frequently hastening her destruction – and those of others.

"They [the musicians] usually arrived knowing it all, poor sods," grimaced Ian Hines as their self-designated Dutch Uncle, "taking no advice that I could offer them and, sure enough, would return to the good old UK with crabs, pox, 'Hamburg throat' – you name it, they had it." All this may have been avoided had they bothered to find out that the "cleanest" tarts were on view in the windows and contact cafes along the Herbertstrasse, in establishments like the Eros Centre and the Palais d'Amour on the Reeperbahn, and in hotels such as Clubhotel, Luxor and the Columbus where commissionaire-pimps in gold braided coats touted for business. Did they really need to be told not to sniff around "kerb-swallows" and females in the cheaper bars? Not only will you catch something, but, whatever delicate attentions you require, you won't get them for the price originally arranged. You might get robbed altogether – and you'd certainly never get your money's worth.

Sometimes, however, you could get something extra that you didn't want. "We spent nearly two months trying to chat up two gorgeous ladies who used to stroll along the Reeperbahn," elucidated Tich Amey. "Just before we returned to England, we found out that they weren't girls at all but two fellows. Thank God none of us succeeded with the chat-up lines."

Had they done so, it's feasible that there would have been no sub-text of financial transaction as there would have been for unlovely old rascals purchasing brief respite from loneliness and frustration. Even if you had a tooth-brace, mottled skin and wire glasses, it was seldom necessary to pay for sex if you were a musician. "We always went to other bars etc, looking for (a) music and (b) females for relaxation on our night off," said Chris Warman, "but even if you looked like the Hunchback of Notre Dame, you could always have a German girl from within the club if you were part of the group. Never did payment change hands, only a drink or two to show off."

Before the breed became commonplace, a British rock 'n' roll conquistador in gregarious mood would be sighted, Cola-Rum within reach, surrounded by a bevy of dolly little darlings aspiring to an orgasm at his thrust. Now more immune to twinges of Christian conscience, he'd got quite used to casual and unchallenging procurement of sexual gratification from almost any one of the females ringing the stage apron to better ogle him with unmaidenly eagerness. The evening's love life could be sorted out by the first beer break with a boyish grin, a flood of libido and an "All right then: I'll see you later".

Without having to display even perfunctory chivalry, you could just snatch a bird by the arm and manoeuvre her into the nearest backstage alcove for a knee-trembler that could be over in seconds or stretched out like toffee, depending on how much it took for your legs to give way – or how much time you thought you had. Sometimes, a group might have to fill in with an instrumental until its flushed vocalist, now an expert at dressing while running, panted on, either zipping up his flies or wiping sticky fingers on his shirt.

Well into his third month in Hamburg, his desire was verging on the satyric, and his boasts about his conquests were not the exaggerations and downright lies they'd been at home. A Roman emperor might never have had it so good. "We had all the girls we wanted: no shortage at all," winked Ricky Richards. "We were beating them off. We used to pay an old lady called Mutti to bring up our breakfast. All five of us would be in bed with birds, and she'd cackle and shout *'Die Fickerie! Die Fickerie'* – the 'Fuckery'. As Colin Milander used to say, 'We live in very enlightened times, don't we?'"

Britain contained only islets of like broad-mindedness such as an English teacher at Aldershot County High School For Girls telling A-level students that her perception of Dylan Thomas's *Under Milk Wood* was all the more acute because of a one-night-stand she'd had with the author. In the early 1960s too, that same seat of learning had contained an elite of sixth-formers who, for reasons lost in the mists of time, sported a Robertson's jam "golliwog" badge to signify proudly that they had "known" a man in the biblical sense.

Their sisters-in-shame across the North Sea were more dauntingly direct even in days before the birth pill. Free-spirited fräuleins, giving in to Nature's baser urges, would simply lock eyes with a selected onstage guitarist with a crotch-level instrument, and point at him whilst jerking a phallic forearm, and hope he got the message that tonight was to be his night.

With increasing frequency, however, the later watches of the night would pass less tempestuously than usual. "To be quite honest, you were so bloody tired after work sometimes that all you wanted to do was get to sleep," yawned Tich Amey. With sex on tap, so to speak, a musician – like a prostitute – was often less interested in the ritual than his bedmate's flat, purse and like material possessions. One of Germany's own Rattles, for example, walked out with a Herbertstrasse inhabitant mostly because he had use of her white Mercedes.

Basic needs of the stomach spurred The MI5's whispered sweet nothings during their period of servitude with the excessively thrifty Manfred Wotilla. "We had a job beginning on New Year's Day in Rendsburg," explained Johnnie Law. "Wotilla said that then we'd start getting the money he owed us. I asked about what we were going to do in the meantime – and you know what one of his suggestions was: 'You all had plenty of girls in Kiel, so do the same in Dortmund. Let them buy you food.' We had enough girls who were okay for buying us drinks and sometimes a meal when we finished."

This scheme was tested in Hamburg too by Tich Amey: "Somebody said that it was a good idea to get in with one of the local girls. I got hooked up with a lady of the night – though I never gave her more than my time. Nevertheless, she thought the world of me. When we finished playing, she used to take me out for dinner."

A lot of these altruists weren't too fussy about who they obliged as long as he was British and in a beat group. Some would transgress the unwritten machismo code instilled into many adult males throughout Europe that condoned their own infidelities, but not those of their women. "It was funny to witness tearful goodbyes," chuckled Colin Manley, "only to see someone's sweetheart holding hands with a member of the next group to arrive fresh from England."

Cognisant of the situation, a musician learnt not to spoil a no-strings dalliance by getting jealous and sulky with a girl who needed someone who didn't care anymore than she did. Indeed, on departure, he himself would proffer his paramour of the previous few weeks to a new arrival as an Eskimo might invite a house guest to "laugh" with his wife. These fraternal gestures backfired on occasions as Beaky Dymond discovered on reading a sarcastic "Thanks a lot, mate!" on a postcard from Cologne, written by a guitarist who reckoned – albeit without specific evidence – that he'd contracted venereal disease from one of the Boston's cast-offs there.

Tich's nose for trouble was sharper than Beaky's where romance was concerned: "Another girl fancied me too. She was there every night, looking up at me. All I'd done was speak to her, but I was walking into the club one night when she collared me with a gun in her hand. I had to pull her into a doorway and talk my way out of it. As I hadn't been interested in her, she was going to make sure that no-one else would have me."

Infatuation was not an emotion denied to the musicians either. The story goes that Dave Dee became enchanted with Gigi, a dashing young lady who, during The Bostons' first trip to Hamburg, had taught him the only German song in their repertoire. One day, as she patiently corrected his pronunciation, he crossed that impalpable barrier between inferred friendship and declared love. Later, she was untrue and they parted. Nevertheless, Dave was quite willing to resume their *amour* years on when he was one of the most renowned names in European pop.

Fame could be a powerful aphrodisiac, but even stars could be cuckolded by the common man. Gene Vincent, for example, accused his wife of a fling with one of the Star-Club waiters. The tense hours that followed culminated in a slanging match you could hear all over their hotel. Yet Gene would be astonished at how easily he could make light of it the next evening at the Star-Club bar, his head thrown back with laughter at some vulgar joke shared with the very waiter concerned, demonstrating to all the world that any bad blood between them had been diluted.

The Great Freedom embraced moral generosity, but, as Dick Taylor noted: "Tolerance has its limits though, and Skip Allen managed to push them when a young fan came up to our hotel room. I am quite sure that Skip didn't realise how young she was until he got dragged off by the police from the ever-busy station across the road. They kept him for several hours, and we were quite worried about who we were going to use as a drummer that night, but they finally kicked him out with a flea in his ear. When he came back, he told us that the cops had actually sent him packing once, but on the way out he had told them, 'Well, I did kiss her!' – and they went back into interrogation mode for another hour or so. As he was still a teenager himself, Skip was terribly shaken by the experience."

Back from his travels, a lad not unlike Skip would revert from the untamed man-about-St Pauli to the tongue-tied boy from the youth club, confused and wracked with guilt. His nearest-and dearest would often guess what he'd been up to from signals that penetrated the tacit vow of silence that has persisted among bands of roving minstrels for as long as *omerta* has among the Mafia. Stray mutterings about amatory adventures in Germany were unsettling for wives and fiancées – particularly those who had to keep up a "just good friends" farce to protect the "available" image of groups that'd set their sights higher than the Hamburg-Butlin's-ballrooms treadmill. When outlines thus dissolved in a compartmentalised life, frank exchanges over table-cloth or counterpane brought to the surface both her noisome home truths about him, and his disobliging comparisons of her with unforgotten fräuleins so self-possessed that they weren't troubled about anything as tedious as his missus or the girl-next-door.

CHAPTER EIGHT

Dr Feelgood

"What with playing, drinking and birds, how could you find time to sleep?"

John Lennon (The Beatles)

The bars stayed open for far longer, and the beer was cheaper and had more of a kick in it. For Britons in Germany, cold lager was easier to like than their own "rough" cider and warm "mild" and "bitter" ales had been for the wartime GIs, unable as they were to order Southern Comfort, El Paso wine – or rum-and-Coca-Cola, a beverage that The Andrews Sisters celebrated in a 1944 million-seller. The revised title in Britain was "Rum And Limonada".

Rarer than winter roses in the Dog-and-Gluepot too were German drinks like schnapps and Korn, a gin-like spirit made from potatoes. These had been the strongest stimulants on offer when The Jets came to Hamburg in 1960. Alcohol was common currency too in other Teutonic reaches of British pop. "I popped a couple of pills to keep going," confessed Ace Kefford, "but we were more into getting legless on German beer." Georgie And The International Monarchs also drank their wages on the Storyville network; some members more than others. Indeed, the Scottish contingent's keen consumption of *stein* upon *stein* of lager became so serious that subsequent dismissals and replacements were to transform The Monarchs – with a new "Georgie" – into an all-Irish concern by the time the season finished.

A harder-living Midlands combo in Stuttgart got on the outside of a whole month's allocation of *gratis* beer in the space of one evening –

while drummer Ron MacKay calculated that interval drinks bought for Acker Bilk and his band during their six weeks in the New Orleans Bar amounted to eighty-six schnapps, three magnums of champagne and over two hundred tankards of beer. "On top of that," added Acker, "we had to buy something to drink on stage. The way we were sweating, we had to keep drinking or we'd have dried up altogether."

Drugs did not enter the equation for the Paramount Jazz Band in Dusseldorf, and nor was it immediately obvious to The Jets that St Pauli was a narcotic ghetto as well as a sexual one. "I never saw any drugs when I was in Hamburg then," insisted Ricky Richards. "No cannabis, no amphetamines, no cocaine, no heroin, no drugs at all – just beer. You didn't need drugs in Hamburg. I feel sorry for anybody who couldn't get a buzz in Hamburg without that stuff. The whole place was a buzz."

Means of sustaining the buzz varied from person to person. As Tony Sheridan explained: "Ricky isn't the sort of guy to get involved in drugs. The Scottish groups tended to be more into alcohol, but The Pretty Things were very much into all sorts of drugs which we weren't. However, after our first two weeks in 1960, we discovered that we ought to eat better, eat more, sleep more and stop messing about a bit more to stay fit – and these pills made us fit very quickly. Preludin would keep you awake for a couple of nights."

Containing amphetamines, Preludin – and Captigun – were brands of appetite suppressants for dieters. Outlawed during the 1950s in the UK, they were, professedly, only available on prescription in Germany. Nevertheless, unauthorised caches could be obtained with ease and it was no hanging matter if you were caught with them. Most Hamburg policemen couldn't be bothered with the paperwork.

A British rock 'n' roller's only previous encounter with non-liquid artificial euphoria might have been when a beard of beatniks paid him the compliment of thinking him sufficiently hip, ie disreputable, to want to be instructed about a post-bellum equivalent of glue-sniffing. Like, you buy a Vick's inhaler from the chemist's, man, and you isolate that part of it containing this really far-out stuff called benzadrine. This you then eat.

Producing a similarly tacky "high" for German beatniks was Nostrilene hay fever spray, but a handful of college students in

Hamburg were using Preludin for all-night assaults on course work. For purposes other than fighting the flab too, supplies came to be stocked for employees' use in most St Pauli establishments that kept Dracula hours – as Dave Dee gathered during his group's first night at the Top Ten: "We walked in, and they said, 'You are onstage in an hour.' We said, 'Oh no, we've been travelling for two days.' This guy said, 'Don't worry about it.' We went on, came off, the other band went on, came off, we went on again. It got to about two-thirty in the morning, and we were absolutely knackered. The guy says, 'Don't worry. I'll take care of things,' and he came up with five rum-and-cokes and these little tablets. I said, 'What are these?' He said, 'Don't ask questions. Just take the tablets. You'll feel great.' We didn't know what they were, and, of course, it was speed – actually Preludin slimming pills – but they did the trick.

"The only problem with that," he warned, "was that when we finished work, we couldn't sleep and went through the next day waiting for the pills to wear off." Unlike booze, onstage perspiration did not diminish their effect. Therefore, after the final session of the night was as energetic as the first at seven pm, a group with eyes like catherine wheels would be ripe for mischief, which might begin with five-in-the-morning bar-hopping and end in a drowsy malaise twenty minutes before showtime. "Of course, we were knackered again," said Dave Dee, "so we asked for more pills."

Frothing over for the second night running, groups became unpredictable. You'd never know if the front line was going to slouch onto the boards to unacknowledged applause to stand immobile throughout the hour with faces like a Berlin winter – or bound on, infused with a fresh fizz, for an onslaught of endlessly inventive cavortings that seemed to burn up months of youthful energy in sixty minutes of metabolic chaos.

Thus began the rocky road to harder drugs for some who continued to keep the company of those with the same destructive tastes. The majority, however, pulled back from the abyss – but many never got the chance. Dickie Pride and, in my researched opinion, Stuart Sutcliffe, are instances of two whose dabblings in amphetamines led to death before the age of thirty. Others reacted by embarking on involuntary voyages lasting decades on shoreless seas of despair: wrist-slashing and overdosing cries for help; worsening blackouts; incarcerations in asylums and an inability to make long term plans. How could they?

Outwardly wasted lives served, however, as cautionary tales. A recurring sentence from Ace Kefford during our first conversation was "my head had gone" as an unarguable rationale for a tragic odyssey that had taken him to the psyche-boggling sensations of LSD – lysergic acid diethylamide – and a consequent downward spiral to a Warwickshire drug rehabilitation centre by 1997. Hopefully, this will mean an end to the constant mental breakdowns that stemmed ultimately from his "couple of pills to keep going" when at the Storyville with Carl Wayne And The Vikings over thirty years ago. As Seneca reminds us: *Pars sanitatis velle sanari fruit.**

Though inconsistent, the more common – and more gentle – after-effects of consuming amphetamines embrace diarrhoea, ringing headaches, hyperactivity, facial tics, indigestion, rashes, nausea, panic attacks, raging thirst, irritability, and long wakeful periods in bed. More sinister are muttered trepidation building to Hitlerian screech; the bawling of purgative obscenities in public (on stage, for example); muzzy eyesight as a harbinger of temporary loss of vision; uncontrollable shivering, dizziness, swaying and staring vacantly as preludes to a convulsive fit; nightmare hallucinations ("the horrors"); suicidal depression, and other disturbances that would reduce a group's live wire to a pathetic isolate. He'd be found sitting alone at the club's most secluded table, lost in melancholy and paranoia, his fingers pushed against his forehead, and his lips pressed together as if holding back pain. When his eyes weren't screwed shut, it was noticed that their twinkle had gone; a burned-out look was emphasised by purple-black blotches beneath them, like mascara that had trickled and dried.

To those back home who could not see his emaciation and the corpse-grey colour that he radiated, the only indication that anything was amiss was in letters that flitted too fitfully from topic to unrelated topic in handwriting that, becoming noticeably larger and more spidery, deteriorated to near-illegibility like Captain Scott's log as its writer died by inches in the Antarctic blizzards.

---

* Desire to be cured is in itself a step towards health

CHAPTER NINE

Lend Me Your Comb

"They wanted to know what made us tick, and we found them entertaining. Rather than associating with the real tough characters, we just sort of fell together"

Tony Sheridan

One man's toilet paper is another man's handkerchief. Rockers, racketeers and like St Pauli fixtures – as well as passing trade like soldiers from the West German *Bundeswehr* with night passes – coveted items that were commonplace in Britain. Pointed-toe shoes with elastic gussets in the sides, for instance, were as prized in West Germany as Levi jeans would be in Soviet Russia. When the British groups dropped in like aliens from a flying saucer, a source of supply stared Hamburg's fashion victims in the face. "We all wore winkle-pickers," said Ricky Richards, "and the gangsters – who couldn't get shoes like that over there – would pay us 200 DM – about twenty quid – for a pair that'd cost us three pounds back in London." Fetching hugely inflated prices for a while later would be denim shirts with button-down collars; hipsters in Billy Bunter check, and ties ranging from op-art slim-jim to eye-torturing kipper as teenage Germany in general tried to stay as few steps as possible behind Carnaby Street.

That they'd ever have anything to do with prevalent pop fashion had been unthinkable for the young aesthetes of Hamburg, Kiel, Hiedelburg and other university towns. At the turn of the decade, collegians of this kidney were more likely to have been "sent" by Lewis, Meade Lux than Lewis, Jerry Lee. With "cool" defined by Jack Kerouac's Dean Moriarty rather than Elvis Presley, their record collections might advertise a pseudo-sophistication that ran from Stravinsky to the most limp and "tasteful" modern jazz. At a pinch, this took in the likes of Ray Charles – black, heroin-addicted, twisted voice of the underdog – and organist Jimmy Smith whose black skin also tipped the balance of a style midway between jazz and pop. Cult celebrities could be forgiven anything but that acceptance instanced when Charles had a 1959 million-seller with 'What'd I Say' and Acker Bilk's 'Stranger On The Shore' appealed as much to the Great Unwashed two years later.

Such "selling-out" was deplored by both German jazz connoisseurs and the trad purists across the Westarweg. There were other points of contact too, if only superficial ones such as sunglasses worn even in a midnight power cut, and the occasional beret. Furthermore, blue-stockinged females in Germany tended not to hide their figures inside holey, tent-like sweaters on permanent loan from boyfriends with bumfluff beards. Neither did either sex go in for duffel coats, desert boots or corderoy trousers that looked as if they'd hung round the legs of a particularly disgusting builder's labourer for the past five years.

It came down to the difference between not so much "trad" and "modern" jazz as being "hot" and being "cool". At students union dances, British revellers would don boaters or top hats, and a hotch-potch of hacked-about formal garb, drink heavily of cider and, when the trad band commenced their puffing and plinking, launch into a curious galumphing motion that blended the Charleston with a variant of the Jitterbug.

The bohemian set at Hamburg's university, colleges and the fee-paying Meister Schule were inclined to hold onto their dignity, their Brooding Intensity. One prominent faction – the "Exis" – allied themselves to the Montmartre existentialists and their "nothing matters" preoccupation with doomed romanticism and man's conquest of a disordered nature through the self-sacrificing detours of art. Its high priestess was svelte and spectral Juliette Greco, the Thinking Man's French actress and singer. With her straight hair, intellectual aura and black-eyed but otherwise skull-white facial cosmetics, her presence was as felt as Che Guevara's would be in the kind of student bedsits where headscarves dimmed table lamps, and skip-read Genet, Nietzsche, Camus and Sartre looked well on bookshelves.

Greco-esque monochrome was the pervading colour scheme of Exi living quarters and sartorial style. In some respects, it anticipated the Gothic look of the late 1970s. Predominantly unisex, the usual fabrics were suede, corderoy and velvet, but Exi women wishing to look more feminine might don fishnet stockings, ballet slippers and shortish skirts. Exi hair was *Pilzen Kopf* ("mushroom head") or "Hamlet" – a heavily fringed cut, uncaked with Brylcreem, that, if widespread in Germany (and France) was regarded as being a bit square in Britain. Though Adam Faith had a similar brushed-forward crop, it was associated more with the outdated Kaye Sisters, a trio who were more the stuff of *The Billy Cotton Band Show* than *Thank Your Lucky Stars*. Worse, the wearing of a *Pilzen Kopf* would label a man as effeminate in the streets of Wolverhampton or Cork.

With sound reason, Exis were almost as afraid of Rockers as British homosexuals were of "queer bashers", but it was perhaps a horrified boredom with Stan Getz, the Modern Jazz Quartet, Brubeck *et al* – that they could barely bring themselves to articulate – that brought Hamburg's academic *crème de la crème* within earshot of the British rock 'n' roll uproar in St Pauli as early as 1960.

Torn between the bravado of being where he didn't belong and a yearning to head for the exit, never to go there again, the poker-faced *Pilzen Kopf* among the pompadours might think better of it, perhaps on the grounds that the more arduous the effort required to like something, the more "artistic" it is – and rock 'n' roll wasn't that. "Artistic" was endless centuries of a film by Cocteau; one of Shakespeare's so-called comedies or the Japanese water-torture effect of listening to some minimalist composer: a cultural duty first, and entertainment frequently a poor second.

Just as you'd lift a pigeonhole flap in a self-service cafeteria to get cheap, predictable food, so you'd go to the Star-Club for cheap, predictable music. However, on observing in Tony Sheridan, Kingsize Taylor and their ilk a certain primitive *épater le bourgeoisie*, and receiving the information that their more rugged brand of pop was "uncommercial" (and, therefore, an antidote to pleasure), such a pioneer would tell his mates where he'd been, describing what happened there in awestruck detail, and delighting in the faint revulsion that chased across their faces. However, not wishing to appear prudish, they'd accompany him – with toffee noses asking to be punched – on his next visit to this low-life gala deep in the Reeperbahn mire

It was a rearing-up of everything they had been taught to despise. Yet when the initial shock was over, they would feel then what he had felt. Losing a little of their cultivated cool, they even started having fun – or at least, via some complex inner debate, gave in to a self-conscious conviviality as they attuned to the situation's epic vulgarity.

Against the feigned indifference and circuitous enquiry that was the acceptable courtship pattern within college portals, how gratifyingly refreshing it was for the young masters to be studied unsurreptitiously by prattles of town girls whose skirts could billow out most fetchingly as they turned back to continue their incessant "ooo, 'e's lovely" (*"Ach, er ist lieblich"*) jabber about this or that British musician.

This would cease when the group sauntered onto the boards to hit all their instruments at once at the staccato "one-two-three-right!" that kicked off an hour of glorious rubbish that bore only the most wilfully shambolic similarity to any other pop presentation ever seen. After the volume that all but precluded conversation, what struck you first about this maddeningly catchy doggerel was the slamming beat and interchangeable cycles of block chords imposed on nearly every salvo of rhyming couplets, neo-dadaist in their boy-girl mindlessness. In between, the louts responsible had a most uncouth manner in addressing the crowd that kept it just short of open riot. Unfettered by slickness, they didn't care how badly they behaved up there – burping into the microphone, flicking vulgar finger-signs, and saying things like "fuck off" and other highly offensive English terms of abuse.

Mein Gott, they were great! Drawn back to another Grosse Freiheit bash before the week was out, what could the dumbstruck intruders do afterwards but thread through to the customary corner where the group had wedged itself, rehearsing mentally what they were going to say by way of congratulations, and the cool way in which they were going to say it. The professionally-minded musician would smother bemusement as these out-of-the-ordinary fans panted out gutteral, tongue-tied gaucheries like *"Goot evenink. I yam called Gunter. I digged very much your music. How iss your brother George?"* to Mike Harrison of The VIPs.

Not surprisingly, many British rock 'n' rollers did not seek the particular company of the Exis and their sort. If preferring a quiet drink with the Faschers, Gerry Marsden would always reserve a little of his personal charm for anyone who entered his orbit, but others had no compunctions about drily snubbing an Exi to his face, deriding him behind his back, and penning a sardonic remark when asked for an autograph.

Nevertheless, bohemian sects were to comprise a pronounced minority in club audiences – but, however high on Captigun a few of them might have been, they did not dance or shout approval to the ceiling at first, preferring to cower near the sanctuary of the stage when, squinting their way every now and then, the Rockers began their nightly brawl. Gradually, the tempest of underlying menace dropped, and the Rockers' collective attitude towards the slumming smart-alecs became not genial exactly but grimly urbane after, say, an especially bravura 'Rip It Up' blew away so many inhibitions that the Exis arose from their seats to flock spontaneously stagewards to join the hip-to-hip Rockers when the group was less than a few dramatic bars into the subsequent 'Whole Lotta Shakin''.

With this breakthrough, the students sat more comfortably, blocking the view for older regulars. As beat groups got more addictive, Exis would neglect their studies and day jobs to be near them throughout the watches of the night in the midst of what could be perceived, with a certain mental blindness, as not so much a district of vice but one akin to Greenwich Village, New York's vibrant beatnik stronghold. Living in the Big Apple himself thirty years after, Jurgen Vollmer mourned his lost youth: "That period I definitely would say was the greatest time of my life. I mean, every day sitting there and having The Beatles right in front of you. I was totally in ecstasy. I didn't think whether they'd be big stars. I just enjoyed that moment."

Jurgen had been the first to hoist a placard – "I love George" – in front of his favourite group. Next, the Exis came up with more in-joking notices. They also ensured that the musicians' birthdays were public events, and, when a group's return to Britain was imminent, made plans to turn the final evening into a farewell shindig.

Many took to going round the clubs in leathery Rocker dress. Some even tortured their *Pilzen Kopfs* into a lubricated cockade – until it drove them crazy, always obeying gravity eventually and cascading forward, and causing spots to explode around the scalp-line.

Humouring the Rockers made it easier to hang around with a chosen group. Their non-specific purpose in doing so undeflected by curtness and bad manners, fustian intellectuals would buy rounds of drinks to oil the wheels of prolonged conversation, willing, even glad to be accepted as unpaid and unrecompensed minions as long as they could be seen nattering familiarly to the new British messiahs of cool. For some, "ligging" during the intermissions came to be the main intention of the evening.

Yet many a weary musician found less crowded hours spent with selected Exis a stimulating change from drawing on a cigarette and nodding in smiling agreement with unintelligible platitudes shouted over the racket of voices in the club. A principal advantage that the Exis had over others as hungry for reflected glory was that most of them "spoke pretty well English that we had learned at school," explained Jurgen Vollmer, "while the general audience – the Rockers – didn't speak English. They were all rather uneducated working class. We were something different."

Vollmer, Astrid Kirchherr, sculptor Detlev Birgfeld and an illustrator named Klaus Voorman were among the least transparent of the Exi clique who wormed their way over to pay artist-to-artist and even highbrow-to-highbrow respects. Certain of the rock 'n' rollers turned out to be great talkers who used long words – in English, mind, but long words all the same – as well as studentish vernacular and restricted code. Another subliminal lure was that Tony Sheridan and members of The Rockin' Berries, Beatles and Pretty Things, for example, had all sprouted from art schools. Just as the likes of Johnny Kidd and Tich Amey were fascinated by the well-read Duchess, so the Exis could have an emotional commonality with this tight-trousered lead singer or that clenched-teeth guitarist who had once aspired to fine art with music as merely an extra-mural pursuit.

Stuart Sutcliffe was one who put action over debate, but most of Britain's lapsed two- and three-dimensional artists in Hamburg went no further than listening wistfully to the likes of Birgfeld and others who still breathed an atmosphere of coloured dust, palette-knives, hammer-and-chisel and lumpy impasto. They spoke the same jargon, and also purported to have let evening become morning during a single reading of Dostoevsky, Chekhov or Rimbaud. After limbering up with maybe a chapter or two of de Sade, Henry Miller or Colin Wilson's *The Outsider*, they had also got to serious grips, apparently, with Kirkegaard, the Danish mystic, and his existentialist descendants, principally Jean-Paul Sartre. British and German alike were also as enraptured with Kerouac and Burroughs and associated Beat Generation bards such as Corso, Ginsberg and Ferlingetti whose works they may or may not have studied.

Dialogue for the purpose of dialogue between Exi and rock 'n' roller was to ensue about, say, the transmigration of souls, the symbolism of dreams, what Sartre wrote about the Soviet intervention in Hungary in

1956 and what Camus thought he meant. Then it might drift off into word
games, free-association poetry – and ego-massaging asides about the
masterpieces an Exi was going to paint, the *avant-garde* films he was
going to direct, the ground-breaking novels he was going to write,
interrupting his new-found British chum's soliloquy about his life, his
soul, his agony – and his bloody bass player's perpetual machinations to
be allowed to sing 'Red Sails In The Sunset'.

 Pretentious and futile they might have been at times, but for Paul
Raven, a lost cause as a schoolboy, his period of afternoon polemics on
the beach at Kiel with lecture-cutting university students represented "the
first time I'd met people like this who were constantly working on new
ideas and questioning what they read. I'd have long discussions on Karl
Marx, Communism and Democratic Socialism, and theories of economics.
It was something I'd never done before, and it led me into reading
extensively for the first time."

A more pragmatic benefit of being on the same wavelength as
students – or pretending to be – was eating in subsidised college
canteens. Another was the increased possibility of getting sex with your
unofficial scholarship after it became chic for off-duty beat groups to be
invited along to bohemian gatherings. Yet it wasn't effortless like it was
with the pornocracy that solicited you nightly at work. You weren't quite
so sure of yourself with ladylike birds from the Meister Schule, more likely
to be won over with the dropping of names like *Bark* and *Vargner* than
Fats Domino or Duane Eddy.

Successful British suitors would find female Exis to be much more
liberated when compared to women back home with whom canoodlings
on front room settees were all you could expect, even when there weren't
third parties ironing, watching television, sweating over homework and
generally hovering around. Lack of privacy to such a degree needn't be an
issue when chatting up one of the posher Exis, but what could be
unsettling was a disarming independence manifested in her own car and
cheque book, and a refusal to be a mere adjunct to a boyfriend who her
"progressive" parents might permit to share her bed.

Proud, even boastful, about interest shown by such classy bits of skirt –
and their male counterparts – rock 'n' rollers would submit cheerfully to
modelling before sketch pad and canvas, and to more realistic portraiture
via the *woomph* of flashbulbs as shown in Astrid Kirchherr's grainy sessions

with The Beatles at the Dom; The Searchers in her silvery-black bedroom, and The Undertakers on the doorsteps of a Freiheit brothel.

The Undertakers did not pose in their expected macabre props but as sartorial magpies in winkle-pickers – perhaps from Cazneau Market in their native Liverpool – roll-necked pullovers and what appear to be corderoy suits as visual proof that interaction between German and British youth in Hamburg cut both ways. Cloth caps with bobbles were *à la mode* amongst both factions – and both sexes. It wasn't unusual either to see an Exi girl sporting her British beau's leather jacket while he wore her collarless blouse with the front tails knotted, exposing the midriff. Round the legs of both would be form-fitting leather trousers just like the ones Eddie and Gene had worn on that fatal 1960 tour.

With a basic pattern lifted from a blue-brushed denim get-up sold in the Hamburg branch of C&A's, Astrid Kirchherr and Stuart Sutcliffe's shared wardrobe contained Astrid's hand-made his-and-hers suits of beige velvet, unusual for epauletted jackets (*sans* lapels) that buttoned up to the throat, and high-waisted trousers with no pockets around tight buttocks. "Wearing your sister's suit then, Stu?" Paul McCartney had quipped when first he saw the now ex-Beatle swanning around in such an outfit in 1962 – but it wouldn't be long before the group popularised it as a stage costume.

Immigrant rock 'n' rollers also took trichological cues from their new admirers – of which the furthest reaching was when three of the remaining four Beatles requested an Exi wielder of scissors to carve a *Pilzen Kopf* from protrusions stiffened by a decade of grease. Each one guessed that it might not tumble naturally down towards their eyebrows for a while, but as it neared completion, eyes had widened and jaws had ceased chewing. Had he and the other two the nerve to keep it like that, even grow it thicker and longer eventually? Just wait till the cowlicked lads back on Merseyside saw this novel "Beatle cut". You'll need a guide dog to stop you bumping into things, they'd say.

CHAPTER TEN

Let's Stomp!

"If my first six years had been an apprenticeship, Germany was my finishing school. I developed my act far beyond the Elvis-Eddie Cochran rip-off it had tended towards, and got to understand exactly how to read a crowd too, to give them exactly what they wanted"

Paul Raven

The Sound as well as the Look was perfected in Hamburg in readiness for what lay ahead. "Germany boosted our morale," reckoned Cliff Bennett. "For the first time, we seemed to be making a solid impression on our audiences." Destined for a walk-on role when British pop shook the world, Cliff would be managed by Brian Epstein, the electrical goods retailer who began representing The Beatles in 1961.

Once also-rans in Merseyside's league division of groups, Lennon *et al*'s trips to Germany had bred a new confidence, even if they were to remain technically immature for some time. "All we really were," admitted George Harrison, "was thump-thump-thump." But, as Colin Manley noted: "By the time they got back from Hamburg, they were different altogether. They'd found their timing and you could see that they were going to happen in a big way."

The Beatles' stage act became worth seeing during a stint at the Top Ten – "a great place for young musicians," enthused Ricky Richards. "It made them three, four times better than when they came in." Here and elsewhere, it was the enthusiasm of the customers that helped foster such improvements – particularly on those occasions when audience and musicians would be as one. "The great thing I picked up in Germany," said Paul Raven, "was this thing of audience participation. The kids in Hamburg used to love to stomp and chant and wave their arms, shouting 'yeah yeah yeah' and all that sort of thing. I worked all this into my act, together with the stage movements you need to go with all that. To get it really right, I used to rehearse two or three times a week, bringing in anything that would make people look at me on stage."

In the manner of a Pentecostal tent revivalist's congregation, onlookers might assume dual roles of rhythm section and accompanying choir, latching onto the *omnes fortissimo* hey-yeah antiphony with the singer on 'What'd I Say', the call-and-response chant that Ray Charles had first improvised in 1959 at a Pittsburgh dance. Depending on the mood, it could last up to a full hour via an open-ended design that no native act had dared, until shown the way by the British invaders. "First of all, we obviously sang better English," said Johnnie Law. "We were natural and had a lot of fun onstage, getting the people going with songs like 'Shout' and 'What'd I Say'."

Tearing chapters from the same book – a very loose-leafed publication – it was a rare evening for certain groups if they did not reach at least one hiatus without giving 'em a prolonged 'What'd I Say', 'Shout' – or 'Whole Lotta Shakin'', 'Money', Little Richard's 'Keep-A-Knockin'', Bobby Comstock And The Counts' 'Let's Stomp', Bobby Parker's 'Watch Your Step', even 'When The Saints Go Marching In' among other high-energy pieces that required little prior instruction beyond, say, the odd "No, not boom blat boom-boom blat. Try boom-boom blat b-boom-boom blat" to the drummer.

Taking primitivism to the limit by 1965, The Pretty Things pared down their show to a continuous performance underpinned throughout by Bo Diddley's trademark shave-and-a-haircut-six-pence rhythm, and Phil May extemporising from full-blooded screech to *sotto voce* intimacy, drawing the listener in and then building the tension to panic.

Even the Irish showbands ceased copying records, choosing instead to pile on the pressure as, amid bellows of encouragement from his boys, a vocalist might exchange preliminary "yeahs!", "heys!", "that's what I wants" (in 'Money') and so forth with all-and-sundry until it reached a point where he could, ideally, take it down easy, talk at the audience and elicit louder participation. When the ear-stinging decibels were about to eclipse even the group, he'd grin and wave at the baying blackness beyond the girls who clustered, tits bouncing, round the edge of the stage. Next, he'd sweep into the wings, leaving 'em yelling for more – or just yelling – long after the last chord of the playout.

"We didn't bother with arrangements or anything," said Paul McCartney. "The main thing was to keep the noise and the beat going." Whoever was at the forefront of an end-of-set raver would also stoke up the first scattered screams that had ever reverberated for him by enhancing it with knee-drops, doing the splits, crawling to the footlights, jumping into the audience, dancing on the tables and general tumbling about. "They go in for movement," observed Spencer Davis, "musical ability doesn't matter so much." Even in the laid-back close of the decade when there was, supposedly, greater respect for instrumental virtuosity, Ozzy Osbourne of Black Sabbath "had the feeling that they didn't care what we were doing on stage as long as something was going on. If we stopped or anything, they used to go mad."

Methods of thus utilising time interestingly varied, but circa 1962, the choreography and music of many acts alluded to the Twist, a US invention reviled by *Melody Maker* as "the most vulgar dance ever invented". Yet it lasted well – for nothing dates a 1960s movie more than the obligatory Twist sequence in which middle-aged socialites rub shoulders with beatniks, all pretending to towel their backs whilst grinding a cigarette butt with the foot.

Just as teenagers in its country of origin had seized upon it, so the depraved Twist took Europe by storm – as La Torsion, Il Torcemento, La Torcedura *ad nauseum* (though the Germans kept it as plain Twist). As a craze, it went as deep as trad had done in Britain alone (as had connected revivals of the Charleston and the Can-Can). Its Acker Bilk was a former poulterer from Philadelphia named Chubby Checker – but his 'Let's Twist Again' was checkmated in France by Johnny Hallyday's bi-lingual cover. Elsewhere, there were expected native reproductions, both on vinyl and dance floor, of alternatives like the Mashed Potato, the Gorilla Walk, the Mickey's Monkey, the Hully Gully, the Fly, the Shimmy-Shimmy, the Locomotion, the ungainly Turkey Trot, the Slop, the Hitch-Hiker, the back-breaking Limbo, the Madison, the Shake and, with no precise instructions detailed in its lyrics, the Stupidity.

Europe came up with its own La Yenka and the Letkiss, but none shaped up to the Twist – for down the Star-Club, a barrage of applause could be perpetuated a split-second before it would otherwise have died by the man on tenor sax blurting the descending four-note intro to Joey Dee And The Starliters' 'Peppermint Twist' as a signal for 'Whole Lotta Shakin''-esque delirium. Whether by exhibition teams or individual mavericks, the group could be upstaged by unabashed demonstrations of the Twist and lesser dance sensations from the States that the average German teenager wasn't supposed to have mastered yet.

Guarding their celebrity with the venom of a six-year-old with a new bike, the group might fight back with a spectacle of its own such as the Double-Decker, a short-lived fad, in which a wailing saxophonist could be piggy-backed around the stage on the singer's shoulders. Johnnie Law would recall that: "One of Paul Raven's showstoppers was 'Land Of One Thousand Dances', doing all the shaking bit, starting at the feet and moving right up the body. I'd tried it myself a few times with no success – so I decided to forget it and be myself." To the delight of the young fräuleins, poor old Pete Best, The Beatles' drummer, was thrust to the front of the stage for an embarrassed demonstration of the Pinwheel Twist, a variation peculiar to the group.

The lads in the audience were more inclined to enjoy what they heard rather than saw. "What I liked was that you didn't have to play the hit parade," said Johnnie Law. "In Scotland, you were in trouble if you didn't play at least eight or ten songs from the Top Twenty." Indeed, the core of many an outfit's far shorter repertoire back in Britain would have been lifted from the current singles chart and classic rock. A 'Hound Dog' prefaced by a verse of 'Que Sera Sera' was idiosyncratic among items that did or did not placate a town hall mob inclined to gripe not only if anything unfamiliar was attempted, but paradoxically if they were given the same old muck in the two or three hours before a dauntless caretaker, anxious to lock up, pulled the main electricity switch because all that awful row had overrun by ten minutes and was degenerating into a late-night Twist session – "late" being gone nine-thirty pm.

It meant nine-thirty in the morning in German clubland – which meant that you had more time to anger patrons by playing a hit to death. "Many numbers had to be repeated at least two, or three times," reasoned Chris Warman, "to get through the six hour stint." However, the long shifts on stage meant that you didn't have to be so wary about surprising people with items from pop's obscurer trackways: side two track four of LPs, B-sides and smashes from the US R&B and C&W charts that had sunk without trace in Britain.

If they hadn't made the German lists either, certain numbers mostly from black America were as well-known around St Pauli as some that did. Off-the-cuff examples are Screamin' Jay Hawkins' manic 'I Put A Spell On You', 1960's 'Think' by James Brown, Arthur Alexander's 'A Shot Of Rhythm And Blues', 'Wild Side Of Life' from Hank Thompson, Brook Benton's 'Hurtin' Inside', 'Spanish Harlem' from Ben E King and 'Twist And Shout' by The Isley Brothers – whose long-players some groups would turn to as regularly as monks to the Bible. European Top Forty entries that couldn't be resisted included King's 'Stand By Me', 'Sea Of Heartbreak' by Don Gibson, Sam Cooke's 'Chain Gang', 'Stay' from Maurice Williams And The Zodiacs, Chris Montez's 'Let's Dance' and Ray Charles' UK Number One, 'I Can't Stop Loving You', countrified, sentimental and the complete inverse of his pulverising 'What'd I Say'.

Mild-mannered interpretations of Charles by Britons of Marty Wilde-Cliff Richard vintage had given way to those never to be dared on vinyl. 'I Gotta Woman', 'Hallelujah I Love Her So', 'Sticks And Stones', 'Hit The Road Jack' and the ubiquitous 'What'd I Say' were attempted by innumerable British groups in Germany, but as sonic vibrations *per se* these may have seemed stilted if heard on tape afterwards – because most of the singers were no more capable of taking on Ray Charles without affectation than Cliff or Marty. However, with a muffled PA system obliterating the more plummy brush-strokes of enunciation and inflection, the effect of even the most frail vocal attack could be made tremendous in the context of the onstage cavortings; the feeling that everything could fall to bits at any second, and the overall infectious atmosphere of a packed-out Reeperbahn club.

In contrast to 'What'd I Say', Chuck Berry's melodies served as support structures for lyrics celebrating the pleasures available to US teenage consumers. If not lending themselves so much to 'What'd I Say'-like dissection and improvisation, 'Sweet Little Sixteen', 'Roll Over Beethoven', 'Carol', 'Rock And Roll Music', 'Little Queenie' and all the rest of them were, if anything, more prominent than those of Charles in the repertoires of almost all young British vocal-instrumental groups in Germany; Berry's incarceration and dearth of major European hits only boosting his cult celebrity.

More popular Yanks dominated British pop, but though combos like Gerry And The Pacemakers prided themselves on embracing everything in each week's Top Twenty in their act, they tended not to lean as obviously on chart material when in Germany. Songs like 'Dr Feelgood', 'Some Other Guy', 'Just A Little Bit', 'Hippy Hippy Shake', 'Kansas City', 'If You Gotta Make A Fool Of Somebody' and any quantity of gutbucket Mississippi and Chicago blues items echoed round St Pauli, but how many clubgoers could name the original artists? How many can you name now?

Some "standards" of this type became synonymous with particular interpreters. Tamla Motown provisioned Kingsize Taylor with 'Respectable' from The Isley Brothers – and their 'Shout' emerged as Alex Harvey's signature tune for a while after he heard it in a cafe in Wick as the sole oasis in the vinyl desert of that particular nickelodeon.

 Not yet powerful enough to go it alone, Tamla Motown and other independent labels relied on lease deals to reach Europe. James Brown, for instance, came via the EMI subsidiary Parlophone in Britain and Polydor in Germany where cunning UK groups had already gone directly to source via mailing list and pen-pal, and were performing arrangements of the sacred sounds before they were even released officially outside America.

Other outfits weren't so quick off the mark. John McNally remembered that, "Chris [Curtis] and I were walking back from the Star-Club one day when we passed a record shop where we heard 'Love Potion Number Nine' by The Clovers. We got that and actually rehearsed it at the Star-Club for a few days. We just played it as we felt it." See, the idea was to make 'Love Potion Number Nine' and all the other set-works *not* sound like any other group's version. Hence the calm precision of The Searchers' 'Twist And Shout' and The Beatles' frantic work-out just one step from chaos. Both ensembles were adept at adapting songs by US female vocal groups of ingenuously fragile conviction. Each, for example, tried 'Shimmy Shimmy' by The Orlons, The Marvelettes' 'Please Mr Postman' and The Shirelles' 'Boys'.

Like nearly everybody else, they also inserted a token song in German into the set. The line of least resistance in this respect was to do 'Wooden Heart', Elvis Presley's European spin-off forty-five from the movie soundtrack of *GI Blues*, a fictionalisation of his military service in Germany. The King acknowledged the melodic debt 'Wooden Heart' owed to the traditional 'Muss I Denn Zum Stadtele Naus', by breaking into German for a couple of verses.

More erudite was a beat group vocalist applying the same technique to, say, Marlene Dietrich's 'Falling In Love Again' (from *The Blue Angel*) or when likewise stealing the show from more extrovert co-stars with Marlene's folky 'Sagt Mir Wo Die Blumen Sind', a translation of Pete Seeger's 'Where Have All The Flowers Gone'.

Doing the rounds too was 'Besame Mucho', a sensuous bossa-nova revived as a 1962 instrumental by Jet Harris to mark the twentieth anniversary of one of these Latin-flavoured ballads that, like 'Begin The Beguine', 'Sway' and 'Perfidia', never seem to go away.* Generally, only the title was sung in Spanish when 'Besame Mucho', a frequent request for the ladies, transported them for a few minutes from the shimmering sea of bobbing heads in the Star-Club to warm latitudes, dreamy sighs and an ocean dawn from the quarterdeck – and then a fluffed guitar run-down into 'Ubangi Stomp' would jolt them back to reality.

Excerpts from stage and film musicals also impinged on otherwise frenetic hours on the boards. 'Summertime' (from *Porgy And Bess*), 'You'll Never Walk Alone' (*Carousel*), 'Til There Was You' (*The Music Man*), 'Hilili Hilo' (*Lili*), you name 'em, all could silence revellers like a mass bell in Rome – especially when emanating from performers not known for musical restraint: hard men with a romantic underbelly.

Conversely, though the overall impression was that they favoured a more subtle approach, The Searchers could rock as hard as anyone. However, The Fortunes, the most sure-footed of three units of that name from the West Midlands, didn't go in for much wild stuff at all. Instead, they chose to follow the principle that no matter what is

---

* It was still going strong in 1991 when sung by Leslie Nielsen-as-Frank Drebin in the comedy film *Naked Gun 2¹²: The Smell Of Fear*

currently fashionable, an audience for the opposite can always be found. "We've got nothing against beat music," elucidated their Glen Dale, "but we prefer ballads and slower, more tuneful songs."*

The Fortunes – and The Bachelors – were to succeed without having to compromise their stylistic determination, but others could not be viewed even in all-embracing Hamburg as either "so square they're hip" or "so far behind they're ahead". Trad had not recovered from being dead there in 1963 when The Swinging Blue Jeans opened at the Star-Club, walking an uneasy line between trad and mainstream pop so bland that it verged on muzak. "We got booed off on our first night," confessed Ray Ennis, "but we changed to out-and-out rock 'n' roll and then it was okay." That the Jeans could adjust so easily is admirable. That they endured as one of the most frantic archetypes of Merseybeat showed that they weren't faking either.

Such a group had to be truly dedicated to its craft to endure hour after hour of reacting instinctively to, say, the singer's prelusive "weeeeeell" that pitched them into another twelve-bar rocker and that changeless four-four off-beat on the snare drum. With glazed listlessness setting in by the end of the first chorus, some stretches went by as total blurs like some run-of-the-mill job you'd done for years. For that very reason, Dave Berry was one who did not toe the party line about Hamburg: "I hated every minute of it. I feel that every stage appearance should be special, but I failed to see how it could be with repeating the same act six times a night."

After a while, it got ridiculous. "We used to run out of things to play," complained Black Sabbath's Tony Iommi. "I mean we didn't have an enormous list of songs we could do anyway, but it wasn't too bad. After we had done three shows though, we began to run out of material, so we used to play songs over and over again or just make a terrible mess of something we never really knew how to play."

The monotony of dragging out a British palais repertoire was sufficient impetus to rehearse strenuously the most obscure material that could be dug up from the common unconscious. Anything went: calypso, barrack-room ballads, Boy Scout campfire ditties, oompah band drinking songs, songs-with-actions, music hall, the Hokey-Cokey,

---

* Proving that aversion to all-out rock was not indicative of any lack of corporate vigour, The Fortunes survived a series of disasters during a lengthy series of engagements – always one week before or a week after The Casuals – in Germany which might have destroyed a lesser group. One van breakdown necessitated a trudge from Frankfurt to Cologne. Another meant a freezing winter's night sheltering in a public convenience

even rocked-up cracks at all the detested trad stand-bys. The hoariest old chestnuts were tried, though preferment was often given to those granted stage and vinyl blessings by rated US artists. Gene Vincent, for instance, hadn't considered beneath him 'Over The Rainbow' and 'Ain't She Sweet' – committed to disc on his debut LP, 1956's *Bluejean Bop*. Little Richard would likewise slip in 'When The Saints Go Marching In' as Fats Domino would 'Red Sails In The Sunset' – and Ray Charles put his seal of quality on 'You'll Never Walk Alone' and 'Without A Song'. Because it had been been recorded rock 'n' roll style by US comedian Lou Monte in 1958, some groups even took on board the vaudeville novelty 'The Sheik Of Araby'.

Inverting the principle that a drop of black makes white paint whiter, neither had they inhibitions about making a run of the most frantic rockers all the more piquant by hanging fire midway and inserting one deadpanned selection from the perverse and antique likes of 'Beautiful Dreamer', 'You Make Me Feel So Young', 'We'll Take Manhattan', 'Tennessee Waltz', 'Danny Boy' and the skiffle weepies, 'All My Sorrows' and 'Nobody's Child'.

Sometimes a number like 'Up A Lazy River' or 'Everybody's Doing It' would be heard all over the Reeperbahn before being dropped quite inexplicably, never to be played again. In the air rather than actually popular too were 'Michael Row The Boat Ashore', 'My Bonnie Lies Over The Ocean' and similar singalongs that could keep restless audiences sweet if, say, an amplifier fell abruptly silent or the rest of the group were trying to sober up the drummer backstage.

"It was still difficult filling out the time by not doing 'Green Onions'-type stuff, just to pad it out," said Chris Warman – but, if the microphones went dead, apart from wrecking your voices working up a communal 'Bye Bye Blackbird', 'Ging Gang Goolie' or 'Madel Ruck-Ruck-Ruck', what else could you do but an instrumental? Unhappily, some groups couldn't prevent themselves from busking a time-consuming dirge that, like Booker T And The MGs' 'Green Onions', lived only in its riff. That a house electrician raised his thumbs to indicate that the problem was sorted out was no grounds to stop just blowing, blowing, blowing – simply to give vent to your own arrogance and spark off tedious long-term imitative patterns: a drummer commanding the Star-Club stage alone under his own voodoo spell for exhilarating minutes on end in 1962 would father the half-hour of obtuse crash-bang-wallop that would still be driving paying customers to drink in the 1970s.

In the early 1960s, improvised lyrics – even in English – were inclined to utilise a listener's time more interestingly than meandering soloing. As a change from spoken continuity, Gerry Marsden used to sing any words that came into his head over lengthy cycles of chords that propelled him into the ice-breaking opening line of a known song. Certain phrases bore repetition, so he wrote them down for revision and ultimate evolution into items that were no longer mere segues.

So began Gerry's songwriting career. Among its first fruits was a paeon to his future wife, 'Don't Let The Sun Catch You Crying', which he and The Pacemakers premiered at the Star-Club the very day it was penned. A creative triumph too for Van Morrison was his donation of 'One Two Brown Eyes', one of the one, two compositions he'd finished by then, into The International Monarchs' onstage *oeuvre* in 1963.

Yet if a group featured more than a couple of home-made songs, it would provoke criticism in an age when reputations were made more easily by churning out the good old ones, current hits and arrangements of the latest US imports.

The development of songwriting to any great extent was also incidental to the common-or-garden pop musician's self-image – particularly when he was in the midst of the distractions of Hamburg. A typical recollection of The Beatles' Freiheit period was of John and Paul composing in a dressing room while George and Pete let themselves be lionised at the bar, draining the *steins* pressed on them by a grateful clientele. A few Lennon-McCartney efforts were unveiled publicly – two in as many hours by late 1962 – but though 'I Saw Her Standing There' became something of a fixture during The Beatles' Star-Club seasons, it hadn't the fighting weight of 'Twist And Shout', 'Shimmy Shimmy' and the other more fervently anticipated crowd-pleasers.

Where did songwriting get you anyway? No-one paid attention to an original. It was the last thing anyone wanted to hear, whether a kerb-swallow relaxing in the Blue Peter or Bert Kaempfert on the prowl on behalf of Polydor for a bargain-bin "Beat *Gruppa*". As everyone knew, if an opus like that was announced, it was seen usually as an unofficial interval, a chance to do something other than dance or listen.

With the demarcation line between artist and jobbing tunesmith persisting well into the 1960s, it was understood that, if a working outfit contained individuals who made up songs, even as a team, it wasn't a caste-within-a-caste so much as an eccentricity, a bit of fun. At most, it was a half-serious contingency plan so that, should the group go sour, it might be possible to get somewhere purely as a composer.

There was, however, fat chance of Frank Sinatra, that jackpot of all songwriters, covering a would-be rock 'n' roll Gershwin's offerings if howls of affectionate derision were all he could expect from his own group – whose critical prejudices brought forth the same hectoring arguments (like hook-lines from diabolical songs): "You can't beat the Yanks at that game anymore than you can at anything else. We don't need more than what we're playing already? If we did, could a twit like you come up with anything of the necessary standard?"

Often, a twit like him would realise that a song was no good as soon as he started coyly chugging its introductory chords, but he'd be handsomely endowed with a capacity to try-try again. More often than not, he'd speak with quiet pride of getting by without being able to read a note of standard music script, and, unimpeded by the formal dos and don'ts that otherwise inhibit creative flow, he'd have so many ideas streaming from him that it was all he could do to write them down.

Shards of inspiration would cut him during the walk to the Hauptbahnhof for *The Daily Herald*. While the others were rampaging round St Pauli, he'd be back in dormitory quietude with the ghost of an opening verse, maybe a sketchy chorus, engrossing him until his scoffing and pie-eyed colleagues surprised him dozing over his instrument, surrounded by cigarette butts, smeared coffee cups and an exercise book full of scribbled lyrics and notation peculiar to himself.

In the teeth of ridicule, grapplings with his muse and an "I'll show 'em" attitude could result in couplets that weren't so McGonagall-esque and, after he ventured into other idioms, tunes and riffs less dependent on the three basic structures that recurred in rock 'n' roll: the "three-chord trick", the twelve-bar blues and, heard most often in smoochers, the I-IV-minor VI-V turnaround. These were complicated frequently by an eight-bar "bridge" passage (IV-I-IV-V) or "middle-eight". Was it so unreasonable to keep in his heart the hope that the rest might consider one of his songs superior to some of the non-originals that'd been in and out of the set since their first hour on a Reeperbahn stage?

For quite a few, it would be a way of imprinting their importance to the group – if they were sure enough of their position to impose unsolicited ideas. Sometimes, they were the quiet blokes who presented no limelight-threatening challenge on the boards to, say, the lead guitarist. However, the concept of his diddle-iddle-iddling being cemented by rudimentary chord-slashing could become rather a misnomer after a few weeks in Hamburg led musicians to anticipate and attend to each other's idiosyncrasies and stylistic clichés – and come to acknowledge their own. As Acker Bilk remarked, "Before I went to Germany, I reckoned I knew a fair bit about my horn – but I'd never been able to get a band together and play away for hours every day. You can have great soloists who make a sound like a bunch of tom-cats when they play together. You've got to integrate yourselves, get to the stage where you know each other's minds – sort of extra-sensory, dad."

In the different framework of a beat group, lead and rhythm guitars would often merge in interlocking harmony; the interaction of *Play In A Day* virtuosity and good-bad rawness compulsively exquisite over the low-fretted throb of the bass. Like Scotty Moore's heart-stopping second guitar break in Elvis Presley's 'Hound Dog' on record, there must have been certain transcendental moments on the boards that could not be recreated, that would look impossible if transcribed on manuscript paper.

For reasons as much artistic as financial, Tony Sheridan was sorry that "no-one taped any of the Top Ten gigs I did with The Beatles" – though Tony could function well enough without a second and third guitarist. So could The Big Three and, during their period of maximum impact, Johnny Kidd's Pirates via their respective guitarists' dazzling lead-rhythm techniques. With the same guitar-bass-drums line-up, Dr Feelgood were to rule the London pub-rock scene in the mid 1970s, and their guitarist and focal point Wilko Johnson was outspoken in his admiration of and debt to Mick Green of The Pirates.

Johnson was to be as famous for his spasmodic movements onstage as his picking. A tenet confirmed years earlier in Hamburg was that a mediocre guitarist could make himself seem outstanding by training himself to turn round abruptly at moments of high drama, and play with the guitar on the back of his neck, above his head or in the small of his back. If the results were likely to be so askew as to be noted by even the most tone-deaf onlooker, he'd settle for stepping forward to solo with grimacing flash, his eyes fixed on the neck of his instrument as if stupefied by his own dexterity.

Guitarists anchored less to underlying chord patterns than the melodic requirements of the song were seen as either anodyne or attractively unfussed. Colin Manley, Tich Amey and Gerry Marsden were three who thus directed their talents to their groups' general good rather than their own self-aggrandisement.

Younger players were, nevertheless, more likely to copy Gerry's stagecraft rather than his fretboard style – or make of guitar. That he used an orange Gretsch was to have less influence on a schoolboy's choice of instrument than the fact that, on his excursion to Frankfurt with Ricky Richards, John Lennon had acquired a Rickenbacker, then the only American electric guitar available in Germany – though it was based on a hand-tooled acoustic prototype by German Swiss artisan Adolph Rickenbacker who, on emigrating to Los Angeles to establish a manufacturing firm in 1925, had marketed the solid-body electric that would stimulate the company's spell of greatest prosperity after John's 1996 Model was rechristened "The John Lennon" in 1964. The arch-Beatle had liked it for its unusual sharp-finned, short-armed shape. If employed but rarely for soloing, its uniquely jangling effect as rhythm *arpeggio* was seized upon most conspicuously by The Searchers – whose endorsement coupled with their chart breakthroughs also swelled Herr Rickenbacker's coffers – just as Hofner had been advantaged by Paul McCartney's televised thrumming of its "violin" bass, bought from a shop on the Reeperbahn in 1961.

By today's standards, electric instruments sounded puny yet harsh and atrociously distorted as they battled with amplifiers of thirty-watts maximum that were sent through speakers known to tear, explode and even catch fire because of power surges and the mismatch of British and German ohms. Paul McCartney would recall that, "If we had troubles with our overworked amplifiers – we had to plug two guitars into the same one – I'd just chuck it all in and start leaping all round the stage or rushing over to the piano and playing a few chords."

The Star-Club's ornate concert grand was to be good enough for Jerry Lee Lewis and Little Richard to punish with parts of their respective anatomies other than fingers, but if you hadn't bought your own keyboards, you usually had to contend with house eighty-eights with maybe up to half the keys missing and the rest out of tune. If you still wanted it to be heard, you could stick an omni-directional microphone near or in it, but a drummer had to fend for himself. "My Ludwig kit had to stand or fall on its own," said Chris Warman, "with no miking-up or clever sounds through systems like they have nowadays."

In the Top Ten, however, the public address speakers, suspended from the ceiling and trained on the dance floor, also faced the stage with the inadvertent but welcome result of giving an instrumentalist, amplified or not, an idea of the overall sound at any given moment. Electric guitarists could then adjust controls accordingly, but before the advent of onstage monitors, programmable desks and graphic equalisers, vocal balance was achieved by simply moving back and forth on the microphone, most commonly the non-detachable heavy-duty Shure type that resembled a small human skull.

You'd be virtually gulping it sometimes as you strained against a house PA constructed originally for oompah bands, and the knock-on effect as a selfish guitarist's volume crept up. Yet breathtaking and intricate three-, four- and five-part chorale was hard-won but honed at all levels, whether "fool" bass rumbling or soaring counter-tenor.

While The Nashville Teens had no fewer than three vocalists unencumbered by instruments, newer outfits were tending, by 1963, to contain no non-playing members – with guitarists (particularly rhythm players), organists and even drummers frequently expected to double on other instruments – as, for example, Beaky Dymond and Paul McCartney did – when required as well as join in on harmonies, vocal counterpoint and even take the lead when the usual front man needed to get his breath back. "Me, Carl and the guitarist Johnny Mann shared lead vocals," said Ace Kefford. "I used to do 'Jump Back' and Brenda Holloway's 'Every Little Bit Hurts', then we'd go back to Carl and 'My Prayer', 'She Loves You' or whatever." Likewise, Beaky and Dozy took over on occasion from Dave Dee, and Bobby Rankine was the ballad merchant in Alex Harvey's Soul Band.

Gerry And The Pacemakers once brought Faron over to Hamburg as guest vocalist. Disposed towards knee-drops and scissor-kicks, the leader of the then-disbanded Flamingos was in his element, along with all the other natural showmen like Harvey, Dee, Rory Storm, Dave Berry – and "Freddie", a former child film actor and sometime member of The

Seniors, who adopted the stage surname "Starr" to avoid confusion (and, possibly, litigation) with Herr Quinn.

Extraordinary onstage vitality was also the calling card of yet another Freddie – Garrity – with Manchester's Freddie And The Dreamers. From the common bedrock of 'Money', 'Besame Mucho', 'Kansas City' and other numbers not designed specifically to be funny, their first Hamburg residency wrought stylised semi-vaudeville routines from what had been informal buffoonery. Owing to the language barrier, these hinged on visuals and repeated catch-phrases – like Garrity's "Just a minute!" – that were light-years from the pop-Dada musical junk-sculptures of the group's younger collegiate blood-brothers, The Bonzo Dog Doo-Dah Band.

Cutting the cackle might have cost Freddie and his boys their job at the Star-Club – because it made up for the deficit of manifest teen appeal in their podgy bass player, a drummer with the oily allure of a backstreet used-car salesman, and two guitarists, one shifty-looking in sunglasses and the other prematurely bald. Finally, there was geeky Freddie himself: Norman Wisdom recast as a pop singer.

None of The Barron Knights were Mr Universe either, but they'd started with relatively straight faces before discovering that making monkeys of themselves onstage was the key to not only survival but prosperity at the Star-Club. To a lesser degree, Screaming Lord Sutch And The Savages had arrived in their morbid way at a similarly expedient juncture – while Dave Dee And The Bostons at the Top Ten sugared their sets with deliberated moments of levity like Tich swinging his guitar neck round on each off-beat to trigger Dave's rhythmic ducking to avoid it clouting him on the head – and it quickly became apparent how much English-speaking seamen appreciated Dee's rich fund of dirty jokes.

Nevertheless, as Tuesday or Wednesday night wore on and the percentage of gawpers thinned, groups were inclined to sacrifice much of the light entertainment for the less exacting task of attending to mere music, perhaps whilst perched, strumming languorously, on amplifier rims. "By two am, except at weekends, things got a bit 'tired'," said Chris Warman. "As a drummer, my timekeeping wasn't affected, but fills suffered as fatigue crept in. It became just a simple backbeat."

While accompanists kept pace with each other's physical weariness during the last sessions, a singer might push his endowed octaves past their limits with a strangled vehemence dredged from vocal cords beyond remedy. Unaccustomed to singing for so long and so often, his voice would weaken to a gravelly croak, bubbling with catarrh. When it got too painful, instrumentals and the waving in of second-string vocalists would give a few minutes relief, but medication and enforced silence in the interim before the next evening's stint was the only cure – and that wasn't always sufficient.

Yet, putting on the agony for up to eight shows a night, he got better at capitalising on, rather than shrinking from an inability to pitch past a growled vocal compass without cracking. Rather than try and fail to hit a high note, he'd ad-lib huskily like a gospel shouter as though a song's sentiments couldn't be expressed through expected melodic articulation. However inaudible without electronic assistance, its sandpapery appeal was such that a fractional widening of vibrato during a quiet verse could be as loaded as the most mountainous roar.

With a side-serving of assorted yelps, hiccups, low grumblings and querulous whinnying, these battered nuances came frequently from some spotty, gangling herbert pop-eyed at the microphone or a baggy-trousered, red-cheeked fatty with all the poise of an otherwise desk-bound head of accounts dancing a flustered Twist with a voluptuous typist at the office party. However, if you closed your eyes, with delicate suspension of logic you could believe that such an unlikely-looking singer had truly got the blues from the chain gang or the ghettos of southside Chicago; that he was world-weary, cynical and knowing beyond his years. From this reserve of lived-in passion, however unsubstantiated, he had learned to slip comfortably from suppressed lust through relaxed insinuation to intimate anguish, sometimes mingling ecstasy and gloom in the same line. Some like Cliff Bennett and The Spencer Davis Group's Steve Winwood became fully capable of taking on the material of any black R&B or rock 'n' roll exponent without losing any of the overriding fervour.

Without a rose-tinted hearing-aid, the spirit was willing but however hard others tried to hack it as blue-eyed soulmen, the outcome was only endearingly ludicrous at best. Yet it was commendable how many untutored beat group singers elected instead to compound a mesmerically hideous charm by warping a limited range, quirky delivery, eccentric breath control or natural coarseness to their own devices. This was certainly the ace up the sleeves of Ringo Starr, Screaming Lord Sutch and, as far as I'm concerned, Chris Farlowe.

Some focused on restraint rather than over-embroidery or beer-soaked hollering. Indeed, it was the very lack of obvious drama that was the key to the stentorian nasalising of Van Morrison and the laconic good humour of Dave Berry – who was also blessed with the presence to elicit anxiety rather than contempt from Star-Club listeners whenever a wounded baritone as distinctive as the mark of Zorro laboured through the nth 'Little Queenie' of the night.

If you lacked the 'image' of one such as the serpentine Berry, all you might have had going for you was a mere Great Voice, albeit as sonorous as that of Roy Orbison or Elvis when he did 'It's Now Or Never'. Often it was one that the long shifts had not robbed of supple purity and unslurred diction, or drained a sound reserve that came not from the windpipe but deeper within. Preserving such attributes could make you someone in a realm where it was reckoned that most pop stars "couldn't sing".

"Real singing" was the drawing card of group balladeers such as Bobby Rankine, Barry Pritchard of The Fortunes, and The Rockin' Berries' Geoff Turton with his pleading falsetto. While Ray Phillips of The Nashville Teens could cut up as rough as anyone else, he won the group's vocal power struggle by melting hearts at the Star-Club with his note-for-note copies of Orbison's 'Cryin'' and 'In Dreams', even the former's nerve-jangling coda with its apocalyptic G sharp.

A fräulein's evening was made if she grabbed, however fleetingly, the onstage attention of hunched-up Phillips – who looked as if he needed mothering – doe-eyed Paul McCartney, or Kingsize Taylor who would sometimes shed pounds of his considerable bulk when goading himself, The Dominoes and, vicariously, the onlookers to near collapse. Certain performers' devotion to duty was such that they'd cry real tears during agonised *lieder* with the aid of an onion-smeared handkerchief. You could also resin your hair with Paraffinol (paraffin oil) which served the dual purpose of adding extra sheen and, as it ran down to soak your shirt, make it look as if you'd worked up one hell of a sexy sweat. With all the exhibitionism of a Johnnie Ray, you could bombard the audience with an arsenal of facial expressions, flickering hand-ballets and other gyrations that brought a song to life and, where necessary, made them less aware of a voice shot to ribbons.

Sometimes, it'd rebel and you'd have to choose between chopping an untidy ending in the air after a muddled verse or two, or, if it was a raver like 'Whole Lotta Shakin'', command all bar the drummer, toiling in the background, to abandon instruments and appeal to dancers to clap along to what they had come to recognise as *mach schau*, a backbeat that an idiot couldn't lose: pounding snare, hi-hat and bass drum in the same lone four-in-a-bar rhythm for chorus after chorus. Willing him on, the jigging crowd would stomp and clap in time until the levelling guitars surged back in again and the snare reverted to its usual offbeat, and the hi-hat to eight quavers a bar while the bass drum continued to clump fours rather than its standard rock 'n' roll on-beat.

Departures from this norm included that "bang bang bang-bang-bang bang-bang-bang-bang bang-bang" beloved of football supporters. Another was hitting solidly and defiantly a fraction slow to stockpile the suspense. This practice also invested more formal pieces with sharper definition.

It has been chronicled (by himself as much as anybody) that Pete Best originated the hand-and-foot co-ordination necessary for *mach schau*. Yet Tony Sheridan has maintained that when he performed with The Beatles, an abundance of rhythm guitar and foot-stamping was necessary "because we had to compensate for the lack of a strong beat". Yet regardless of the whoevers and howevers of *mach schau*, it would not be presumptuous to say that the subtleties of rhythmic developments in Hamburg were to alter pop drumming procedures forever.

The Beatles were also among suggested root causes of factions within succeeding Hamburg audiences sparking off orgies of unison *mach schau!* chants (later corrupted to "lets go!") to spur a group's inert front line into stark sensationalism. It was first taken up, reputedly, after a shirty Allan Williams' yelled "Make a show, lads!" at the petrified young Liverpudlians during their first weeks at the Kaiserkeller.

Yet it would be Dave Dee And The Bostons who would defy all-comers as St Pauli's most proficient "makers of show" – partly because, unlike The Beatles, it was a fallacy that they'd arrived as provincial clodhoppers. Nonetheless, it was through the hothouse emergency of *mach schau*-ing for hours on end that Dave and his Bostons – rather than The Beatles – evolved into, perhaps, Hamburg's best-loved musical attraction.

CHAPTER ELEVEN

The Green Green Grass Of Home

"When we got back to play places as far apart as Elgin in Scotland and Penzance, we were a better band. Thirty-six hours a week of working together in Germany saw to that"
Chris Warman (The Lonely Ones)

L ike a chrysalis changes into a butterfly, so encounters with the Fatherland wrought workmanlike groups even from raw beginners by the time they returned with the outsides of their vans defaced with the fräuleins' affectionate messages. As late as 1970, sending groups to Hamburg for a three month stretch was still considered a foolproof way of toughening them for less demanding if more reputable tasks in Britain. Jim Simpson, manager of Black Sabbath, reasoned that it was "rather like training a thousand-metre runner by sending him on five-thousand metre courses".

It also brought any scum to the surface, musical and otherwise. Behind the public intimacies of off-mike comments and momentary eye-contacts, close proximity to each other in bandroom and sleeping quarters could initiate explorations of territory impenetrable to outsiders: jokes side-splitting to nobody else; the open-state of masochistic warfare between two guitarists who both want to play lead; a singer who is everybody's best pal onstage but otherwise shunned by his backing group who move to another table when he joins them in the Blue Peter afterwards; a drummer's heart feeling like it would burst through his rib-cage when the saxophonist smiles at him; and a tacit implication in a seemingly innocuous remark that sparks off a hastily unplugged guitar and a slammed backstage firedoor.

Complications of personal alliances included a case of two homosexuals who ended up in the same group after carnal self-interest had been a factor in the transfer of one from another outfit also resident in the same Hamburg club. The Alex Harvey Soul Band and The Bobby Patrick Big Six each contained brothers, but sibling rivalry – and personality clashes between non-relations too – could resolve into a brusque empathy for the sake of the group.

So it would be too that worms would turn, and a gentle drummer's barbed rejoinders to ritual antagonism would turn him from a "sitting duck" into a jovial straight man in Ted, the group loudmouth's running commentary on the daily grind of stage, bar and bunkroom. Sardonically amused by everything, Ted held forth at every opportunity, splitting the concentration of bass player Graham, lying on his bunk, seemingly too involved in filling in all the "Os" on the front page of an old *Daily Mail* to want to listen. For idle hours like this, he'd brought a challenging book but it would occur to Graham that he'd scarcely peeked at it the entire trip, mainly because he couldn't get Ted to shut his fucking gob for five minutes. You couldn't switch it off like a radio. You'd fall asleep within earshot of Ted's twittering, and yawn and stretch to it too. Graham would be noticed staring hard at Ted sometimes, looking as if he was about to swing off the bed with John Wayne deliberation and do something. Sometimes he did.

As well as the drip-drip from hovering aggravations, there were fulminations that had simmered from specific incidents back in Britain, only to boil over in Hamburg. "Tony Sheridan and I were like chalk and cheese," said Ricky Richards. "One time, he was standing there with his brand-new guitar, taking the piss out of me when I was singing at the 2I's in 1959. That was like a red rag to a bull to me – so I lashed out with my foot at him, and kicked a hole in his guitar instead. In Hamburg, we had a run-in about something or other, and I knocked one of his teeth out with a right-hander. Horst Fascher came in to separate us, and he was in tears – because we were gods to him, and he couldn't stand us fighting each other."

All the bitter discord and intrigues that make pop groups what they are would become all the more piquant through living up each other's armpits in Hamburg. Two members of his backing group came in giggling drunk and ate everything in the absent Paul Raven's larder. Ricky Barnes was revolted by John Lennon's sick jokes.

There were professional problems too. Beset with dark nights of the ego, a lead singer in the wings notes with trepidation the screams that the two guitarists' Everly Brother-ish duet of 'Besame Mucho' evokes. If I have to, he'd think, I'll make President Kennedy vote Communist to prevent that happening again.

Then there was Ned, the new bass player, attempting to foist revolutionary doctrines – namely the rotten songs he wrote – onto the status quo and the various creative monopolies. If he didn't resign himself swiftly to just fretting in grey mediocrity beyond the main spotlight, he'd have to go as soon as someone meeker came to light. There were a lot of really good guitarists over here from the Midlands – Alvin Dean, Dave Mason from The Hellions, either of them could step in – but if Ned was dumped, would we lose his fans? Would the other fellows be willing to carry on without him? What if there was a *coup d'état* and they got rid of me instead? Worse, what if they decided that someone else ought to give the orders – or that the group ought to have no demarcated "leader" at all? How would it feel if they were moved to another club, and I wasn't the one that decreed who slept where, ensuring that I had the least crowded bedroom? Who'd be kipping down on the floor if we were a bed short? It was too ghastly to contemplate, the affront to my supremacy as much as the discomfort.

The same questions came up over and over again as the often barely tolerated leader's private hell and the plottings of his underlings punctuated a group's history with unresolvable feuds, whispered onstage spite, prima donna tantrums, backstage post-mortems, *ménages à trois*, homoerotic horseplay and interminable petulance over the most trivial matters. Someone forgets to sing the middle eight of 'She's The One For Me', and then hums it all the bloody time for the next three days. "We got on each other's nerves," admitted Tich Amey. "If you put down a comb, and turned round and looked for it, perhaps Dozy had picked it up, done his hair and stuffed it in his pocket. Silly incidents like that would become major issues, but we stuck together – and that's what made a lot of groups at that time a proper unit – a month in Hamburg. Being on the road in bed-and-breakfast places was one thing, but to be in the dormitory of the Top Ten was another."

Bickering helped pass the time. So did poking ruthless fun at whoever seemed most likely to rise to it. Teasing would increase in frequency during the residency and beyond, by degrees less subtle and less good natured. Intermittent retreats, as if to a prepared position, were as disconcerting as the insults. So were sudden episodes of aggressive friendliness that obliged the acceptance of over-hearty back-slapping, nose-pulling and affectionate punches with a forced smile, and suspicion that they were laced with intense and covert character assassinations over venomous lagers in the club's murkiest corner. Someone would go too far, and there'd be slanging matches and even fisticuffs before an ebbing away that left the combatants, livid with hatred, glowering at each other from the opposite ends of a dressing room, muttering conspiracy to respective sidekicks.

Even those who studiously avoided confrontation would have their fill of the glory and stupidity of being in the group. They all had – because there was no reason for any let-up in the malcontented shiftlessness, the underhanded manipulations, the verbal and emotional baiting, and the general temper-charged ugliness, visible and invisible, back in digs that were worse than ever for all the cursory clearing away of junk food leavings, overflowing makeshift ashtrays, old newspapers, used rubber "johnnies" and congealed vomit.

"With a handful of pills and three bottles of brandy," Paul Raven held it at arm's length: "I could stay awake for a week. Quite often I did – because anything was better than going back to our room. Two of the band wore the same clothes for five years. We cooked in there too, so the place smelt absolutely terrible."

Back in London, his marriage was muddling on towards divorce, but Paul stayed on in Germany like so many others who, despite disturbing erosions in relationships within and without, remained bound to a group by common ordeal one minute and jubilation the next. However, the more serious-minded musician's hand in the on- and off-duty frolics was frequently a duty rather than a pleasure. Neither did such a person contribute much to the group's restricted code, superstitions and folk lore. On the periphery of their private jokes, and as reliable as he was mature, there was no denying that he was a bit, well...you know.

One who didn't quite fit was Stanley Poole, drummer with Dave Dee's Bostons. He was older than the rest, and had a wife and children.

Like Paul Raven, he had to send most of his money home. Though they could ill-afford it, the others still liked Stanley enough to help out with tithes from their own wages. Yet it wasn't to be Dave Dee, Dozy, Beaky, Stan And Tich after it was suggested in 1964 that the outfit rename itself using everyone's nicknames. "Stan ummed and ahed, said 'I'm leaving' and then didn't," Tich Amey explained, "and in the end, we gave him an ultimatum – so he went."

A beat group without a permanent sticksman was no good to anyone. As it was everywhere outside London, drummers were vexingly few and far between. Just ownership of a full kit was sufficient for the striking up of overtures for your services from groups all over the district. For The Bostons back in Salisbury, there was a chap Dozy knew in Amesbury called Mick Wilson who'd blown cornet in the Salisbury Silver Brass Band. More importantly, he also had an old drum kit on tripods, but it was sturdy enough; the cymbal stands didn't keel over, and the bass drum didn't creep forward. No-one knew what Mick was like on it, but he wanted to bash it for a living. Anyway, beggars can't be choosers, can they?

Dave Dee, Dozy, Beaky, Mick And Tich didn't lose heart, and slogged their way to stardom, but that first season in Germany finished The MI5 who left Johnnie Law onstage at the Big Apple as resident singer, fronting visiting groups like The Shoes from Holland and Germany's own Bats; each of whom had seized upon whatever aspect of British beat they felt most comfortable – The Shoes going in for Spencer Davis Group imitations. Their blithe dedication to their craft was refreshing, "but they couldn't compare to the British," said Johnnie. "Yet they were gentlemen, neither of them made me feel uneasy, but I was missing The MI5 – except for the little arguments we used to have. Now I was on my own, I watched all the other groups having the same little arguments – and I had nothing to do with them."

As well as nebulous "musical differences", groups had to contend with a guitarist deciding to shampoo his hair five minutes before showtime; a drummer on another planet with amphetamines; a saxophonist in the same state who screeches through the set semi-comatose on his back; and members uniting with the club manager on the last night of the season in roundabout persuasion and then naked pleas for the singer to return for an encore, no matter how ungraciously it was bestowed, in order to forestall a riot. Defiance, hesitation and final agreement might chase across his face, but if he got as far as the wings, there was no guarantee that he wouldn't bolt at the last second.

Nobody would be on speaking terms as each tore the cellophane from several packets of duty-free cigarettes during infuriatingly slow departures *en route* to the Hook of Holland and the ferry to Newhaven. A few hours later, the old home town looked the same when they stepped down from the train.

The steam was still hissing from the undercarriage as the members of the group went separate ways, one or two with a mumbled "Never again". Certain gluttons for punishment, however, might have added a tacit "until the next time", having reached a conclusion – perhaps wrongly – that they stood more chance of livelihoods as journeyman musicians in Germany than persisting with a spent force like this lot.

Travelling round the Federal Republic during the cruel winter of late 1962 in The Don Adams Band's small, heaterless van, Albert Lee recalled that, "We had to huddle round a tiny Primus stove in the back. We almost froze to death – and almost wrote ourselves off when the van turned over on the ice. I was glad to come home after that one – but I flew straight back out there to play with this German band, Mike Warner And The Echolettes, for three months. Mike Warner dumped us and it took me ages to scrape up my fare home."

A year later, The Krew Kats were stranded too – until repatriated by the British Consul who gave then their tickets and five shillings each after they'd signed forms promising to repay it all. The Consul had done the same for The Undertakers after their eight weeks in Hamburg over the summer of 1962 had ended with two members behind bars – while a trip to Berlin two years later was to climax in an eighteen-hour interrogation at Checkpoint Charlie.

With an entry in the lower reaches of the UK Top Fifty then, most of The Undertakers had sufficient incentive not to return to Straightsville via application form and supplicatory telephone call, just as a hand-to-mouth existence as maybe a jobbing commercial artist in the bohemian district of Liverpool Eight had not beckoned John Lennon. Yet a musician in the next group, wrestling with occupational as well as personal stock-taking, had gazed glumly from the train window, storing up mental pictures of a country that he assumed he'd never see again – because, for all the startling moments on the Hamburg stage, the writing was on the wall for, if not the group, then his continuance of his own career in music.

To his loved ones, he looked just like a refugee from the war-torn Europe of the 1940s. He'd lost weight, and had the sapped colour of one who'd eluded sunlight and was nourished exclusively by those squalid snacks that he was able to keep down. Yet stung by "I told you so" recriminations within minutes of dumping his cumbersome luggage in the living room, the prodigal might launch into exaggerated if selective accounts of his exploits and his familiarity with Dave Dee, Kingsize Taylor – what a character! – and the chart-riding Undertakers.

In his own little room again that night, he'd determine to cling on in showbusiness somehow or other as a more committed "entertainer". Seeing that the group boom was here to stay, he'd find one that was more a financial venture than a bunch of blokes playing together for the hell of it. He'd expect them to channel a percentage of their earnings into new gear, stage clothes and transport as a matter of course, and do whatever willingness and energy would do to push them further up the ladder of success – all the way up if the time came.

Yet, in the factories, offices and college staff rooms of Britain today, how many are the middle-aged employees who, following a spell in Hamburg, had offered instruments taking up cupboard space, and monolithic speakers serving as room dividers to the very music shop counter assistant who'd sold them, when less the worse for wear, to lads for whom the two contracted months at the Star-Club would be, they reckoned, the first step towards world conquest? Well, all they'd recouped were memories that would become more golden in flashback when, all pals again, they indulged in orgies of maudlin reminiscence about the group that had had everything it took back in 1961 when the Earth was young.

However, far from being crestfallen, one of the selfsame group had returned with a new assertiveness. His family weren't sure that they approved of it, and they'd got swiftly onto the inevitable bit about it not being too late for him to resume an apprenticeship, snare some cushy office job, or go away to college. Ostensibly uninviting prospect it might have seemed, but the latter was on reflection almost a cheering thought: anything to get away from the prying about what he'd got up to in Hamburg, the reproaches and the comparisons with children who were a credit to their parents. Finally, being back in Germany seemed the lesser of all evils what with his so-called "steady" wondering when they should name the day; the HP firm about to repossess the amplifier, and a galvanising letter from Alex Harvey offering twenty pounds a week to fill a space soon to be vacated by a Soul Bandsman looking homeward to Glasgow.

All signposts had pointed back to the Fatherland for Howie Casey after Kingsize Taylor found room for him in The Dominoes, following the series of small peaks and deep troughs that had led to the end of The Seniors. It had started when a fire in a Liverpool club took with it all their equipment. This setback was alleviated in 1962 when the outfit – with Derry Wilkie sharing vocals with the man who became Freddie Starr – was booked for an opening season at the Twist At The Top (formerly the Room At The Top), a club in Ilford.

Their "three month stint at the Kaiser Keller" (sic) was mentioned on the jacket of the long-player (attributed to *Wailin'* Howie Casey And The Seniors) of Hamburg showstoppers taped at the Essex venue by Pye who'd visualised them as an English "answer" to Joey Dee And The Starliters whose residencies at New York's Peppermint Lounge had also merited a "live" album of similar material, and enthusiastic press response – though a notice in the *Ilford Recorder* hadn't the impact of one in *New York Cavalcade*. Yet Howie's band still made "Twistory" – as the sleeve notes had it – as the first Merseybeat act to have a record released, a fact not greatly appreciated at the time, least of all by Pye whose patience snapped after none of *Twist At The Top*'s three spin-off singles garnered enough airplay to get near the charts.

Like Howie, other ex-Seniors did not spurn work in Germany for all the harsh precedents of 1960. Groups tended to be housed nowadays in hotels like the Pacific which, if crowded at times, was a far cry from the stinking bunkers of yore. Moreover, though there was still a lot of hanging about between sets, the actual hours spent playing were generally much reduced too.

Nevertheless, after she penetrated 1965's German Top Twenty with the self-composed 'Terry' – about a biker who zooms off to a moonlit end of squealing brakes and gore-streaked tarmac – Twinkle's unnerving spell at the Star-Club, where the hard-faced Rocker coquettishness and leather-jacketed virility implied in 'Terry' was all too real, caused even this prototype "wild child" to retire as a full-time entertainer at the age of seventeen.

It had been, perhaps, too much of an adventure for Lynn Annette Ripley. Pet-named "Twinkle" from the cradle, hers had been a privileged girlhood of chauffeurs, maids and meeting royalty at Ascot. She'd known few who'd lived much differently from her own people in genteel Kingston Hill where Surrey merges with London. However, since finding herself microphone in hand one evening at London's unlicensed Esmerelda's Barn (part owned by the Krays), blonde, personable Twinkle had been allowed a weekly two-song spot with the resident Trekkers before Daddy's Bentley arrived to carry her home at midnight.

A recording contract and transient fame followed, and when she began touring with the likes of The Rolling Stones and Wayne Fontana And The Mindbenders, her parents insisted on the offstage omnipresence of a uniformed nanny to guard their gifted daughter's innocence. Sometimes, however, it was all too much for Nanny. "Hamburg was the first place I ever went to without an escort," cried Twinkle. "I went on with a pick-up group, and it was a nightmare – mainly because I thought I'd have to do one set. I did several, doing the same numbers and wearing the same outfit. I gave up performing then and there."

A singer from Sheffield, Joe Cocker was as defeated – so much so that it was fanciful for him to look to future triumphs when stacking and loading newspapers in a WH Smith warehouse after disbanding his Big Blues outfit – who'd almost starved during three months of hard graft round US air bases in Europe. The Dominettes – who had regrouped as The Ugly's (sic) – had had nearly as hard a time of it during ten 1964 weeks at the Klub Kon-Tiki in Munster.

Neither a hypochondriac nor malingerer by nature, Paul Raven also came close to packing it in after singing for five nights with the double-pneumonia that would see him on a Hamburg infirmary's danger list. Disease nearly finished Harrow's Episode Six too. "A month's club work in Germany turned into a terrible sweat shop thing," elucidated their Roger Glover. "I contracted acute peritonitis there, and ended up in hospital."

After a subsequent two months in the Lebanon – "playing background music to the clatter of one-armed bandits" – Episode Six became, like every other act that spent lengthy sojourns abroad, an unknown quantity locally. Some groups did not remain so for long after casually cataclysmic performances that had been forged, often unknowingly, from the *mach schau* fracas, day in day out, week upon week. "You don't know it's happening to you because you get tired," suggested Dave Dee, "but when you come home, you aren't half tight – musically tight."

Before the stage lights, you sounded Big Time now – and behaved as if you were too. As you'd been shown by someone like Tony Sheridan, you carried on as if you were up there just having fun amongst yourselves. Yet whereas the customers might have Twisted to the other outfits on the bill, there'd been a spontaneous rippling towards the stage a few thundering and startling seconds into the first number.

If they took exception to the onstage cigarettes dangling from lower lips, and, of course, the horrible row, it was food for thought for other local musicians who witnessed it – because no-one could deny its impression on the crowd who remained spellbound until the coda of the final number and the long moment of shell-shocked hush before a spatter of clapping crescendoed to a bombardment of whistling, cheering, stamping pandemonium.

Who were they then, this new group? It was an easy mistake to think that they were foreign on the strength of pre-engagement publicity. "A lot was made of our 'tour of Germany' when we came back," noticed Dave Hill, but no-one was remotely fooled when his In Betweens unfurled their broad Black Country accents between songs. Gerry And The Pacemakers, however, had been popular on Merseyside before they'd even left for Hamburg, and during their first booking on returning to home turf, Gerry was at a loss to understand why his announcements were drowned in jeering: "It took me a few seconds to catch on. Then I realised what it was all about: I was still introducing the numbers in German."

Yet Marsden could not rein the salty vocabulary that had pocked his onstage continuity at the Top Ten. Liverpool didn't mind, but bad language from Hamburg shellbacks kindled extreme reaction in other areas. Much of it came from the Teddy Boys that had remained at large despite the slings and arrows of fashion. Striking a blow for decent entertainment for decent folk was an excuse to have a go at these twerps with their poncy haircuts. Post-performance punch-ups apart, displeasure was most painfully expressed in a shower of pre-decimalisation pennies cascading stagewards, carrying on after the lacerated musicians evacuated the boards and throughout the master-of-ceremonies' attempts to restore order.

Though they'd never admit it, the Teds couldn't really fault the musicianship or the group launching into unashamed classic rock from the 1950s if it felt like it – because German teenagers, as Kingsize Taylor observed, "were a bit behind the times. They go for the old Little Richard gear and stuff like that." In the Bobby era too, a homecoming group had seemed even more like a throwback now that pop was at its most innocuous. Dance crazes generally indicate stagnation in pop, and Britain in 1961 was certainly heaving with that. Yet dire though they were, the Twist and its off-shoots were all there was if trad was too mellow. The search for anything more riveting on the wireless was fruitless as both the Light Programme and Radio Luxembourg were overflowing with slop-ballads that made your granny smile, from Craig Douglas, Jess Conrad, Mark Wynter and further blow-waved domestic heart-throbs in the US Bobby mould.

If that's what the young wanted too, what was the point of trying to get up onto the next level? Maybe Mum and Dad were right. Perhaps a steady job, a mortgage, maybe wedding bells were worth considering after all during the days of inactivity when a group wasn't back on the time-honoured grindstone of bookings in Britain. It was possible to keep up an illusion of professional employment for years on a road that was obscure and quiet, a dusty, wearisome road that didn't look as if it led anywhere important – but there was always a chance that it might. You only had to be in the right place at the right time like The Seniors at Twist At The Top. Look at Cliff Bennett and his Rebel Rousers who had an EMI single out as early as 1961, or The Jaybirds who'd snare a recording deal of sorts with Embassy, Woolworth's budget label, to run off carbon copies of the hits of others.

The Barron Knights, The Swinging Blue Jeans and Bern Elliott had all got as far as studio auditions in London, and it disturbed others that the fish weren't biting for them as well. To Dave Dee, it appeared that, despite his group's St Pauli repute, "Every other band that worked with us [in Hamburg] all got recording contracts. We went round to most major record companies more than once, some of them three times, and we were told to sort of go away and chop up our instruments."

Summoned to Germany or Butlin's for another few weeks, who could blame one such as Dave shaking a frustrated fist in the direction of London while putting off making any unretractable life decisions as he carried on drifting from pillar to post, from bandwagon to unsatisfactory bandwagon, all arriving at the same commercial impasse?

"We were working a holiday camp at Clacton," Dave Dee continued, "but on Thursdays we had an evening off. So we were able to moonlight and do gigs outside. We went down to this ballroom in Swindon to support The Honeycombs, a band that had just had a Number One record. We had to do one hour either side of their spot, and the singer, Denis D'Ell, saw the first part of the act. He went backstage, dragged his managers out, and said, 'You should come and listen to this band. They're pretty good.' The managers, Ken Howard and Alan Blaikley, approached us during the interval and said, 'Look, we think you're great. Would you come up to London and we will get you a recording deal.'"

Tich, Mick, Beaky, Dozy and Dave Dee were, indeed, a hard act to follow. They listened politely to this new offer though, heaven knows, they had been disappointed enough already to be doubtful about Blaikley and Howard. Sodden with bitter ruminations, it seemed daft for the Wiltshire lads to be anything but pessimistic.

On the firmer ground of the teenage clubs, they'd noted that the repertoire of outfits like theirs who'd had the German experience were being copied by others. Fans too were intrigued about the sources of the sounds that had nothing to do with the current hit parade. A significant date in the life of Dundee schoolboy Donnie Coutts (later drummer in The Syndicate) was a night in 1960: "I went to see a marathon Twisting competition. When The Johnny Hudson Hi-Four started, this was it! They were doing the stuff they had learned in Germany so since I worked at Low's Record Shop on a Saturday, I began looking out for records. I discovered that Motown was released on Oriele – The Contours, Barrett Strong, then The Impressions – so I started passing on the material to Johnny to learn."

Back at the Scala ballroom in Dartford, Bern Elliott And The Fenmen had also cut most of the previous Cliff Richard And The Shadows niceties in favour of seemingly archaic rhythm-and-blues – and, doing likewise in Southampton, Buddy Britten And The Regents were no longer Buddy Holly And The Crickets clones now that R&B could stretch to a wide spectrum of blues-based forms from Louis Jordan to Chuck Berry to Joey Dee And The Starliters. Purists preferred a definition sufficiently narrow to exclude anything with a horn section or the phrase "rock 'n' roll" in the lyrics, but "The best R&B bands I ever saw," pronounced Mike Hart of Liverpool's Roadrunners, "were The Beatles, The Big Three, The Bobby Patrick Big Six and The Alex Harvey Soul Band, but they weren't boring enough."

A lot of the groups themselves were dispirited on returning from the open-all-night frenzy of Hamburg to slate-grey Britain where the last chip shop closed at ten o'clock at all points outside the geographical pool from which the British entertainment industry in London was prepared generally to fish for its talent. On the plus side, there was a full workload within easy reach, and it was quite common to cram in three separate engagements from an array of parochial jive hives over a solitary weekend evening – and, during a month underscored with recurring run-of-the-mill dates, there'd be side trips to maybe a golf club dance in the next county – or a spot around the middle of the bill at a theatre with tiered seating.

The running order at these events was seldom a matter of conjecture. Pop meritocracy had less to do with ability as chart seniority. If you hadn't even got a record out, a lousier act that had would headline over you. Further down the scale, provincial pop was so inward-looking that there still seemed to be few realistic halfway points between obscurity and the Big Time – and a policy of territorial defence was epitomised by a closed shop of venues in England's westward regions where, visitors of hit parade eminence notwithstanding, work tended to be given only to groups from the area such as The Betterdays who were to Plymouth's Guildhall what Bern Elliott And The Fenmen were to the Dartford Scala, The Gentry to the Flamingo in Ballymena, The Corncrackers to Llanelli's L-Club and on and on and on. All pop groups are the same. Why import them when our own boys can do the job just as well for a fraction of the cost?

It must have been tempting to fling all of it back in the faces of palais promoters and record company talent scouts alike, who, old and square, ignored grassroots alternatives to dull mainstream pop, quite happy as always with the tried and trusted formulae of catchy tunes, harmless fun, pretty faces, stage costumes, dancing to the Madison, and themselves raking in a bit of cash at the end of the day. Why not thumb your nose at all of them and turn it in? Let's cheat them of another group to milk dry and use as disillusioned scapegoats when they're overtaken by the next bunch of poor souls.

Sod the record industry's shortsightedness, its mental sluggishness, its cloth-eared ignorance! Who needed the time-serving incompetence, the fake sincerity, the backstabbing and the contradiction of excessive thrift and heedless expenditure? In what other sphere of the most corrupt business could you sink into such a deep cesspit of embezzlement, arm-twisting and concealment of guilty secrets?

Getting shot of it, you could still get your kicks in some weekend combo proud to have such a distinguished man-o'-the-boards in the ranks. At dinner parties and during coffee breaks, you'd have the opportunity to be attractive in your down-to-earth reasonableness – casual but not falsely modest – about disengaging yourself from a life that was exciting but unfulfilling. Folk might deduce from the odd secret smile and what has been left artfully unsaid that you had an "interesting" past. Some would even believe that you had, indeed, Hit The Big Time in lands afar.

The children would brag in the school playground about their once-famous Daddy, and workmates would be less inclined to rib you about the aberrations of a flaming youth after they'd seen you perform at the social club on Saturday. Belying your daytime occupation as stock-controller, welder or bus conductor, the volume of applause had risen momentarily when, like you'd planned, you'd stubbed out your cigarette and ambled calmly on stage three seconds after the rest. Those who imagined they were in the know had convinced themselves that they could glimpse a profile once defined by the footlights at the Star-Club, and the years had fallen away.

CHAPTER TWELVE

All Around The World

"I remember how excited The Beatles were to meet Richard. In Hamburg, they'd always be with him, asking him about America, the cities, the stars, the movies, Elvis and all that"
Billy Preston (Little Richard And The Upsetters).

So frequently did they make the trip that groups were greeted like old friends by a customs official who'd remark if a guitarist had grown sideburns or a drummer had gained weight, and ask after a sacked lead singer. What he wouldn't do was make the token fuss about the *carnet* for the van like he had first time round. That was when he gave clearance for it to be loaded just minutes before the ferry cast off, just to put the wind up this silly little shower gibbering with childish excitement and stopping just short of open insolence.

They weren't such kids anymore, but they were still raring to get back. In that resolve, they were in empathy with the title song of Freddy Quinn's musical, *Homesick For St Pauli*, that German milkmen were whistling throughout spring 1962. By then, Hamburg clubs were offering more powerful incentives for the most in-demand British talent; not least of which was *flying* to Hamburg-Fuhlsbuttel air terminal rather than crawling to Germany by land and sea. Certain individuals were able to demand even more. The Top Ten's proprietor, Peter Eckhorn, hadn't quibbled, for instance, when Ringo Starr, asked for thirty pounds a week and the use of a flat and car to transfer from Rory Storm's to Tony Sheridan's backing group.

If the undisputed king of the Reeperbahn, Sheridan faced tough opposition whenever UK stars of the same vintage were brought over – among them Johnny Kidd, Vince Taylor, Emile Ford – and Screaming Lord Sutch with his simulated slaughter and mutilation that nearly went horribly wrong one night at the Star-Club when Freddie "Fingers" Lee, his pianist and "prostitute", forgot to put the protective wooden board in his blouse for the "Jack The Ripper" sequence, and his screams were all the more blood-curdling as the dagger brandished by the unknowing, cackling Lord punctured his flesh.

With Freddie out of action, the ruler of horror-rock was left, so it seemed, without anyone to "murder" and in danger of being murdered himself by a let-down audience. However, as his next set of the night coincided with the Dave Dee group's beer break at the Top Ten, Sutch procured Stan Green who, because the wooden board was nowhere to be seen, was throttled rather than stabbed.

David Sutch's reputation preceded him when Manfred Wotilla booked him and The Savages for the Starpalast for a weekend to headline over three other groups. Johnnie Law And The MI5 – who appeared second-to-last – remembered his Lordship breaking five microphones at the Barrowland club in Glasgow months earlier. Foreknowledge of Wotilla's cash-conscious foibles, however, prevented history repeating itself in Kiel. "Lord Sutch was pretending to cut a microphone cable," noticed Johnnie, "and he stopped and said, 'Oh, I'll have to be careful or Manfred will cut my money.'"

Sutch went down well in France too, even when it was challenging British dominance of German club pop with *yé-yé* entertainers such as Les Chats Sauvages, Les Chausettes Noires and a Parisian Elvis in Johnny Hallyday, a blond youth whose singing and passable mastery of the guitar had earned him a virtual residency at Le Golf Drouot. Most of Vince Taylor's Playboys were absorbed into Hallyday's backing group after one unhinged evening at the Paris Olympia when old Vince had floated onstage in atypical white vestments to preach a repent-ye-your-sins sermon to a mystified then furious *yé-yé* audience.

Little Richard had got religion too. He'd recorded little but sacred material since enrolment in a theological college, and had, in 1961, embarked on a gospel tour of the world. Nevertheless, it had become a straight rock 'n' roll presentation containing hardly anything but his old smashes by the time it reached Europe where Richard and his band, The Upsetters plugged gaps in the itinerary with German dates not at the Ernst Merck Halle, Hanover's Sportspalast or the Kellesberg auditorium in Stuttgart, but the Star-Clubs in those same cities.

British musicians there for the season were as starstruck by the celebrated Richard as their own fans were by them – for the "Georgia Peach" in billowing drapes and overhanging pompadour who'd captured their adolescent imaginations, was still discernible in the soberly attired, bristle-scalped exquisite they met backstage, and later saw on stage when he shrieked his head off and hammered the piano, just like he had in *The Girl Can't Help It* when it had reached European cinemas in 1957.

Emulation of heroes is a vital part of growing up, affecting the clothes you can't afford, the hair style you're forbidden to have, and the manner in which you mouth into your fist in front of the bedroom mirror. As a schoolboy, the self-image of many a UK rock 'n' roller was formed with Little Richard lurking in the background. To Gerry Marsden, warming up the audience for him was "like an audition before God", and Richard himself would inform his biographer, Charles White, that "Paul [McCartney] would just look at me. Like, he wouldn't move his eyes – and he'd say, "Oh Richard, you're my idol. Let me touch you.' He wanted to learn my little holler, so we sat at the piano going 'Oooooooh! Oooooooh!' until he got it."

Like Caesar deified by the Gallic peasants, Richard would offend none by refusing gifts pressed upon him – like one of Paul's best shirts. The US legend's graciousness did not seem, however, to rub off on John Lennon who, having made up his mind to be the hard man he never would be, preferred to exercise an observed disrespect in the presence of a star. Calling Richard "Grandad" and telling him to shut up was the least of it, but Lennon was as diligent as everyone else in making myriad private observations of his idol's performances for incorporation into his own. "He really got into my bones," agreed Paul Raven after catching Little Richard at Berlin's Stattehalle, "and he got me stamping and jumping, and I decided afterwards that I really had to go back to rock 'n' roll."

To do so then would have placed you so far behind that you'd be ahead of 1968's rock 'n' roll revival in Britain – which would see a reissue of 'Rock Around The Clock' in the Top Fifty. Yet in Germany, Bill

Haley had never been away, and, while this portly old smiler could no longer raise riots, he played before a crowd of thirty thousand in Berlin in June 1964, and was better received than the co-headlining Manfred Mann, even though he hadn't had a record in the charts for years, and the English group were on the crest of 'Do Wah Diddy Diddy', their third European smash and first million-seller.

German demand for Haley showed no signs of slowing down two years later when he shared a dressing room in Kiel with a disconsolate Paul Raven who, unlike Bill, was tiring of his particular musical rut. Unlike Haley, he also hadn't had hits. He never would either, he told Bill ruefully, despite the years he'd spent trying. The older man made encouraging noises about carrying on regardless, don't let anyone stand in your way, you'll get there in the end...

Paul would remember the conversation years later – and was surprised when Bill did too. Ray Charles' more general recollection of socialising with the British pop contingent in Germany was that, "We would sit and say we loved each other's music – the typical thing that people in our musical brotherhood all do." Yet no matter how ordinary – even boring – the likes of Haley and Charles might have appeared, you'd pinch yourself to check you weren't dreaming that you were keeping your end up when hanging about with those who'd been impossible yardsticks of aspiration and escapism during the drudgery of 1950s schooldays.

On a backstage staircase, you might be passing the time of day with Pat Boone, Chubby Checker, Jerry Lee Lewis, Brenda Lee, Ricky Nelson or Little Eva, propagator of the Locomotion and the Turkey Trot. In the wings, you'd stand next to a squat, rather tubby old bloke who'd waddle onstage to metamorphose into Fats Domino. Afterwards, you'd hand a camera to Alex Harvey to take a souvenir photo of you with the great American. You wouldn't think to ask Fats to snap one of you with Alex.

US luminaries had become affordable when the Star-Club gave no quarter during a ruthless if costly campaign to outflank all rivals as the Reeperbahn's premier music venue. A desperate tactic of the less wealthy Top Ten was to bill a Glaswegian duo who xeroxed The Everly Brothers as the real thing for two months while the *real* real thing managed only four evenings at the Star-Club.

Manfred Weissleder also won the lesser bidding war for the most dependable UK talent, beating by twenty-five per cent Peter Eckhorn's offer of three hundred marks each for The Beatles, then on point of lift-off. Yet even a British group of this calibre would be expected to provide accompaniment if required for passing US solo artists like Davy Jones, who, on the strength of a big moment with a disc entitled 'Amapola', had gained well-paid work in Europe that he was able to sustain through an easy professionalism that cut less assured acts to pieces. Among those privileged to back him were Johnnie Law and his MI5, The Bobby Patrick Big Six – and the aforementioned Beatles who likewise served Gene Vincent when his usual group, Sounds Incorporated, were delayed and missed his opening night at the Star-Club in the summer of 1962.

Many a British outfit would so impress a US vocalist that he'd hire them on a semi-permanent basis. Thus Philip Goodhand-Tait and his Stormsville Shakers, a Midlands combo, landed a prestigious job backing Larry Williams throughout Europe – and, after greeting Chubby Checker at Hamburg airport with a publicity-earning guitar fanfare, Kingsize Taylor And The Dominoes were present at every stop during the Twist potentate's quasi-royal progress round West Germany. Jerry Lee Lewis was to record an in-concert album in 1964 with The Nashville Teens at the Star-Club* – while Gene Vincent had Sounds Incorporated constantly on the move during the European legs of too many unbroken years of relentless touring.

So popular was Gene – the "Screaming End" – in Germany that a banner with his name on it hung across the Reeperbahn announcing an imminent appearance at the Star-Club where he'd have pulled a capacity crowd through word-of-mouth even after finding himself in Hamburg time and time again. Like London buses, if you missed one Gene Vincent show, there'd be another along if you waited.

However, rather than play backstage host to a residue of stargazers, Gene and those of similar standing had opportunities to form genuine friendships with managers, staff, patrons – and, especially, fellow musicians. In either the heat of performance or the cool of bar-stool gossip afterwards, eyes would meet through the cigarette smoke. Thus George Harrison hit it off straight away with Billy Preston, The Upsetters' fifteen-year-old organist, and Dave Sampson became particularly friendly with Ricky Nelson (and was to be deeply saddened

---

* Selections included 'Money', 'Long Tall Sally' and 'What'd I Say'. It sold well in Germany and France, but legal problems stood in the way of US release. In 1964, the Teens also backed Jerry Lee on a lip-synched song in a low-budget UK movie, *Be My Guest* starring David Hemmings

by his sudden death in 1985).

Few of the new-found chums in Hamburg had any way of knowing then to what extent their lives would interweave. They seemed only likely to meet again if the Yanks' booking schedules brought them back in Europe, but then came the pop watershed year of 1963 when the visitors were infected directly with the bacillus of British beat, much of it made contagious in Germany. It was spreading throughout Europe, and the North Americans were able to make educated guesses that – with The Beatles as principal carriers – it was likely to prove as unstoppable and incurable in their own continent.

CHAPTER THIRTEEN

Liebestraum Twist

"It was a really bad song, but we gave it a dynamite instrumental track. We needed the money; you do when you're drinking your pay every night"

Van Morrison (Georgie And The Monarchs)

With but a few months to go before the coming of the first of these upstart beat groups in the hit parade, The Shadows ruled Europe throughout 1962's windy spring with 'Wonderful Land'. Its reliance on massed violins upheld British record industry bigwigs' suppositions that outfits with electric guitars were *passé*. With the exception of The Bachelors, such vocal units as there were in the UK charts – The King Brothers, The Kaye Sisters, The Springfields, The Viscounts and precious few others – were unlikely to be caught titillating Grosse Freiheit fancies with their polished harmonies and rehearsed patter.

Since amplified groups were unfashionable, their records were viewed as small time in comparison with earnings on the boards in somewhere like Hamburg. Yet the commercial discographies of many British beat groups either began or were perpetuated with releases via the record firms, production companies, pressing plants and publishers centred in a city that accounted for over fifty per cent of the total disc output of West Germany, the third largest such market in the world.

A lot of Hamburg's pop output came to be produced under conditions interrelated with the free-and-easy attitude of its red-light district. Until then, a typical session had been tethered by Musicians' Union regulations. These were weighted on the side of any malicious fourth row violinist who yelled a gleeful "time's up!" in the middle of a take in an age when artists were expected to finish within ordained periods divided by tea-breaks and an hour off for lunch during conventional office times or an evening period with the studio janitor turfing everybody out well before midnight.

Such rigidity had not been conducive to the freshest possible performance from a Reeperbahn nightbird like Ricky Richards whose debut single was issued in early 1961. His Jets were still holding their own at the Top Ten when Ricky gave 'em something from the German hit parade, namely 'Fräulein' by Chris Howland, the games show host trying his hand at pop. During the next intermission, Richards was invited by a Gerhard Trede to join his party at a *stein*-laden table. A producer for the Philips label, middle-aged Herr Trede was there to rub a professional chin during The Jets' recital, and had decided that Ricky rather than Tony Sheridan was just what was required for a couple of jazzy backing tracks awaiting a lead vocal in the studio attached to Trede's riverside abode in Fuhlsbuttel. Shall we say ten o'clock in the morning?

The appointment made, Gerhard finished his drink and left, and the chosen one returned to work. When The Jets wound up at three am on the Big Day, Ricky wondered whether to snatch a little shut-eye – though he didn't feel like bed yet – or miss out a whole day's sleep and hope for the best. This internal debate was enough in itself to banish rest, and so he killed time in a bar, a walk round the fish market and on to breakfast at the Seamen's Mission before hailing a cab to take him to the airport suburb six miles north of the city centre.

After paying the fare, Trede conducted Ricky into the studio annexe. It had been assumed that Richards would be able to sight-read the sheet music to the two songs, 'OK Madame' and 'Tanz Mit Mir Dixie' ('Dance With Me Dixie'), but only the chord letters beneath the staves made any sense to the self-taught guitarist. Could he not take the music back to the Top Ten bunkroom, figure out the tunes, and get his tongue round the German lyrics? We could have another go tomorrow. No, said Gerhard, just keep listening to the backing tapes, and pick it up by ear. I've got faith in you.

By early afternoon, Ricky, despite his fatigue, had learnt each opus well enough for what he imagined was a cautious test recording. There followed an ominous silence of many weeks from Trede. Meanwhile, The

Jets disbanded and Richards threw in his lot with the troupe entertaining the troops round Frankfurt. It was from one such base that he made an enquiring call to the producer about whether the disc was ever going to be recorded. Recorded? You've done that already, Ricky. 'OK Madame' coupled with 'Tanz Mit Mir Dixie' is a week away from the shops.

If nonplussed that his bleary-eyed efforts – credited to "Rick Hardy" – were about to be unleashed on the German public without his knowledge or permission, the young man's excitement that he might be now on the way to Freddy Quinn-sized stardom was not tempered by catty remarks from jealous fellow artists – who were no doubt delighted when this one-off forty-five was cast adrift and lost on the saturated radio wavelengths of northern Europe.

It had had as much chance of being a hit as a message in a bottle has of reaching its addressee but, to the mild amazement of everyone concerned, another item tossed as recklessly onto the vinyl oceans washed up in Frankfurt's local Top Twenty during summer 1963. The group was Georgie And The Monarchs; the company was the German division of CBS – whose Ron Kovacs was barking orders from behind a glass-fronted booth of editing blocks and compressors after the thrilled young Irishmen arrived at a complex in Cologne.

Selected by Kovacs, the A-side of a proposed single was 'Boo-Zooh', a semi-instrumental with a voice carrying the melody line. It would need an explanatory '(Hully Gully)' after its title on the label – so that the cats would know with what permutation of the Twist they were supposed to cut a rug. The boys did what they could with 'Boo-Zooh (Hully Gully)' and were rewarded with what both they and CBS recognised as an unrepeatable freak occurrence, a novelty in similar vein to The Singing Dogs or 'Woo Hoo' from The Rock-A-Teens.

Van Morrison's 'One Two Brown Eyes' was not lent critical ears by Kovacs – though some numbers penned by members of The Beatles had been worthy of Bert Kaempfert's attention in May 1961 when, for a flat fee of three hundred DM, the standard union rate, the group backed Tony Sheridan on his first single, 'My Bonnie', and other items. Their only previous recording experience as a group in a *bona fide* studio had been a bit of a lark in 1960 when, minus Stuart Sutcliffe and Pete Best, they had pitched in when a couple of Rory Storm's Hurricanes had taped three ballads in the minuscule Akustik studio into which extraneous sounds from the adjacent Hauptbahnhof would infiltrate if the door was left ajar.

The following April*, The Beatles and Hurricanes had been thrown together again in Hamburg, this time at the Top Ten with The Jaybirds, performing in rotation both their own spots, and those in Tony the Teacher's timetabled master classes. The star pupils were The Beatles, who Sheridan chose to be with him onstage when Alfred Schlacht, a publisher associated with Deutsche Grammophon dropped by.

At Schlacht's urging, Bert Kaempfert looked in too. Though approaching forty, Kaempfert did not look as out of place in the club as Gerhard Trede had when checking out The Jets. Resembling Craig Douglas's slightly older brother, Bert was no longer just the supplier of songs and orchestral backwash to such as Freddy Quinn and Ivo Robic. He had surfaced as something of a pop personality in his own right following a recent global smash with his arrangement of 'Wonderland By Night', a sound portrait of Manhattan. Though this, his most enduring recording, was the work of another writer, Kaempfert was to be foremost among German pop composers who made headway in English-speaking territories. Off-the-cuff examples are his co-writing of Presley's 'Wooden Heart', Nat "King" Cole's 'L-O-V-E', his own 'Bye Bye Blues', 'Danke Schoen' for Wayne Newton – and Frank Sinatra's chart-topping 'Strangers In The Night'.

This excerpt from Kaempfert's score to the spy film, *A Man Could Get Killed*, lay five years in the future when he entered the lives of Tony Sheridan and The Beatles. "Bert came in for several nights," recounted Tony. "He'd been trying rock 'n' roll with young German artists like Tommy Kent, but it had sounded ludicrous – because you can't sing anything approaching rock 'n' roll in German. He was impressed, therefore, with what he thought was our authenticity – which was, of course, second-hand American music infused with elements of our own which were authentic.

"On stage, it was a free-for-all. I was doing most of the lead guitar – though if, say, John wanted to take a solo, he'd be halfway good because it came out of the rawness in him. George was young, inexperienced and a bit over-awed by the whole thing – but very keen to learn. Bert made no comment on this."

As it had been for Ricky Richards, the artists were hastened to the

---

* By coincidence, Brian Epstein was attending a Deutsche Grammophon course in record retailing management in Hamburg that same month – though his path did not cross those of either his future clients or Bert Kaempfert then

studio by taxi mere hours after the last major sixth of the night had reverberated in the Top Ten. They puffed apprehensive cigarettes, gnawed chewing gum and tuned up in the hollow chamber which Tony Sheridan learned was "the British Army Radio Station – where Alexis Korner had worked when in the army – which was in a big assembly hall within the Friedrich Ebert Halle, a school in Harburg, just outside Hamburg. There being no afternoon lessons in Germany, Polydor used it for their pop acts prior to leasing a studio in Tondorf later on. We used the same equipment at the back of the stage that was there when the British occupied Germany in 1945. Yet the German method of recording music – especially classical and all the Freddy Quinn stuff – was very competent."

While 'Wonderland By Night' might not have been to Tony or The Beatles' taste, they were in awe of the man who'd breathed the air round the King, and been voted "Bandleader Of The Year" in *Cashbox*, the US music business journal. Yet for all this, Bert was neither imperious martinet nor condescending intercom voice. Instead, he acknowledged freely that he was more at home with light orchestral outings. He even admitted that he'd have preferred Sheridan to have been framed in that fashion, but it was a combination of the budgetary restrictions of Bert Kaempfert Produktions and his own puzzlement about why his inhibited attempts at German rock 'n' roll hadn't left the runway that had dictated the employment of a British Beat *Gruppa* to punch out each song in three takes at most behind an acoustically separated Sheridan.

"The attitude was: 'Let's put a single out from the sessions and put the rest on an LP if it does well'," remembered Tony. "Bert was quite happy to leave it all to us to play 'live' – like we did at the club – after discussing the choice of material with him. I'd heard Gene Vincent do 'My Bonnie' – very differently – and later on, I heard a Ray Charles version. Long before we'd even thought of recording it ourselves, we'd done a Jerry Lee Lewis-type arrangement, but without piano. The B-side was 'The Saints', which was a rocked-up signature tune of my old skiffle group."*

Tony Sheridan was the man of the moment in 1961, and The Beatles merely one of two outfits, both to be called "The Beat Brothers" because, as George Harrison reminds us, "'Beatles' was too close to *die pedals* – whatever little kids' terminology would be for it – that's German for 'prick'." The art student in Sheridan was unimpressed too: "Polydor

---

* The Beatles also recorded 'If You Love Me Baby', 'Sweet Georgia Brown', 'Why' and 'Nobody's Child' with Tony Sheridan

couldn't use 'Beatles' on the record label because it sounded slightly rude and, optically, it looked like nothing. I used to think the name was rotten."

The other Beat Brothers was a more amorphous affair with ex-Jet Colin Milander the only mainstay. "He'd be on all my other records," said Tony Sheridan, "and a tour of Israel until 1964 when he returned to England to become a decent citizen. He and I recorded with whoever was around. Roy Young came in. So did Ricky Barnes – and Alan Hawkshaw who was on keyboards with Emile Ford's Checkmates, and several drummers including Tony Newman from Sounds Incorporated, and Gibson Kemp – who was to succeed Ringo in Rory Storm And The Hurricanes. Sometimes we used two drummers at once. Once, we were about to do a version of 'Ruby Baby', and Joey Dee And The Starliters were performing that same number in the Star-Club – so we took them into the studio to do the backing vocals (with Bert Kaempfert playing these wooden blocks out of rhythm)."

Bert had considered a single release without Sheridan by this Milander edition of The Beat Brothers to be a worthwhile exercise. In selecting a "Hully Gully" arrangement of the children's play rhyme, 'Nick Nack Paddy Wack' as the A-side, he imagined he couldn't go wrong if only because plundering public domain music (deemed to be "traditional") – as well as the sections everybody knows from classical music – meant that you could cream off composing royalties.

That this has always been an intermittent ploy in European pop is exemplified by Sounds Incorporated's German single, 'Wilhelm Tell (Twist)', and, six years previously, Danyel Gerard's rock 'n' roll adaptation of 'Billy Boy', a huge seller in France in 1958. A few months after that, Kaempfert's British compeer Cyril Stapleton had even cracked the US Hot Hundred with an upbeat muzak medley of the same sort of doggerel – that included 'Nick Nack'. Why shouldn't the grafting of a robust Chuck Berry backbeat onto it not be just as commercially potent as doing likewise to 'My Bonnie' and, during the same Sheridan sessions, 'Swannee River'? Hell, what did it matter if the original time signatures were different?

Kaempfert thought twice about The Beatles' similar go at 'Ain't She Sweet', but it was not to be issued until it had acquired historical rather than artistic importance. While Lennon and McCartney weren't obvious no-hopers as songwriters, Bert heard nothing from them that was in-keeping with contemporary trends. However, 'Cry For A Shadow', a George Harrison instrumental, sounded enough like The Shadows for it to be immortalised on tape before everyone packed up for the day. After destiny had taken The Beatles' hand, Kaempfert would recount that, "It was obvious to me that they were enormously talented but nobody – including the boys themselves – knew how to use that talent or where it would lead them."

Issued in June 1961, 'My Bonnie (Mein Herz Ist Bei Dir Nur)' would be incorporated into The Beatles' act – with Lennon assuming Sheridan's lead vocal – to emphasise the group's association with a disc that, like 'Boo-Zooh', had lodged itself in a parochial chart, *viz* Hamburg's Top Ten of Twist singles where – though an explanatory "Rock" was printed between the title and the writer's credit (translated as "Trad arr Sheridan") on the Polydor label – it nestled amongst a domestic cover of Joey Dee's 'Peppermint Twist', 'Liebestraum Twist' by a certain Charly Cotton, 'Steller Zahn' by Oliver's Twist Band as well as the usual Chubby Checkers. For whatever reason, disc-jockeys in other areas started spinning the Sheridan forty-five too, and cash changed hands for twenty thousand copies within a fortnight.

After it came to rest at Number Five in the West German charts, it was Tony's correct assertion that, "The initial success of 'My Bonnie' had nothing to do with The Beatles, but it was a stepping stone for Brian Epstein to come into the picture." The Liverpudlians' final weeks at the Top Ten had become very long, itching as they were to get back home to crow about their marvellous achievement. When they did, fans would ask for 'My Bonnie' in the department store where Epstein was a bored and frustrated sales manager. Thus his fate was sealed. Something lured the tragic Brian to a Beatles lunchtime bash at the Cavern and awoke in him a desire to be their Larry Parnes.

His clout as a major record retailer in northern England was to impel Polydor's UK outlet to release 'My Bonnie' – by "Tony Sheridan And The Beatles" – in January 1962. The *New Musical Express* reviewer Keith Fordyce was generous ("worth a listen for the above-average ideas") but, unaired on either Radio Luxembourg or the Light Programme, the disc died its death – just like it did that same month when it appeared in the USA where a three-line news snippet in *Cashbox* made a lot of the

'Wonderland By Night' hitmaker's part in it.

If he wasn't to be an Elvis in the wider world, Tony Sheridan restricted himself to staying adored as one in Germany. As it turned out, 'My Bonnie' would bring him to a prominence that he might not have warranted in the ordinary course of events. Though later recordings were of greater musical merit, 'My Bonnie' was to be as synonymous with Tony as, say, 'Rock Around The Clock' to Bill Haley, 'Be Bop A Lula' to Gene Vincent, and 'A Whiter Shade Of Pale' to Procol Harum.

The most immediate outcome was a 'My Bonnie' EP in September 1961 as a taster for an album freighted mostly with tracks by Milander's Beat Brothers. These encapsulated a musical inventory of Top Ten audience expectations: a huge helping of classic rock in 'Whole Lot Of Shakin' Going On', 'Ready Teddy' and 'Hallelujah I Love Her So'; corny old 'You Are My Sunshine' and 'Swannee River', and bang up to date with 'Let's Twist Again'. It also contained 'Skinny Minny' (sic), an obscure Bill Haley And The Comets title, that as a single would restore Tony to the national hit parade.

For good measure, the LP also embraced 'I Know Baby' and, in homage to the place, 'Top Ten Twist' – two originals dragged from Sheridan who then "saw no future in writing songs myself because Bert Kaempfert wanted ballads to be in German. He came up with 'Ecstasy', a Ben E King number. Lee Curtis did it too."

Though Sheridan – like big-voiced Lee Curtis – could emote a *lied* almost as poignantly as Ray Phillips doing Orbison, his forte on vinyl in the early 1960s was condensing his uptempo crowd-pleasers into the two to three minutes that was the *de rigueur* length of pop tracks then. Yet while his post-'My Bonnie' overhauls of such as 'Let's Dance', Lee Dorsey's 'Ya Ya', 'Kansas City' and – as inevitable as Valentino's seventy-eight rpm reading of 'Kashmiri Song' – 'What'd I Say' were pleasant enough, the slick exactitudes of the studio adulterated the *au naturel* power that in its full flowering could exact hey-yeah submission from the most ill-disposed audience. Tony himself would glower that, "I've never been very happy with the music I recorded in the early days. We could have done much better stuff."

"We" would come to mean Sheridan and The Bobby Patrick Big Six, a known recording entity in its own right, albeit with releases sprinkled over several labels including Polydor who were quite amenable to the Six

George, Stuart and John at the Dom fairground

Pete (extreme left) and Stuart (extreme right) stand aside as George, John and Paul await their walk with destiny

The Fab Five at the Top Ten

(L-r) The Bostons' Beaky, Dozy and Tich at the National Beat Contest finals

Ricky Richards was the first UK rock 'n' roller to release a forty-five in Germany

Graham Bonney – one-hit-wonder at home but enormous in Germany

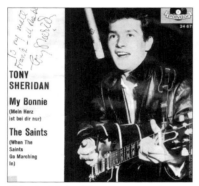

This single's backing group gave it historical importance

The only occasion when Spencer sang lead on one of his own Group's A-sides

Gene Vincent

Bill Haley (right) and two Comets

With Searcher-in-waiting Frank
Allen on bass, The Rebel
Rousers back Bo Diddley at the
Star-Club, 1963

Backstage at the Star-Club,
Jerry Lee Lewis (left) holds
forth to Cliff Bennett

Ray Phillips, the only remaining original
member of The Nashville Teens

Bert Kaempfert

With the sundering of Paddy,
Klaus And Gibson, Klaus
Voorman (flute) landed on his
feet as one of Manfred's Menn

Lord Sutch screaming

Tich (left) and Dave Dee

In the 1980s, Horst Fascher was a
wanted guest at Beatles conventions

Johnnie Law (seated) And The
Tremors in the 1970s

Ricky Richards' passport, bloodstained after his 1960 road accident at Luneberg Heath

Screaming Lord Sutch And The Savages, 1995: the author is on keyboards and Tony Dangerfield on bass

Former Searcher Tony Jackson in the nineties, in affectionate mood with fans in Swinging Sixties garb

Dozy, Beaky, Dave Dee and Tich, 1985

Geoff Nugent fronts The Undertakers, 1989

The Pretty Things, 1997, consisting of Dick Taylor (extreme left), Phil May (centre) and three of Bern Elliott's former Fenmen

amalgamating with Sheridan. "Polydor regarded us as a novelty," said Tony, "that they didn't want to drop as long as we made enough money for them to register at least a small profit."

Many of the company's Hamburg signings – including Alex Harvey – chose to record in a studio that Peter Eckhorn had had built at the rear of the Top Ten. On the rebound from a night on stage, a musician's adrenaline could be pumped more profitably onto a spool of tape rather than into after-hours pleasures that might poleaxe him with a hangover or gonorrhea. It also meant that you could follow creative instincts that would raise the eyebrows of any middle-of-the-road producer aiming for moderate success with moderate records of Bobby blandness.

Contractual problems obliged some of the works of Harvey and his Soul Band – mostly discs solely for the Top Ten juke-box – to be issued under pseudonyms like "Bruce Wellington And His Robber Band". Even an eponymous 1964 LP from the club studio could not feature Alex's usual combo but one culled from the ranks of Kingsize Taylor's Dominoes – who were already Polydor artists. Nevertheless, this – and *The Blues*, a semi-acoustic album made the following year in Hamburg with younger brother Leslie – hinted at what the former "Tommy Steele of Scotland" was to become in sterling trawls through 'Framed', 'I Just Wanna Make Love To You' (both still in Alex's act a decade later) and various urban and rural blues – and instances of his predilection for messing with iconoclasm in renditions of such as 'Waltzing Matilda', 'The Big Rock Candy Mountain' and 'When I Grow Too Old To *Rock*', an adaptation from a Rodgers and Hammerstein musical.

From plug-in to final mix, it took only twelve hours to tape *Alex Harvey And His Soul Band* but that was nothing against Kingsize Taylor And The Dominoes banging out an entire LP between four-thirty am and eight am one morning for a remuneration that worked out at one pound per minute of needle time. Among the busiest of all the British outfits that recorded commercially in Germany, the group began as accompanists to another Polydor act, Audrey Sarno, whose singing of her A-side, 'Bitte Bleib Doch Bei Mir' ('Please Stay With Me') was all the more affecting for her being told about her father's death just before the session.

The single was attributed to *Audrey Arno die Tony Taylor Band* (sic). Not such a mistake, however, were the diverse aliases Kingsize used to shelter from the blizzards of writs that might have settled if it had been discovered that he was on the books of Polydor, Philips, Fontana and Decca at the same time. "Kingsize would sign anything," sighed his bass guitarist, Bobby Thompson, "and I had terrible visions of being sued. I don't know how many records we made, but it has to run into a couple of hundred individual tracks."

Form tended to overrule content, and most of the numbers were common property of scores of other groups. 'Twist And Shout', 'Dizzy Miss Lizzy', 'Hippy Hippy Shake', 'Dr Feelgood', 'Money' – all the old warhorses were smashed out, one take each, by Kingsize and his ever-changing Dominoes, and issued on an abundance of vinyl formats. Outlines would dissolve between each via inclusion of the same tracks on compilations and repackagings – like 1963's chart-topping *Let's Do The Slop, Twist, Madison, Hully Gully With The Shakers*, reissued as *The Shakers' Twist Club With Kingsize Taylor And The Dominoes* after one of the record companies rumbled that The Shakers and Taylor's group were one and the same.

Kingsize would have no reason to be distressed about the proliferation of these grippingly slipshod products, but the two hours of in-concert recordings that The Searchers made for Philips at the Star-Club in 1962 would come back to haunt them after their UK chart breakthrough a year later. These had even contained a nascent version of 'Sweets For My Sweet', the song that had done the trick, but it was a single, 'Sweet Nothin's', that threatened – ineffectively as it happened – to damage sales of the official follow-up, 'Sugar And Spice'.

Three more ancient tracks from the same source would rear up on a *Twist Im "Star-Club" Hamburg* LP by Philips. The club was also the location of the Teenbeat series of EPs from Ariola-Eurodisc as well as discs on its own independent Star-Club label by residents such as The Liverbirds, Shorty and Them and The Roadrunners. For Lee Curtis and Ian And The Zodiacs, it was a springboard to deals with Philips and their entertaining hopes of chart success; Curtis seizing on Marty Wilde's 1962 revival of Frankie Laine's 'Jezabel', and slugging it out with Tony Sheridan over 'Ecstasy'.

Recorded in Hamburg too under the aegis of house producer Siegfried Loch, a 1962 xerox of The Marvelettes' 'Beechwood 4-5789' was the first manifestation of Ian And The Zodiacs' practice of heisting the overseas hits of others wholly for the domestic market – just as The

Casuals were to do in Italy, and with similar effect. Thus The Zodiacs and Ian were to checkmate Adam Faith (with 'Message To Martha') and Sounds Incorporated ('Spartacus') in the German Top Twenty.

Fame in the Fatherland was not as qualified for Neil Christian after he surfaced as a Presley-like figure in German pop. Long absences from Britain to consolidate this may explain why, after he notched up but one chart entry ('That's Nice') at home in 1966, such fans as he had there would learn of a Christian record on the Deutsche-Vogue label that they were never likely to hear climbing high up the West German Top Twenty.

Even his backing group – as Christian's Crusaders – were allowed a Germany-only single in their own right, and the guitarist Ritchie Blackmore's *entrée* into Polydor studios in 1965 as a session musician was partly on the strength of his having been a Christian sideman. Unable to recreate that 'That's Nice' miracle elsewhere, Neil would spend the rest of the decade racking up further German smashes of which 'Two At A Time' – all oompah brass and quasi-military drumming – was typical.

A Londoner of the same 1966 one-hit-wonder standing in Britain as Christian was former actor Graham Bonney. As a singing guitarist, he'd joined The Trends and then The Riot Squad before turning to session work. After he was heard on records by The Ivy League, Julie Rogers and Jet Harris, he had found himself in 1965 in the backing group of Michael Chaplin when this son of the famous Charlie fancied his chances as a pop singer. Having a go himself, Graham met with fractionally more success than Chaplin at home with the self-penned 'Supergirl' tip-toeing into the Top Twenty – just – before it rocketed into the stratosphere in Germany. After 'Supergirl' slipped from its six weeks at Number One, Graham – *und die Jive Five* (his backing group) – elected to concentrate on goods intended purely for Germany.

As implied in titles like 'Das Girl Mit Dem La La La' and 'Aber Nein Nein Nein', Bonney went the whole hog, more or less, by singing in the same language as his consumers. To a lesser extent, Lee Curtis and Tony Sheridan were to succumb too – and, though Germany wasn't all they had going for them, both The Beatles and Searchers would release German-language arrangements of certain of their hits; the latter group under the supervision of Deutsche-Vogue's producer and lyricist Laurence Yaskiel – who would translate 'Sugar And Spice' as 'Sus Ist Sie' ("she is sweet") and 'Needles And Pins' as 'Eintousend Nadelstiche' ("a thousand needle pricks").

In 1966, The Spencer Davis Group were to make use of their leader's German degree on the sole occasion when Spencer was better equipped than Steve Winwood to take lead vocal on an A-side – albeit only in Germany. Its *bierkeller* joviality anchored by a maddeningly familiar riff on fuzz-tone guitar, the Group's medley of Walter Kollo's 'Det War In Schoneberg' ("He was in Schoneberg") and traditional 'Madel Ruck-Ruck-Ruck' ("Maiden, come closer") was seen as either an aberration or a breath of fresh air in an unremitting stylistic atmosphere of popped-up R&B. Davis was to record another forty-five in German – of 'Aquarius' from the musical *Hair* – perhaps to subsidise a stay in Berlin after a cryptic 1968 press release had announced that "Spencer Davis has left The Spencer Davis Group".

Years earlier, Johnnie Law's own period of vocational reflection, fronting pick-up groups at the Big Apple, had ended with his acquisition of the nucleus of a more fixed set-up in The Tremors – a bass player and guitarist from Scotland plus a Hamburg drummer – who backed him on two German singles for the Philips subsidiary, Fontana: 'Sing La La' and 'Ring-A-Ding-Dong'.

From the titles, you may be able to imagine what they were like, but for what it signified rather than its sound, even a foreign record release was a yardstick of achievement back home – though less so than in the bad old days when trad had held the whip-hand with regard to bookings. However, in the space of a solitary season in Hamburg in 1963, many a local outfit had been astonished to return to a scene that had been turned on its head.

As it had been in Germany, trad bands were now the ones desperate for work as, with each passing week, another jazz stronghold either closed down or adopted new guidelines that enabled young rock combos to defile its stage. More and more church halls, social clubs, village institutes, pub functions rooms, ice rinks and even riverboats were offering pop evenings now. To the chagrin of trad-loving impresarios, the entire country was crying out for these bloody beat groups as the Olympic flame of this Merseymania or whatever it was called was carried to its every nook and cranny.

CHAPTER FOURTEEN

Just A Little Bit

"People think they're listening to the Liverpool sound, but what they actually hear is the Hamburg sound because this is where it was created"

Kingsize Taylor

You didn't have to look far for the principal blueprint at a time when The Beatles could have topped the charts with 'Deutschland Uber Alles'. Back-of-beyond youth club quartets from Enniskillen to Great Yarmouth wore shiny collarless suits, cheeky grins and *Pilzen Kopf* haircuts that looked like spun dishmops whenever they shook their heads and went "oooooo" like Paul McCartney-via-Little Richard. They each had an unsmiling lead guitarist who, in his own mind at least, picked a black Rickenbacker just like George Harrison's. Some of them even went through a phase of putting on tortuous Scouse accents for onstage announcements, *thank yer very mooch.*

In Liverpool itself, those too young to have spent lunchtime sessions at the Cavern with The Beatles huddled in blankets for days outside the club to be sure of being first in when the group came home. With two smash hits in rapid succession since their disc debut that summer, The Searchers were causing Lennon *et al* nervous backward glances. The Beatles may have ruled the Cavern, but The Searchers' status in the similarly mildewed Iron Door was such that it hosted their fan club convention in January 1964. This drew coach parties from distant London, but only three of their idols attended as Tony Jackson was stranded on the wrong side of the North Sea.

The UK chart offensives of both The Searchers and The Beatles had been disturbed by disinclined obligations to honour outstanding Star-Club engagements, contracted when each was renowned only within the hinterlands of the Mersey and the Elbe – and before their respective managers had coaxed them to forsake leather cosh-boy gear and the grosser extremities of *mach schau* for mohair suits, playing to a fixed programme, "back-projecting" rather than fixing on front row *fräuleins*, and not cursing or mucking around onstage half as much.

If a group had gone smooth or was full of any prima donna attitudes that often came with such preparations for fame, a couple of weeks in Hamburg could take them down a peg or two. As The Beatles' first *bona fide* forty-five, 'Love Me Do', had lost its tenuous grasp on the British Top Twenty, they were considered by Star-Club staff to be no more deserving of red carpet treatment in December 1962 than Kingsize Taylor And The Dominoes, Cliff Bennett And The Rebel-Rousers, and The Carl Fenn Combo: the other acts also second-billed to headlining Johnny And The Hurricanes.

In time, The Beatles could be bigger than Hitler, but it was the here-and-now that mattered. The audience was getting restless, The Nightsounds had just started their set at the Top Ten, and The Beatles weren't on stage yet because their new drummer, Ringo Starr, had gone missing. Of them all, he'd been the most resentful about being away from home over Christmas. Nevertheless, he excused himself with a joke when fearsome Horst Fascher came upon him back at the digs, pedantically "collecting sticks or changing cymbals – so I told him that if he wasn't on stage on time, I would kick him up the arse".

For The Searchers, an equally onerous return to the Star-Club exactly a year later had hidden long term blessings that emerged from social and musical intercourse with Cliff Bennett And The Rebel Rousers. By the time the Liverpudlians got back, a sparser arrangement of a Bennett showstopper was to become their second UK Number One and the song that most people would associate forever with The Searchers. "At the Star-Club, we stole 'Needles And Pins' from Cliff Bennett And The Rebel Rousers," admitted John McNally. "We found out that Jackie de Shannon did the record, so we got it and learned the song. We performed it with Tony Jackson singing lead but when it came time to record 'Needles And Pins', the lead vocal just didn't happen. In the end, Mike Pender sang it because it needed a softer voice. We'd have lots of situations where a song goes down a storm on stage, but when it comes to record it, it doesn't seem to happen – so you have to make a few adjustments."

The upshot was an irrevocable schism in the ranks – and the most major personnel change of the Merseybeat era. The decision that Pender should be to the fore on 'Needles And Pins' was made by Chris Curtis – because "if anyone was the leader," Jackson conceded, "Chris was. He was the spokesman, did all the interviews. In Hamburg, his drum kit was positioned at the front. He used to play standing up."

Outsiders like Frank Allen of The Rebel Rousers noticed that Curtis in Hamburg was "the supreme showman and a hideous singer, though his recording voice was melodic and atmospheric. I enjoyed their company [The Searchers], particularly the caustic quick wit of Chris Curtis. Mike and John were very much my kind of people too. Neither of them drank to any extent, and most of their spare time was spent writing long letters home to their girlfriends."

Yet it was southerner Frank's friendship with Chris that was to have an important bearing on the group's future after internal tensions worsened, and the alienated Jackson collected his cards. After giving first refusal to Jackie Lomax of The Undertakers, The Searchers alighted on Allen who would inform Cliff Bennett that he was leaving The Rebel Rousers.

It was regrettable but not disastrous, and Cliff understood perfectly that Frank could not, as he put it, "blow the chance of a lifetime" as The Searchers, exemplifying ideally the two-guitars-bass-drums archetype of the Merseybeat explosion, had been second in the "British Vocal Group" section of 1963's popularity poll in the *New Musical Express* after closing the gap on Gerry And The Pacemakers as leading pretenders to the mantle worn by The Beatles – who had won it with more readers' votes than everyone else put together.

This had rounded off the year of their conquest of Britain via hit parade Merseybeat, Beatlemania and the Royal Command Performance. A postscript was added in a prosy *Sunday Times* article lauding Lennon and McCartney as "the outstanding composers of 1963", and the commission of the first of more Beatles biographies than anyone could have comprehended then.

This publication, Billy Shepherd's *The True Story Of The Beatles*, contained a drawing of John, Paul and George with *Pilzen Kopfs* and stage outfits strolling down what can be assumed to be a St Pauli *strasse*, judging by the questionable caption: "The boys loved every minute of their life in Hamburg and were the best-liked British group there." Only a half-leer on the face of "George" hinted that there'd been anything untoward about the group's conduct during their seasons in the clubs along the Reeperbahn, described by Shepherd as "a street of wild beat dives, crazy strip clubs, loud noise".

Long before this rewriting of history, Manfred Weissleder had anticipated the trend that would motivate it by sending Roy Young and Horst over to Liverpool in January 1962 to winkle out more Merseybeat performers with the same tang of star quality as The Beatles, Kingsize Taylor and Gerry Marsden to likewise get the crowds slopping over onto the pavement at the Star-Club. Among those who satisfied this requirement were The Searchers, The Big Three, The Mojos, The Undertakers (billed as *Die Totengraber*), The Strangers, Lee Curtis and, after a bad start, The Swinging Blue Jeans. However, rather than magic, most of the rest were only capable of music, albeit played with guts, like.

The high summer of Hamburg's musical love affair with north-west England's grimy pivot of Victorian commerce peaked in August with the Star-Club's week-long "Liverpool Festival". When The Big Three began a second residency in November, the foyer was still decorated with copies of *Mersey Beat*, Liverpool's fortnightly pop journal, and its editor Bill Harry was contributing a regular column to the club's own *Star-Club News*. It was small wonder, therefore, that the place was now nicknamed "Manfred's Home For Wayward Scousers".

Musicians from the area were so rife in St Pauli that bar staff's pidgin English was infused with Scouse slang – "fab", "gear" and so forth plus obscurities like "duff gen" (false information) – and, even before Young and Fascher's expedition, there'd been rumblings that once you'd heard one "Merseybeat" group, you'd heard 'em all. "They'd got to the point where they were copying each other all of a sudden," thought Tony Sheridan. "The drummers were very similar," agreed Chris Warman. "I think they were frightened to change the style."

By 1963, Weissleder would be hiring only one Liverpool outfit at a time – with acts from other regions encouraged to drop compromising fab-gear dialogue onstage. Even The Beatles hadn't been immune from sanctions. A story goes that, because the flat provided for them looked as if someone had thrown a hand-grenade into it within a day of their coming, Manfred had been on the verge of sacking them until Henry Henroid convinced him that their promises to be tidier in future weren't empty.

All was forgiven, and the group had played their allotted hours in the Rock 'N' Twist-Parade 1962 that had followed the Liverpool Festival. The line-up had included Gerry And The Pacemakers – and Tony Sheridan who "wasn't impressed with the majority of groups from Liverpool. They were playing for reasons that didn't command respect from non-Scouse musicians. Though they were extremely attractive and charming, the music didn't come up to expectations. It was an affront to watch some of them when there were people like Alex Harvey who came to the Top Ten with the first true rhythm-and-blues band that I'd ever seen live on stage. That knocked me out completely."

The Soul Band was the meat of other discerning musicians too. "Alex Harvey was way ahead of the competition, both as an experienced player and for his feel for the blues," said Ricky Barnes. "None of the Liverpool groups had it – and I mean none of them – they were more like showbands. Alex built an atmosphere. It was a driving, swinging thing and you could see the excitement on the faces of the crowd."

Yet when the Merseybeat madness that was harrying the British charts rebounded on Germany and elsewhere in Europe, sound financial sense kept its representatives pouring in, even those not actually from Merseyside – particularly as so many groups had traced the Beatle scent all too well. This was demonstrated by the moptopped Dominettes who, breaking a journey back to the Midlands in Paris, had passers-by wondering if they really were The Beatles, then braving a season at the Olympia. On hearing The Dominettes' Brummie accents – indistinguishable from Scouse to most non-British adolescents – libidinous females clustered round the group like a pack of friendly but over-attentive hounds.

Yet, though The Dominettes – after rechristening themselves The Ugly's (sic) – landed a Pye recording contract, they were not among the Second City's precious few hitmakers, even though Ray Thomas of The Krew Kats, back from the Fatherland in November 1963, had been stunned to find the local scene "in total chaos. There were about two-hundred-and-fifty groups, half thought they were Cliff Richard And The Shadows and the other half thought they were The Beatles." Partly because it had mushroomed within months of the Merseybeat breakthrough, "Brum Beat" lacked the same cohesion and depth, matured over years of sub-cultural isolation. "A lot of the bands in Birmingham had the same repertoire as those in Liverpool," noted Denny Laine (who was to form The Moody Blues with Ray Thomas and others). "A lot of it came from Germany with people bringing stuff back. Some of them used to put stickers over record labels so that rival groups wouldn't know what they were."

All over Europe, there was a propensity of local heroes with sheepdog fringes who had the word "beat" in their titles* or used insectile appellations. They also played 'Twist And Shout', 'Money' *et al* – items that now bored any self-respecting R&B aficionado. From out of the sub-cultural woodwork in Paris, for example, had crawled legion two-guitars-bass-drums outfits like Les Cyclones and Les Sunlights while a veritable German megastar, Roy Black, had functioned as a member of an Augsberg beat group until he was signed to Polydor as a solo balladeer.

Thus it occurred to certain St Pauli entrepreneurs that it might be possible to find or even manufacture such a parochial alternative that could sound as identical to a Liverpudlian group over the house PA system as Eckhorn's ersatz Everly Brothers had to the genuine Don and Phil, and be cheaper and easier to deal with than a foreign group.

As usual, Manfred Weissleder's was the most profitable venture into Teutonic Merseybeat. Guided by him, four Hamburg teenagers became The Rattles, a name with the same scansion as "Beatles". Modelling themselves in the British beat image, they reached a high enough standard by late 1962 for Manfred to let them share bills with the likes of Sheridan, Cliff Bennett, The Beatles, Kingsize Taylor and The Searchers, and make in-concert recordings from the Star-Club stage. Later, in a kind of cultural exchange, The Rattles' morale was boosted by a successful fortnight's residency in the Cavern, and appearances on British television to plug 'The Stomp', a single promoted mainly through the imprint of the notion that its makers were the German wing of the Merseybeat movement – to be stressed even more in the

---

* Like The Beatmen whose converted bus was still going carrying them to and from Germany, and who had released a debut single, 'You Can't Sit Down'

title of their Ariola LP, *Liverpool Beat Live At The Star-Club*.

The same commercial pragmatism afflicted Bern Elliott And The Fenmen whose version of 'Money' scrambled to Number Fourteen in the *NME* Top Thirty – the climax of the group's chart career – after a publicity campaign that emphasised that they'd won their spurs in Hamburg and had thus caught that chartbusting Beatle lightning. They even recorded "live" at the Cavern, giving as good an account of themselves as the best regular attractions who'd also had first grabs at the R&B motherlode still echoing round St Pauli, just as 'Love Me Do' had been at the end of 1962 when The Beatles were expected back at the Star-Club.

Some felt that they'd been protesting too much about leaving Britain at such a supposedly important juncture. With 'Love Me Do' creeping to Number Seventeen, The Beatles had done well for first timers, yes, but how could anyone have presumed that they were anything other than a classic local group that'd got lucky. Indeed, because of the inward-looking nature of home-reared pop, The Beatles were unknown even then to groups of like repute in other British shires. Dave Dee had, apparently, never heard of them until the news of the impending arrival of a Liverpool outfit at the Star-Club was imparted by one of The Jaybirds in the gents toilets at the Top Ten. "And what are they called?" inquired Dee. "The Beatles? What a bloody silly name that is." He did not consider the conversation worth mentioning to the other lads when they convened for the night's toil, but: "You make a statement like that and you always remember it – then, of course, we ended up with a name like Dave Dee, Dozy, Beaky, Mick And Tich."

Because they'd never been in Hamburg at the same time, members of The Beatles and the Dave Dee group were not to meet until both were longtime chart contenders. "I first saw McCartney in Cromwell Road in London," said Dozy. "All he said was, 'Oh, I've seen you lot on the telly,' and we said, 'We've seen you on the telly as well.'" This is another example of the degree to which those who happen to be in the same profession know each other, but, back in 1963 when it appeared that The Beatles were going to stay lucky, Dave Dee and his boys had familiarised themselves quickly with Beatle hits as well as the likes of 'Sweets For My Sweet' – forever on German radio during the group's residency at the Hanover Top Ten – like they had already with less specific Merseybeat pieces.

"We used to do 'Love Me Do' and 'Please Please Me' after they were hits," recounted Tich. "We also did 'Some Other Guy', 'Mashed Potatoes', all the Liverpool music." Likewise, by the time Georgie And The Monarchs finished in Frankfurt in autumn 1963, every other request from *Mittelstand* teenagers on the dance floor seemed to be for 'She Loves You' or, when some idiot's girlfriend wanted it, 'Do You Want To Know A Secret' with its *"I yam in love with yooooooou"* falsetto hookline.

Now that German audiences had become as well-versed in Beatles album tracks too, "We learnt all the songs off *With The Beatles*," said Dave Dee, "and all President Kennedy's fleet were coming into the Top Ten – it was the year he went to Germany and did his *'Ich bin ein Berliner'* line – and they came up to us and said, 'What is this music you are playing?' We told them it was Beatle music, and they said, 'Gee, why don't you play it in America? It would go down really great.' I guess they were the first Americans that ever heard of The Beatles and of Beatle-type music."

When an opus like 'I Saw Her Standing There' or 'Sweets For My Sweet' was performed, it was heard by many older club-goers as a regretful salaam to groups seldom seen in Hamburg since they'd hit the Big Time and betrayed their grassroots following by condescending to slot in no more than maybe a night at the Star-Club in between far bigger dates on a European tour. You'd slip quietly to the dressing room to say hello afterwards, but it would be as deserted as the Marie Celeste – though you might catch the back of the getaway car being chased out of the Reeperbahn by clamorous teenage fans. When you tried again if they came back for a second set, you'd be part of a backstage crush, and they'd probably look through you like fakirs in a trance.

Still, there were other groups you could see for less than half the cost and discomfort. At the Top Ten, Dave Dee's lot were just as they ever were for all the new songs they'd taken on board. As always, they were wringing the audience with earthy patter and larks like playing dead and jumping up suddenly during 'Watch Your Step', and the old routine of Dave dodging Tich's guitar. With the exception of Freddie And The Dreamers, it seemed that comic capers were always moderated or dropped altogether when you had a hit as Falstaff was by Madcap Prince Hal while Henry IV's corpse was still warm.

Perhaps it was a compulsory criterion for reshaping rough diamonds into what a good pop outfit was expected to be in those naive times. Pye executives had been aghast when it came to their ears that The Undertakers, true to their name, rolled up in a hearse to take the stage in commensurate costumery. It was, therefore, deemed necessary for them to mothball the black-creped top hats, frock coats *et al*, and abbreviate their name to just "The Takers" in order to plug the follow-up to 'Just A Little Bit', their sole UK chart entry, on *Thank Your Lucky Stars*. As 'If You Don't Come Back' was a bit near-the-knuckle anyway in its narrative of lovesick insanity, nothing could be left to chance.

'If You Don't Come Back' had been recorded originally by The Drifters. Likewise, The Big Three rifled the North American R&B vaults for their first single, Ritchie Barrett's 'Some Other Guy', recorded in Decca's West Hampstead complex the morning after the trio's final date of a month in Hamburg. "We were croaking like old frogs," complained Johnny Gustafson, but worse was to come when a second forty-five, 'By The Way', made the mighty Big Three sound uncannily like every other group. Neither did anything else they taped in a studio ever approach the excitement they could generate on the boards at the Cavern or Star-Club.

Furthermore, according to Gustafson, Brian Epstein was to sack them eventually for "unruly and rowdy behaviour". Yet, however loathsome it was to them, the Three had been trusted to give "good copy" – ie quirky wit delivered in thickened Scouse – in media interviews; effect what were intended to be smiles in photo calls, and restrict their public expletives to the admissible "cr*p" and "bl***dy" of the most plain-speaking Pacemaker, Beatle or Searcher.

Though The Bachelors had had their fun in Hamburg too, they put themselves across as nice chaps to whom nothing potentially damaging could stick. They were so unbesmirched by off-colour publicity that, like The Beatles had been the year before, The Bachelors were chosen to be token pop group in 1964's Royal Command Performance. While it was nowhere as droll as Lennon's chirpy "rattle yer jewellery" ad-lib, the three provoked puffy smiles amongst the stuffed-shirts when they turned to the Royal Box for an amended opening line – "We wouldn't change you for the *wurrrrld*" – of their most recent smash.

The Bachelors were inclined to win polls in Ireland as The Beatles did in England. Within a narrower parameter, The Mojos were regarded by many – including themselves – as "Liverpool's Yardbirds". Musically, they bore a closer resemblance to the Surrey hitmakers at their most blueswailing than The Bachelors did to The Beatles – because, unlike most Merseybeat combos, they veered towards the more ethnic R&B of Muddy Waters, Willie Dixon and Howlin' Wolf rather than Motown and further developments of what was becoming known as "soul music". Their very name was in obeisance to Waters' 'I Got My Mojo Working', and, in 1964, they were the first UK beat group to record Dixon's 'Spoonful' – which was to be the virtual anthem of the "blues boom" of the later 1960s.

However, The Mojos' commercial testament was the cynically self-penned 'Everything's Alright'. Taped in Hamburg, it contained, expounded guitarist Nicky Crouch, "the most popular beat, the most popular riff, and the most popular concept for a pop song". So it rose with almost mathematical precision into Top Twenties throughout Europe despite the circumstances under which it was made. "We'd been in a drinking house on the Reeperbahn," said drummer Bob Conrad, "and were in no fit state to record. Terry [O' Toole, pianist] rushed off in the middle of a take to be sick."

Pragmatism ruled too for Johnny Gustafson after the exit of their bass player on 29 February 1964 couldn't have come at a worse time for The Merseybeats, rare among Liverpool's more successful groups in that they were denied the Hamburg experience. Their biggest smash, 'I Think of You' – in their trademark wistful style – was pondering at a UK Number Five when the vacancy occurred. Located in Frankfurt with The Seniors, Gustafson dived on a plane to Gatwick on the morning of 2 March. Once there, he hastened to the next flight to Newcastle where he stumbled into a theatre dressing room at seven-thirty pm to honour his first engagement as a Merseybeat. "The Seniors had been playing stomping rock 'n' roll in crazy madhouse clubs," recalled Johnny, "Which suited me perfectly. I didn't like the watery style of The Merseybeats at all – but money flashed before my eyes."

The same could be said of The Dowlands with their unwilling cover of The Beatles' 'All My Loving'. Fellow protégés of console boffin Joe Meek, The Ramblers added vocals to an otherwise sax-dominated instrumental repertoire on returning from a long spell in Germany. Then there was Paul Murphy's production exercise with, allegedly, a pseudonymous Alex Harvey on a comedy disc about Merseybeat – while Ian And The Zodiacs (as "The Koppykats") knocked out an album of Beatles hits on the budget Wing label. Could you tell the difference between these and the original recordings? Indeed you could, but it was to be the group's best selling UK release.

Striking while the iron was lukewarm too, Philips, Ariola and Decca commandeered the Star-Club's recording facilities to rush out as much product in the Merseybeat fad's first fiscal year as the traffic would allow via LPs such as *Liverpool Beat* (with Kingsize Taylor And The Dominoes and The Bobby Patrick Big Six), *Rock 'N' Beat Bands Competition* and *Star-Club: Centre Of Beat*. These and other labels also latched onto British groups and individual musicians that meant little at home but were worth exploiting in Germany, even to the extent of warranting an album release. Hence the appearance over there of the likes of Ricky Brown And The Hi-Lites' *The Liverpool Beat*, *Presenting The Crescendos* and an eponymous offering by Casey Jones – alias Brian "Cass" Cassar – And The Governors.

Having sustained a worrying hat-trick of comparative flops, Adam Faith and his investors had also paid heed to the new trend by switching without a pause to Merseybeat by hiring a visible guitar-and-drums backing group, and Chris Andrews, a songwriter who, as "Chris Ravel", had sung in the Hamburg clubs with an ensemble called The Ravers. Chris, therefore, knew the field, and could provide made-to-measure hits driven by walloping drums, clangorous guitars and call-and-response vocals almost as loud as Adam's own wobbly singing as heard on his Top Twenty restorative, 'The First Time'. However, Chris Ravel And The Ravers' cracks at ersatz Merseybeat in 1963 – summarised in the B-side title, 'Don't You Dig This Kind Of Beat' – fell on stony ground.

When Dave Sampson was confronted with the rearing monster of groups, he – like old rival Cliff Richard – didn't even bother to compete. Nevertheless, whereas the Bachelor Boy was to shovel out a greater proportion of potboiling ballads until the peril had passed, Dave, without even a recording contract by then, had accepted gladly a residency with the house band at the Top Ten in Hamburg where he administered the hundred per cent rock elixir with which he'd always scored onstage, if not on disc. During his year there, Sampson was to share the dormitory with old pals like Baby Bubbly and Johnny Kidd who'd likewise seen what was coming, and were dealing with it in their different fashions; Kidd fighting back into vogue and the UK hit parade with jaunty 'I'll Never Get Over You' at Number Four – though his next forty-five, 'Hungry For Love', ran aground at a mere Number Twenty, much sales potential being drained by a version by The Searchers.

Sampson was also around during the game of musical chairs involving The Searchers, Cliff Bennett And The Rebel Rousers – and Kingsize Taylor who lost his bass guitarist to Bennett as Cliff had lost his to The Searchers. Personnel upheavals had always been an occupational hazard for both group leaders who, more than just front men, had the same all-powerful hold over the others as Alex Harvey had on his Soul Band. A firm believer in the values of punctuality and discipline, Bennett once fired a horn player for drunkenness on stage – and God help you if he caught you with drugs.

As well as empathising with Cliff's enforcement of order, Brian Epstein recognised him as the group's X-factor. Yet, though the management agreement may not have covered the ever-changing Rebel Rousers, Epstein's entrepreneurial muscle assisted the passage of their seventh single with Cliff, 'One Way Love' (another blueprinted by The Drifters) into the British Top Ten in October 1964. This, Bennett's first big smash, was to be his last for two years with only one of the forty-fives released in between so much as scratching at the Top Fifty.

After two years in Germany, The Rockin' Berries dismissed a pair of saxophonists on a worthwhile return to native soil that was marked too by much the same oscillating pattern of chart strikes as Bennett. After Geoff Turton's high tenor rather than the usual lead singer, Clive Lea's grittier baritone carried 'He's In Town' to Number Three in 1964, the next one, 'What In The World's Come Over You', was a relative miss before paradise was regained with 'Poor Man's Son', also their final glimpse at the Top Twenty.

The Nashville Teens also checked in at British customs in 1964 prior to registering two respectable hits – 'Tobacco Road' and 'Google Eye' – and then tailing off with a string of lesser chart entries. Yet at least they, The Berries and Cliff Bennett had been on hand to put effort into giving each release the best possible chance with scrupulous TV plugs and a renewed omnipresence on the UK ballroom circuit.

When Kingsize Taylor's definitive 'Stupidity' was a "turntable hit" on Radio Luxembourg in 1964, he was not as well-placed to likewise make the most of it as he had elected to consolidate rather than advance his career by remaining in Germany where well-paid work, generally within easy reach, was still guaranteed. He'd get nothing like the same wage or respect in any of the unsalubrious beat clubs that could be found these days in the the most remote British towns.

Bookings were there for the taking but not the cash now that curmudgeonly promoters had put inbred dislike of teenagers and pop on ice after smelling the money to be made from all these young – and often marginally competent – outfits happy just to have somewhere to make their noise for the many stupid enough to pay to hear it. Take care of the pennies and the lads can take care of themselves, as Larry Parnes used to say before he moved from pop to the theatre. If you took sixty pounds net for a dance, you'd only have to fork out fifteen for up to four groups who could argue amongst themselves how it was to be split. A strict-tempo bandsman wouldn't stand for it, but the average turnover per week for a member of a semi-professional provincial beat combo was slightly more than thirty shillings (one pound fifty), no matter how representative he was of the given "Beat" or "Sound" that nearly every municipality and county within these islands was supposed to have in the early 1960s.

By the middle of 1964, British beat of every regional shade was exported to the United States after The Beatles made themselves available for engagements there. As is their wont, our colonial cousins, convinced of the incredible, had exhibited an enthusiasm for the group that had left British Beatlemaniacs swallowing dust. The rest of the world followed suit, and Beatles singles – even the antique Sheridan sides – were swamping global Top Tens five or six at a time.

At the first signs of wavering at home, The Searchers and Freddie And The Dreamers kept a foreseeable demise at arm's length with heftier triumphs over the Atlantic – though Gerry And The Pacemakers were slow to gain ground. Eventually, 'Don't Let The Sun Catch You Crying' – the one he wrote at the Star-Club – came to rest at Number Six, a giant step forward bolstered by repromotions of earlier British hits. The Swinging Blue Jeans and The Nashville Teens had briefer moments of US glory – and so did Pete Best when one of his post-Beatles groups was brought across the ocean for a sell-out North American tour at odds with fading interest in him, even in Liverpool and Hamburg.

Pete had turned up his nose at offers to join, first, Rory Storm's Hurricanes and then The Merseybeats before room had been found for him in Lee Curtis And The All-Stars, a club draw both on Merseyside, and the Grosse Freiheit where the first coachloads of Beatle worshippers from outside the city had pulled up in 1963. Outside the Star-Club too, Mercedes were now disgorging famous sightseers like Freddy Quinn and Leni Riefenstahl. Next came camera crews stockpiling footage for television documentaries. As late as 1966, during Welsh combo, Smokeless Zone's solitary month at the Top Ten, "We saw these cameras coming into the club," exclaimed vocalist Plum Ellis, "but didn't know they were there to film us. Then this character told us we were to be featured in a documentary about The Beatles. What a gas!"

CHAPTER FIFTEEN

You Better Move On

"We had already had a riot when we played in Holland – so I think we started to twig that Europe was quite a hip place as far as we were concerned"

Dick Taylor (The Pretty Things).

Record companies have to keep pace with the times – which meant matching the profitable discoveries of rivals. This Liverpool nonsense, therefore, had sent even the slowest-witted talent scout to the north-west of England to plunder the musical gold.

After the Merseybeat ferryboat beached on a mudbank, other "Sounds" and "Beats" came and went and, with far-sighted provincials like The Beatles now based there, direct control returned inevitably to London. For its journalists, this signalled a convenient finish to traipsing up past Birmingham for pop news – and, with their very accents millstones round their necks, certain northern groups even endeavoured to pass themselves off as either Eton-educated lispers or growlers of an imagined *gorblimey* dialect that'd stick in the throat of a genuine East Ender.

Recording managers, still seeking that Next Big Thing, had instructed A&R outriders to fan out beyond England. There was a particular note of urgency in expeditions to Germany where the myths about Hamburg and The Beatles had been believed, and the guts had been ripped from old factory premises, cellars cleared and bars extended to make venues for beat groups with long hair, no matter how awful they sounded.

Whether local entrepreneur or prowling music industry big-shot, each wanted to come upon if not *the* New Beatles then *a* New Beatles, even if he didn't understand what precisely he was looking for any more than his 1970s' counterpart would be when searching out a New Sex Pistols. All he knew was that a club was packed; there was an electric atmosphere and, as it was with EMI's precious Beatles, the phenomenon hinged on the enigma of untouchable boys-next-door.

Although he wasn't a group, Polydor had started with the obvious. Thus far, however, the label's very own Tony Sheridan had resisted tempting incentives to work a passage round the globe on The Beatles ticket than others less qualified would. Months passed. Groups that had once looked up to the Teacher conquered the UK charts, and The Beatles spearheaded the "British Invasion" of North America. Yet nothing would draw Tony from his Teutonic haven until a repromoted 'My Bonnie' – this time by "The Beatles With Tony Sheridan" – spread itself thinly enough to sell a purported million by 1964 without climbing higher than Number Twenty-Six in the States and spending only one week in Britain's Top Fifty. In its wake came the resurrection of associated royalty-earning items thrust out on rush-released albums with titles like *The Beatles' First*, *Ain't She Sweet* and *This Is The Savage Young Beatles*.

There were also sufficient resulting offers and promises from seemingly frantic offices in London for Sheridan – encouraged by his new producer, Paul Murphy – to brush his now grey-flecked hair forward and go to Britain to promote a new LP, *Just A Little Bit Of....* "I wasn't after fame at home," insisted Tony, "particularly as I had so much recognition and warmth when cocooned in Hamburg that there was no question of dropping what I had there – but for a short time, there was a bit of interest in Britain even if, as it turned out, nobody was pushing me very much."

He was "special guest" on a tour with The Searchers, and was one week's pop act on the ITV children's series, *Five O'Clock Club*, hosted by fellow 2I's stalwart, Wally Whyton, and a house band led by Alexis Korner, surely the strangest symptom of the British R&B movement's new acceptability. Indeed, the memory of Whyton's glove-puppet compere, Pussy Cat Willum's introduction of Korner's gritty rendering of 'See See Rider' is more difficult to forget than Ollie Beak's preamble to the Rosco Gordon-Undertakers item that was the title song of Sheridan's album.

During the visit, Tony renewed his acquaintance with The Beatles, meeting them – for "talk of old times, laughs about some of the German raves and best wishes for the future", so he told *Melody Maker* – at Brian Epstein's London apartment after a shoot for their first movie, *A Hard Day's Night*. This hail-fellow-well-met reunion, however, was not repeated a few months later when the group and Tony – with backing musicians from Sydney – were benighted in the same hotel during the Australian leg of The Beatles' world tour. To the one newshound who asked him why not, Sheridan said he "wasn't trying to jump on their bandwagon" – though he continued to look up individual members, bar John Lennon with whom he was never to speak again after 1964.

While it had been his old Hamburg accompanists that had brought about exposure beyond Germany via the 'My Bonnie' windfall, Tony was uneasy about the rest of the Beatles items with him that Polydor were planning to doctor for rush-release. However, it was to his advantage to stay malleable for the time being by, say, re-recording his vocal to 'Sweet Georgia Brown', inserting Beatle references after the Kaempfert backing tracks were, allegedly, tidied up with help from such as New York session drummer Bernard Purdie. "I got terribly screwed financially over the Polydor material with The Beatles," claimed Tony. "If 'My Bonnie' and its spin-offs had truly sold what they were supposed to have sold, I should have been a millionaire two or three times over. Also, 'If You Love Me Baby' had an extra guitar part added in New York and a couple of words cut out because they were blasphemous – 'goddam' or something like that. I had no idea that that sort of thing was going on."

He was dizzied, perhaps, by the sweep of events that had him zigzagging hectically across Britain after his adventure Down Under: "For a while, The Bobby Patrick Big Six and I lived in Manchester. We were playing one-night-stands – but we never made anywhere near the money that could have been made in Germany." Once, Tony was required to drop everything to fit in a *Saturday Club* where, before unseen millions, he pitched into not the intended numbers, but some unknown to his backing trio, Paddy, Klaus and Gibson who, though formed in Hamburg only weeks previously, knew Sheridan well both personally and as an erratic if brilliant rock 'n' roll musician.

The "Klaus" was Klaus Voorman who had forsaken the security of graphic design to thrum bass with his old girlfriend's new husband Gibson Kemp on drums, and ex-Big Three guitarist Paddy Chambers. Managed by Brian Epstein, the three secured a contract with Pye – The Searchers' label – and a residency at the Pickwick, a fashionable night spot, frequented by London's "in-crowd". In with the most exclusive in-crowd of all, Voorman was to land the plum job of designing a Beatles LP sleeve, but his liaison with Gibson and Paddy was nowhere as lucrative. Three consecutive flop singles contributed to the break-up of the trio in May 1966 when Kemp returned to Hamburg and Astrid amid false speculation that Paddy and Klaus would continue as a duo like Johnny Gustafson was as "John And Johnny" with drummer John Banks now that The Merseybeats were in abeyance too after 'I Stand Accused' had waved them out of sight of the UK Top Fifty forever.

Gustafson's old Big Three colleague Chambers then joined The Escorts* – though there had been an open invitation for him to re-enlist with the Three if ever circumstances permitted. Neither party had then regarded this eventuality as improbable, but by 1965, autumn leaves were falling on the group. After the first set one evening at the Liverpool club where the Three had risen from the ashes of Cass And The Cassanovas four years before, another drummer took over when Johnny Hutchinson collected his pay and went home – and that was it, more or less.

Lacking a fourth part of the common-or-garden beat group's two guitars-bass-drums too, some people thought that there was also short weight in the music of Paddy-Klaus-and-Gibson and The Three Musketeers, formed in Hamburg by Ritchie Blackmore in 1965. Yet "power trios" were to be "it" a couple of years later when the likes of Cream, The Jimi Hendrix Experience, Blue Cheer and Rory Gallagher's Taste would hark back to the test cases of The Big Three, The Jaybirds and, predating both of them, The Tony Sheridan Trios.

Hendrix's future bass guitarist had been in Germany in 1965 with south-east Kent's The Loving Kind – while a teenage Gallagher had brought a trio over to Hamburg after he had tired of the inordinate amount of old stuff that still remained an integral part of the act after

---

* Whose bass player was to replace Klaus Voorman in The Hollies after the German proceeded quickly into the ranks of Manfred Mann

Cork's Fontana Showband belied the modernisation inherent in renaming itself The Impact. Rory was not to be generous in recounting how he'd mastered his craft on the podium with various well-paid showbands: "You'd get a really great jazz saxophonist having to play 'Let's Twist Again', and a drummer who really wants to be in a ceilidh band, or someone like me who just wants to play Chuck Berry – but you'll do it for a laugh at a certain point although I knew from Day One that I was only passing through."

Initially, it was as an escape valve from The Impact that Gallagher coerced its bass guitarist and drummer into forming a splinter group, The Fendermen. These were, nonetheless, to disconnect from the main band altogether after being noticed on a Radio Telefis Eirrann television programme performing a Gallagher original, 'You Fool Me All The Time' – though it had been necessary, as Rory would report, to persuade "a friend to pose with a Vox Continental organ" to conform to the stereotyped four-piece image.

Then came a trip to Hamburg that included a spell at the Big Apple with Johnnie Law who was delighted by not only the young Irishman's fretboard dexterity, but also his painstaking dedication to the job in hand, and his expert knowledge of the obscurer trackways of pop: "What a worker Rory was! He never wanted to finish. He was only eighteen then, but he knew every song I wanted to sing – you name it, anything from Buddy Holly, Chuck Berry, Bob Dylan..."

The fizzling out of The Fendermen, however, after they returned to Cork forced Rory back to the old routine of tape-recording *Pick Of The Pops* off the Light Programme every Sunday and figuring out which Top Twenty items were likely to come up as he picked up whatever jobs were going in parochial showbands, and wondering on the night if he'd remembered to collect the eiderdowns from the dry-cleaners as, on automatic, he strummed 'Que Sera Sera', 'Sparrow In The Treetop', 'Noreen Bawn' and all the other corn that had kept its popularity with the old folks since Lord knows when.

All he was doing there was ageing too – and so it was that he tried again in Hamburg. "He returned in November 1966," said Johnnie Law, "and had changed his group's name to 'Taste' – so I sang with Rory for another month, and then in February 1967, in a club called the Oasis where I worked for six months."

The Oasis, the Crazy Horse, the Funny Crow, the Tabaras and the Tinalou were but a few of many new (and frequently short-lived) venues that had sprung up in Hamburg – along with late-night watering holes like the Beershop and the Blockhutte – as places like the K52 had in Frankfurt, a new Star-Club in Bochum, the PN club in Munich, the Kaverna in Mannheim, the Big Ben Club in Wilhelmshaven on the Weser estuary, and the Tanzbar Cascade in Cologne – where The Swinging Blue Jeans were to record an in-concert LP – all catering for bright young things clothed by Swinging London-style boutiques now operational in Germany's city centres as a world pop scene started to flower.

Differences between "Mods" in London, Paris, Vienna and Bonn had so diminished that each European capital west of the Berlin Wall fostered the same male sartorial conformity hinged vaguely on Cuban-heeled "Beatle boots" – like blunted winkle-pickers – hipster flares, a corderoy jacket and either roll-necked pullover or denim shirt with button-down collar and tie.

Mod clothes weren't much more than gang uniforms that distinguished you from Rockers – though such enmity as there was between the two tribes was not brought to public attention by a German tabloid press less prone to exaggeration than its British counterpart. Besides, you were a "good kid" at heart, weren't you? At least you were made to look like one – because no amount of backcombing, pulling or application of thickening gel could disguise the haircuts still compulsory for boys out in the sticks. To their mothers and *schlager*-cut fathers, anything longer than a Prussian all-off was still considered unmasculine. Your short-back-and-sides variation of a *Pilzen Kopf* or worse was still there for all to see, however much you might be able to get away with approximations of either the latest Carnaby or biker gear, or pooch out your lips like Mick Jagger's.

Once, you'd gazed with yearning at the shadowy jacket of *With The Beatles* – if only Mutti and Papa would let me have my hair like George's then I wouldn't go on about it any more – but by 1965, the ultimate objective was to grow a severe moptop into a feather duster to look like Jagger or Brian Jones, the two most androgynously hirsute Rolling Stones, now running a closer second to The Beatles than Gerry or The Searchers ever had – and, arguably, overtaking them intermittently as Europe's top group.

The Rattles had witnessed the scream-rent beginnings of this ascent when a last-minute addition to the Glasgow date of a round-Britain package tour in 1963, headlined by Little Richard. Low on the bill, the Stones – whose maiden forty-five, 'Come On', had seized up just outside the Top Twenty – had been granted only a few more minutes than themselves to gouge a sub-cultural wound.

As The Rattles progressed from 'The Stomp' to a cover of Manfred Mann's 'Do Wah Diddy Diddy', so the Stones did from 'Come On' to a Number One slightly over a year later with an unrevised 'Little Red Rooster'; its blues pedigree traceable to a first recording by Howlin' Wolf in the late 1940s. Until then, the very idea of making a living from a brand of R&B more specialist than the mainstream pop of Merseybeat was taken seriously by few until the Stones managed it by thus sticking to their erudite musical guns and without compromising a motley, gauche image, apart from donning quasi-Beatle uniforms to mime 'Come On' on their first TV appearance.

Manfred Mann and The Animals had charted again too; The Kinks had arrived with a vengeance in August when 'You Really Got Me' kicked off a run of smashes that adhered mostly to similar jerky riffing, and The Yardbirds' time was about to come too. This gave much cause for optimism for outfits like The Spencer Davis Group, Van Morrison's new outfit, Them – and The Pretty Things who were advantaged by being in the right place, ie London, at the right time.

There was a period circa 1965 when even The Beatles were seen as a far lesser threat to the Stones than the Things as hairy monsters abhorred by grown-ups but as rabidly worshipped by the young. Yet because they were active in the European charts for a full year before the Things had so much as a sniff at the Top Thirty with 'Rosalyn' in mid 1964, the Stones had transcended the ballrooms, and were provoking running battles inside and outside German theatres that rode roughshod over the most violent stop on the Bill Haley tour.

Panicking city councils and cancellations by hoteliers expecting trouble were the least of it as predominantly male ticket-holders (whose short haircuts broke their hearts) snapped fifty rows of tip-up seats off their spindles and reduced them to matchwood in Dusseldorf at the end of a show in which their foot-stomping and bawling of the lyrics to 'It's All Over Now', '(I Can't Get No) Satisfaction' and so on welled up to a pitch where the walls trembled and the Stones themselves drowned in noise. In a audacious display of bad taste, Jagger goose-stepped off-stage during the play-out, leaving the place in turmoil. What is this? Do I like this? Is it serious? Shall I clap or boo? What's everybody else doing?

Everybody else had realised that there wasn't to be an encore, and ugly scenes loomed while the Stones were in groping flight along an underground tunnel that led from a World War II bunker beneath the auditorium to woodlands two miles away from the gathering mob. Bereft of the good nature and reserve that had hitherto tinged the milling around after concerts by earlier beat groups, the havoc embraced fire hoses, broken police barricades, scores of overturned cars, and train carriage interiors wrecked totally during the course of a single journey to the suburbs. Any pretensions of being "good kids" evaporated through breathing the air round the Stones as dawn broke with catcalling youths still looking for things to destroy, people to beat up.

We could speculate endlessly, but, in a parallel dimension, The Pretty Things could have been the ones raising Cain, and the Stones working up lesser riots – but riots all the same – when scrimmaging round northern Europe's clubs and dancehalls as patron saints of legion also-ran R&B combos who'd ditched stage suits and big smiles for miscellaneous sullenness and earnest attempts at emulating the various Sonny Boys, Blind Lemons and Howlin' Wolves of black America. Some German R&B devotées were derisive about the Bo Diddley and Chuck Berry copies that had freighted the first albums of the Stones, Things and their kind, and were not put off by the middle-age, obesity and glistening baldness of its older white performers such as those who made up Alexis Korner's Blues Incorporated (from whence The Rolling Stones had sprung). Yet though there was talk of residencies in Hamburg and Weisbaden, Korner was not to visit the republic as a professional musician until long after the impure Pretty Things made their Star-Club debut in 1965.

Even if the floor contained a proportion of curiosity-seekers with only the foggiest idea about the music they had paid to hear, the quintet's notoriety ensured a full turnout that night. Indeed, they had been accorded something of a heroes' welcome when fans converged on the upper terraces of Hamburg-Fuhlsbuttel airport to catch the group's plane from the previous night in Amsterdam. Shadowed against the clouds, it had descended from the skies just as Hitler's had done at the start of the ferocious pageantry that was *Triumph Of The Will*, Leni Riefenstahl's propaganda film of the 1934 Nuremburg Rally.

"After it came into land like a Stuka," said Dick Taylor, "I think the fact that we actually had a reception committee of fans was a bit lost on us, but it is something I do remember – and it's an indicator of the difference that a few years had made. We weren't pioneers, just part of the British invasion. We seemed to have been taken to heart by a particular section of fans – and we still meet some of them today."

However, reaction to the Things that evening was not as mindlessly uncritical as it had been for The Jets in 1960 when a British rock 'n' roller wasn't a commodity so easily obtainable. "German bands like The Rattles were getting better and better," explained Taylor. "The audiences were also becoming more and more sophisticated, apart from the tourists who probably came more to be at the Star-Club than hear some particular band. The locals were probably the hippest crowd we would be playing to – so going to Hamburg always kept us on our toes. It still does. We felt a bit nervous about playing the Star-Club for obvious reasons, but we psyched ourselves up by mocking the 'wooden' German groups who were on before us, who were probably just fine really. When we did get to play, the reception was just fine."

If he'd heard of them, John Citizen was not so impressed. "Though they were The Sex Pistols of their day image-wise," reckoned Lord Sutch, "it was too much for the general public in the mid 1960s. The Stones just about walked the line; The Pretty Things went way over it." If children had to like these *Britisher* beat groups, reasoned adult West Germany, let it be ones like The Beatles. As it was with The Bachelors, no nicotine-stained fingers could type out lurid coverage of behind-the-scenes sordidness for next week's *Deutsche Allgemeines Sonntagsblatt* – because any soiling of their impish but innocent public personas was untimely then. "They were regarded as clean-living lads during the time they were getting established," confirmed the late Harold Wilson, "whatever may have gone on later" – or before.

Save the scandal for The Rolling Stones, The Pretty Things and anyone who was either beyond the pale of decency – or too unimportant to matter as shown by a write-up in *The Daily Express* about some of The VIPs, a bunch of pop reprobates from Carlisle, who'd been in the dock for criminal damage to British Rail property.

The VIPs broke the rules in Hamburg too. To the amazement of Johnnie Law, "They started with a slow song, 'Georgia On My Mind'. This was strange because I thought – and still do – that the way to do a show is to start with a few rocker-type songs, go down a little bit and then build it up again – but after 'Georgia', they got a standing ovation.'

They were as captivating to Chris Blackwell, The Spencer Davis Group's manager, when he checked out The VIPs during that earlier season at the Star-Club in August 1964.* "They were un-be-lievable," he'd raved, "impossible to handle or control." Yet handle them he had after signing up The VIPs too. However, on a first-come-first-served basis, they had been left to ginger up on the Grosse Freiheit as Blackwell gave more immediate attention to his Spencer Davis Group's first A-side, a stab at 'Dimples' that was more dramatic than the stumblings of John Lee Hooker on the original.

Give him credit too, Tony Sheridan had stood as tall as a Caucasian bluesman on Jimmy Reed's 'Take Out Some Insurance On Me Baby', but, following the flurry of activity in Britain and Australia, he and The Bobby Patrick Big Six were beginning to absorb some of the self-immolatory tendencies of some of the doomed black icons whose music they played. Causing most concern was the unit's mixture of stimulant intake. Giggling drunk or real, real gone on more than one night, it'd look as if they'd never totter on stage,

Sometimes it might have been better if they hadn't – though they didn't so often nowadays that Sheridan was becoming a booker's risk. The lad himself would admit that it was a case of "'Tony Sheridan? Be careful, he might not turn up.' Polydor was getting sceptical about us too because, though we were very good on good nights, we were a bit wild, fighting on stage, getting drunk, misbehaving generally. Once, we were supposed to be opening for Chuck Berry at the Olympia in Paris, but by the time we got there, we'd drunk all the wine we'd acquired from the previous night in Oppenheim, and we were incapable of playing a single number. We also ended up in jail for a few hours because we wouldn't leave a restaurant after it had refused to serve us. Word about that sort of incident got around."

What corrupts any once up-and-coming act to participants in a

---

* Where they'd trodden the boards with The Nashville Teens, Kidderminster's Shades Five and The Hellions as well as The Spencer Davis Group. In 1966, Jim Capaldi and Dave Mason of The Hellions were to form Traffic with the Group's Steve Winwood

subsidised debauch is when dreams of overnight stardom fade to a stark realisation that, finding yourself back at the same venues time and time again, you were taking up conversations begun the previous year with waiters and stage hands, and that you knew Hanover, Stuttgart, Zurich and every other oft-visited city better than many of its inhabitants.

As for the music, indolence engendered aversion to venturing far beyond the boundaries of an existing style. Why bother doing otherwise for a consumer for whom information that the show they missed this time was just like the one they saw last time is praise indeed? After all, you're not getting any younger; performing on stage is your only saleable trade, and yours is much the same endless highway dilemma as olde tyme rockers like Gene Vincent with no choice but to go right on performing just to maintain a tolerable standard of living. No wonder Gene held his discontent at arm's length by boozing; a consumption that seemed to have increased every time he came back to Europe. It'd kill him in the end.

For those without a backlog of hits like Vincent's, it was disenchanting to be the same age or older than those with one. Someone who'd cadged a cigarette off you the previous month would be pictured in a music paper with his group, posing round a fire escape or copying the mid-air jump patented by either The Rockin' Berries or The Beatles. Approaching your late twenties, you were venerable, a Grand Old Man who would or would not be revered by young sprogs as certain as your former self had been that they were about to soar to the very pinnacle of pop. Surely it was only a matter of a few months at most before they Made It. It'd be like that clichéd movie sequence of dates being ripped off a calendar to a background of clips...Hamburg...the ballrooms...*Saturday Club*...record deal...*Top Of The Pops*...*Sunday Night At The London Palladium*...Shea Stadium...

There were groups that carried that self-belief even as the HP company carted the gear away. In 1965, the *Herald Of Wales'* pop column would carry an article about The Jets – a Swansea group nothing to do with Ricky Richards *et al* – who were "having a ball in Germany" – like all the other poor sods – "playing from seven pm to one pm during the week and six pm to one am at weekends". They had been plucked from a residency at Oystermouth's Big T ballroom for a club tour commencing in Munich, just as their local rivals, The Blackjacks, started a similar three month stint in France.

Around the same time, The Casuals, after coming up for air back in Lincoln, began a year in a Milan night club; The Sorcerers, toast of Cirencester, went over to the Storyville in Frankfurt, and The Medium left Welwyn Garden City for Munich's PN, "just for food and a place to sleep," said guitarist Alan Williams, later of The Rubettes.

He, The Casuals and drummer Cozy Powell of The Sorcerers were among the few trudging round Europe in the mid 1960s who were predestined for record success. So too was Stan Webb, future leader of Chicken Shack, but then just parted from Shades Five after being considered too young to accompany them to Hamburg.

Nowadays, you see, the law was no longer as lax as it had been about minors in Reeperbahn clubs giving Wee Willie Winkie apoplexy. Spot checks by *Der Auslander Polizei* were more frequent and more thorough, and a group's junior members became as resigned to the scream of a squad car taking them to sudden deportation as a trench soldier had been to a stray bullet at the Somme. "When I was first in Germany," elucidated Paul Francis of The Vibrations, "I had to alter the date of birth on my passport as I was officially under age. Every time I was asked to produce the passport, I was sure someone would twig."

Francis had drummed with Rolf Harris And The Kangaroos before joining The Vibrations, southerners all – and backing group to Tony Jackson who, during a six month lay-off following his split from The Searchers, had had his nose remodelled, and auditioned advisedly for musicians "who I felt could live in the cauldron of travelling together. I didn't want friction or any disruptive element within the group. I wanted four guys who would gel socially as well as musically."

For Paul, it had seemed like a plum job at the time as his new employer had sung lead on both The Searchers' first hits, and what was to be their biggest US smash, 'Love Potion Number Nine'. Prospects continued to look good as Tony Jackson And The Vibrations notched up a fast Top Forty strike in Britain with Mary Wells' 'Bye Bye Baby' in which keyboards and a female chorale framed a radical departure from what Searchers fans might have expected.

However, after the follow-up flopped, a workmanlike 'Love Potion Number Nine' was chosen as a third forty-five. "I wanted 'Fortune

Teller' on the A-side," insisted Tony, "but the head of Pye, knew that my old group was in the *Billboard* Top Ten with 'Love Potion Number Nine', so he chose that instead." After a seventh single made its depressingly familiar journey to the bargain bin, what was now called The Tony Jackson Group vanished into an oblivion of European one-nighters that was to finish in disbandment after the release of an EP available only in Portugal.

Jackson's old antagonist's post-Searchers career was ending ignominiously too. A world tour had removed the urbane mask from Chris Curtis, and the strain had shown. Shattered and neurotic, he'd left the group, and, before quitting showbusiness altogether, had made a failed solo single – appropriately titled 'Aggravation' – and had dabbled in record production. Now he had snared an unlikely role as lead vocalist in Roundabout, whose manager had found them an isolated rural retreat in which to rehearse. The outfit was to grind to a halt by 1967, however, and three of its number become the nucleus of Deep Purple.

Another founder member of this prominent heavy rock amalgam was Ritchie Blackmore who was in the middle of the second of two protracted spells in Germany as Roundabout entered its death throes. On an earlier occasion in 1964, he'd been making ready to go there with a group organised as haphazardly as the Kaiserkeller Jets had been. Matthew Fisher, yet to metamorphose into the cowled organist of Procol Harum, "had just left school, and a guitarist called Roger Mingay [who was in Screaming Lord Sutch's band] and a drummer named Ian Broad were trying to get this band together to play Germany. I was going to play bass; Ritchie was to be the lead guitarist, and they were trying to get Freddie Starr to sing. Freddie blew up my mother's car on the M1 and we didn't even get the gig."

After this setback, nineteen-year-old Blackmore was to spend not quite a year in the Fatherland, mostly freelancing in St Pauli clubland following a stint as a Jerry Lee Lewis sideman that had culminated in a booking at the Star-Club in summer 1965. Christmas came, and he was one of The Three Musketeers who began their act by prancing onstage, sword-fighting. When this intriguing trio's contract was terminated after a week at Bochum's new Star-Club, an Essex group called High Society played the rest of the scheduled bookings after giving

Blackmore a lift back into Hamburg where he waited, like Mr Micawber, for something to turn up – which it did in the form of a post in Neil Christian's Crusaders.

Christian's previous accompanists had become redundant soon after he'd scented stardom in Germany. "All I did was mime to my records in this club," he explained, "take a break to sign autographs, and then mime a bit more. Then I got the urge to go on the road again – so I formed a new band with Ritchie Blackmore and Carlo Little." Having made the error of favouring the security of Lord Sutch's Savages over staying the course with The Rolling Stones, Little was not prepared to spit out another bite of the cherry, even though "Christian said, 'Here's ten quid. I'll see you in Berlin.' That was ten quid to cover the band and the van getting from Wembley to Berlin." Yet once the Crusade got underway, you were guaranteed a decent wage for as long as you were needed. "Neil Christian provided a few months of stability," averred Albert Lee, "paying me fifteen pounds a week whether we worked or not, which was pretty good."

At the end of his tenure as a Crusader, Ritchie Blackmore chose to remain in Hamburg for eight months. "All I did was practise guitar," he said. "The only serious endeavour – a group called Mandrake Root – folded up without playing a single gig. Then I received a telegram asking me to audition for a new group which turned out to be Deep Purple."

The tide was turning too – albeit with majestic slowness – for Dave Dee, Dozy, Beaky, Mick And Tich. An appearance on ITV's *Ready Steady Go* pop magazine in 1964 had been the first that Britain at large had seen of the group, whose first single, 'No Time', was a curious waltz featuring whistling and Teutonic overtones. It went straight in at Number Five – Number Five in the *Salisbury Journal*'s chart that is, with advance orders for seventy-five at Messrs JF Sutton in the high street. Though it was nearer to what they were to become, the bulk of sales of the follow-up, 'All I Want', were restricted likewise to loyal Wiltshire.

"We were a working band with two records out, travelling up and down the country," related Dave. "Everything we owned was on hire purchase. All our contemporaries were making it. It appeared that they were making fortunes, and we were absolutely broke. We sat in a little cafe in Manchester, and we had two bob [ten pence] between us. We bought two cups of tea, one cake, and we had one cigarette between us. We passed them round, and we said, 'That's it.' We then drove to London, parked the van, went to a phone box, and called Ken Howard and Alan Blaikley: 'Look, it's all over. We're broke. We can't stand it anymore. We're locking the van up. We're going down the road to the police station and leaving the keys with them. Just tell the HP company where the van and all the gear is.'

"They said, 'Don't move! Stay where you are. We're coming over. In six months, it could all be different.' We said, 'Oh yeah? We've had five years of promises.' They sat with us for about three hours and brainwashed us into sticking it out, and, sure enough, they were right. I reckon it must have been about four months until we actually had a hit record. I think it entered the chart at Sixty-Four or some ridiculous number – but that was enough just to know that we actually got one on the move, and it changed everything really."

Ian And The Zodiacs were also on their last legs when things started moving for them. The US release of a German LP track, a version of Dave Berry's 'The Crying Game', caught on in Texas through the plugging of an enthusiastic disc-jockey. Dollars danced before their eyes, but visions of cowboys yelling "yee-hah!" and firing six-guns in the air in appreciation of their in-person presence on stages in Houston or Dallas faded as The Zodiacs and Ian continued to slide towards poverty-stricken dispersal back in Hamburg.

Already Bern Elliott was no longer fronting his Fenmen. Tearing a leaf from Lee Curtis's book, he was hoping for a fresh start as a Sinatra of the Medway, but this flight from his Hamburg-wrought *zeitgeist* did not yield hits. Without him, The Fenmen were as unlucky – even with the arresting 'Rejected' picking up plays on pirate Radio London. Throwing in the towel, half the group would be absorbed into a Pretty Things in uncertain transition after personnel upheavals and a goodbye to the UK singles Top 50 with 1966's 'House In The Country', a xerox of a Kinks LP track.

Paradoxically, Dick Taylor and Phil May had found their feet as composers by then, and the Things' raw R&B was to defer to subtlety of structure and studied artistic progression. Moreover, there was to be a stronger emphasis on vocal interplay via the enlistment of the two

Fenmen, bass guitarist Wally Allen and former drummer John Povey on keyboards. The Things' valedictory LP for Fontana, *Emotions*, would be layered too with unauthorised brass and string sections by producer (and ex-Hollywood actor) Steve Rowland as a dry run for his grandiloquent scorings from late 1967 for Dave Dee, Dozy, Beaky Mick And Tich. Only a move to EMI would allow The Pretty Things the increased artistic freedom, manifest in 'Deflecting Grey', a consciously "weird" single that paved the way for *SF Sorrow*, unquestionably the first "rock opera" (though, technically, a song-cycle).

Regression was, however, the order of the day for The Nashville Teens who, possessing neither the contradiction of the Things' repellent lure nor The Beatles' Midwich Cuckoo regularity, had only Ray Phillips' Viking cheekbones to save them from quasi-anonymity image-wise. 'The Hard Way' would wave them out of sight of the UK Top Fifty in February 1966, but they'd glance back with 'Revived Forty-Five Time', vignettes of the classic rock that had got them through long nights at the Star-Club and a troubled UK tour with Chuck Berry in 1964.

Lower on the bill had been Kingsize Taylor And The Dominoes – who, whilst growing fat on the Star-Club circuit*, had, conceded Kingsize, "been out of the country at the wrong time". Nonetheless, an engagement in Liverpool during one of his group's infrequent forays home had sparked off a commendatory *Melody Maker* feature, the Berry job, and the drawing-out of Taylor's sporadic recording career after he'd beaten a retreat back to Germany where it'd be "Kingsize Taylor And His Band" for the next two or so years as he continued working according to the lodged conventions of his kind.

Incorrigible old rock 'n' rollers like Taylor, Johnnie Law, Tony Sheridan and Dave Sampson were still able to make any big name who had once deferred to them look tame as they knocked 'em dead with material that had been in and out of the set from the beginning. Running through your best-loved numbers for those who loved them – and you – best of all in an out-of-the-way palais in continental Europe wasn't such a bad place to be in the mid 1960s. Perhaps the saga of a lot of acts should have ended there because they were now as good as they'd ever get.

---

* Taylor would play an estimated five-hundred-and-forty-two nights at Hamburg's Star-Club, compared to Cliff Bennett's one-hundred-and-seventy-four, and Lee Curtis's one-hundred-and-twenty-six

CHAPTER SIXTEEN

Keep On Running

"One thing I don't like is being out of the limelight. I love it all"
Spencer Davis (Spencer Davis Group)

Hamburg's part in the world's preoccupation with UK pop in the mid 1960s was epitomised by the Anglophile "garage band" culture so widespread that you'd be waiting at a bus stop in Laramie or Canberra and hear the same three-chord group rehearsing in a house extension opposite. They'd grown out their crew-cuts and, as with The Rattles and like German outfits before them, had borrowed from all manner of British idioms ranging from Them's instrumental directness and oddly attractive lead vocal whine to The Searchers' fusion of Merseybeat and contemporary folk, developed most spectacularly by The Byrds who had also paid studious attention to the uniquely circular effect of fingerpicking two electric guitars, a Searchers trademark that could be broadened by using twelve-string models like George Harrison's Rickenbacker, heard in the resounding *bis* passage in 'A Hard Day's Night'.

For *Beatles For Sale*, the LP that followed the album-of-the-film, the group, visibly tired on the sleeve photographs, had interspersed Lennon-McCartney originals with items from the annals of classic rock that would conjure affectionate recollections of a wild evening down the Kaiserkeller for tens of thousands more than could have actually been there.

There was nothing for Germans to recall about first-hand contact with The Beatles between 1962 and 1966 – because concert appearances in the Fatherland had been curtailed, owing, according to local opinion, to the possible repercussions of a Hamburg fräulein's claim that one of the four had fathered her child. After all, a summons to a paternity hearing had been thrust into Elvis Presley's hands when, as was his extravagant habit, he feigned collapse and crawled to the lip of a stage during some tortured ballad or other. More recently, a wailing baby had been held in the upstretched arms of a girl, flanked by her grim-faced parents, within feet of a well-known English lead guitarist performing with his group in a theatre in Denmark.

Worries about embarrassing – and financially draining – litigation brought up the same misgivings again and again for many a jittery romeo who, prior to his first hit record, had played the field in Germany. Bouncing his thoughts off his manager, he'd grope for reasons why such-and-such a case would or would not be pursued, and try to convince himself that either the woman concerned couldn't be bothered or hadn't enough evidence to justify making a fuss. With no word from her or her lawyers as the months slipped by, perhaps he was panicking unduly, but, as the saying goes, better safe than sorry.

Whatever the causes, The Beatles' in-person absence from Germany, year upon year, meant that they were never booked for *Beat Club*, one of the most atmospheric pop showcases on television in the 1960s. Transmitted from Hamburg, it was as vital in its way as *Ready Steady Go* – and, unlike its older UK counterpart, the first series in 1966 was not marked with besuited middle-aged interlocutors and similar unhip distractions. Moreover, it was inclined to discriminate positively towards domestic acts like The Rattles, The Rivets, The Lords – and Roy Black, very much a prize exhibit in national charts in 1966 with his 'Ganz In Weiss' ("all in white") at Number One for six weeks, and his second album amassing advance orders of fifty thousand.

Yet *Beat Club* was a crucial inclusion on the European itineraries of hitmaking foreign outfits. Chief among those who were able to come across as well on screen as they did on the boards were Dave Dee, Dozy, Beaky, Mick And Tich. A third single, 'You Make It Move', recommended in *Record Mirror* for its "great big backing sounds behind what sounds like a massed vocal front line", had inched into the UK Top Twenty. Next, a plainer *mach schau*-football chant crash had powered 'Hold Tight!' which got to Number Four.

Tich and Dozy were to agree that a bottom-of-the-bill performance in Munich's Circus Krone in 1965 was the pivotal event that spurred greater record success in Germany. With no preconceptions about them from an audience awaiting The Spencer Davis Group and then Herman's Hermits, the Wiltshire lads stole the show just as they had from The Honeycombs at Butlin's in 1964. "Without sounding big-headed," said Dozy, "I have to say that no-one could follow us. That was the first time we'd witnessed enthusiasm from an audience that size. The hits just seemed to happen from there on in." As well as higher chart positions in Germany for 'You Make It Move', 'Hold Tight!' and subsequent riff-based British smashes like 'Hideaway' and 'Touch Me Touch Me' – plus UK album tracks released as European A-sides – there was a point where the quintet had no fewer than five simultaneous entries in the national Top Twenty.

Going with the territory was the irritation and flattery of attempted pre-emption by local hopefuls such as The Sean Buckley Set on Polydor with 'Hold Tight!', and – sounding even less like she understood what she was singing – Deutsche Vogue's Pat Simon with the same song. Mispronounced lyrics also marred (or brightened) The Image's 'Hideaway', 'Hard To Love You' by Dave Gordon And The Rebel Guys, and, in late 1966, The Four Kings' coupling of 'Nose For Trouble' (also from the Dave Dee outfit's debut LP). It was the same with 'Save Me', a single that, clattering with polyrhythmic percussion, stabilised Dave Dee, Dozy, Beaky, Mick And Tich's shedding of the 'You Make It Move' blueprint just as they'd shed all the Dave Dee And The Bostons preferences for recording purposes – though you'd catch the odd 'Dr Feelgood', 'Watch Your Step' or 'Land Of 1,000 Dances' filling time on *Saturday Club* and like radio sessions.

'Save Me' had been preceded by the *accelerando* of 'Bend It' – decorated by Tich's gimmicky balalaika – which had itself come out before a comparative failure in Britain in 'Touch Me Touch Me', the final experiment with the 'Hold Tight!' formula on an A-side. In Germany, however, 'Touch Me Touch Me' tramped a well-trodden path to within an ace of Number One, and Dave Dee, Dozy, Beaky, Mick And Tich were received on the necessary promotional visit with the accustomed cameras clicking like typewriters and stick-mikes thrust towards their mouths in hopes that they would crack back at the now stock questions about long hair, Mods-and-Rockers, mini-skirts and all that with a combination of zaniness, unblinking self-assurance and the poker-faced what-are-you-laughing-at way they told 'em.

When they made a triumphant debut at the Star-Club – where they'd never played before they'd had hits – the group had become big enough to lord it over the likes of Cream and The Jimi Hendrix Experience in Stadthalles all over West Germany. They were also the well-spring of incidents like the one that took place in 1966 in an arena in Hamburg designed originally for Wembley-sized championship sports galas.

A balcony at the back of the stage contained a noisy young man so overcome by the jubilee atmosphere that his constant cry of *"Dave Dee, I luff you!"* filled one of those sudden lulls that can punctuate such proceedings. Everybody laughed. "Next minute, he's hanging over the balcony," exclaimed Tich in Runyonese present-tense. "Then he falls twenty feet, knocks over a couple of the speaker columns on the stage, drops ten feet from the stage to the floor, and gets a hiding from The Spencer Davis Group's two roadies for knocking over the equipment. He's covered in blood, and he's sitting on a stool backstage in the first-aid area when we come off, and he's still yelling, *'Dave Dee, I luff you!'*"

This was the year too when the adored Dave and his boys racked up their heftiest achievement in overseas climes when they beat The Beatles by over three thousand votes to win the German pop magazine *Bravo*'s Golden Otto award – the equivalent of being Top Vocal Group in the *New Musical Express* poll (where they would be always outside the leading ten).

The Spencer Davis Group figured in the *Bravo* tabulation too, albeit badly behind The Rolling Stones, Beatles and, of course, Dave Dee and Co, but ahead of The Who and Small Faces, acts "senior" to them in Britain's pop hierarchy. The Group had returned to Germany in triumph with 'Keep On Running', a hit that, like 'Hold Tight!', had a no-frills four-in-a-bar beat, and was electroplated trendily with a foot-operated fuzz-box that distorted the lead guitar. No matter how much their longtime partisans refuted the suggestion, the Birmingham R&B outfit were now as much of a mainstream pop group as Dave Dee, Dozy, Beaky, Mick And Tich – with the pace even more hectic in Europe than it was at home after 'Somebody Help Me', another swift chart-topper, had Spencer and his merry men before the cameras for a TV special in Hilversum, after which they played an Amsterdam all-nighter. A televised concert to six thousand in Bremen the next afternoon was followed by two sets at the Star-Club a few hours later.

As lead singer on all the Group's German hits (except the 'Det War In Schoneberg'-'Madel Ruck-Ruck-Ruck' medley), seventeen-year-old Steve Winwood may have been the darling of the ladies there, but Davis with his excellent German hogged the press. His awareness of West Germany's political extremities had prompted some unfortunate remarks to *Melody Maker* about the election of the "new Nazis" in Bavaria. However, having let slip his Hertfordshire address, Spencer precipitated an avalanche of fan mail on its publication by *Bravo*.

Within a year, the journal would be announcing Winwood's "amicable split" with The Spencer Davis Group, and the name of his new outfit – which included members of The Hellions. During the same 1964 sojourn at the Star-Club where the seeds of Traffic had been sewn, other Hellions had socialised with those VIPs with whom they would amalgamate in Spooky Tooth, a "band" (not "group") of similar "progressive" bent as Traffic, and signed to Island too – though to the label's supremo, Chris Blackwell, they "were never as good as The VIPs".

When The VIPs had finished in Hamburg, they – like myriad other mid 1960s beat groups – had been as likely to plunge into the works of James Brown or Wilson Pickett as Ray Charles or Chuck Berry. As well as 'Papa's Got A Brand New Bag', 'In The Midnight Hour', Eddie Floyd's 'Knock On Wood' and similar discs saturation-plugged on pirate radio into European Top Fifties, those R&B musicians keeping eagerly abreast with black American styles were also *au fait* with both the back catalogue and the latest by even old timers such as The Drifters, Little Richard, Fats Domino, Bobby Bland and Chris "Land Of 1,000 Dances" Kenner – as well as newer entries in the US soul charts like The Soul Sisters' 'I Can't Stand It,' 'Harlem Shuffle' by Bob And Earl, Brenda Holloway's 'Every Little Bit Hurts' and gems as erudite by Kim Weston, Don Covay, Betty Everett, Doris Troy, Little Stevie Wonder and others that were infiltrating the repertoires of R&B units in Europe trying on soul for size.

Phil Upchurch Combo's 'You Can't Sit Down' was a single by The

Beatmen as The Capitols' 'Cool Jerk' was for north London "Mod" combo, The Creation, and James Brown's 'I'll Go Crazy' for The Untamed – who did their bit in Germany in 1965. 'I Can't Stand It' and 'Every Little Bit Hurts' had been consecutive Spencer Davis Group A-sides – with the former stretched into a five-minute piledriver as opening track on an LP by Cliff Bennett (who was to make as satisfying a meal of Sam And Dave's 'Hold On I'm Coming') – while 'Every Little Bit Hurts' was unrecorded but featured onstage by Carl Wayne And The Vikings.

Their version of The Temptations' 'My Girl', however, was issued in North America, just after they got back from Cologne. Yet within months, the group was no more, and Wayne, Ace Kefford and Bev Bevan were three-fifths of The Move. This new group was to acquire the same manager and record producer, and follow the same route (a season at London's Marquee, a Decca contract) to success as The Moody Blues – who had "nicked members from the five top bands in Birmingham," smiled Denny Laine, who'd started rehearsing in May 1964 with pianist Mike Pinder and general factotum Ray Thomas from The Krew Kats, fresh from Germany, whilst picking and choosing from prime local groups.

An apogée of Brum Beat had come when both The Moody Blues and The Rockin' Berries appeared on the same edition of *Ready Steady Go* in January 1965 when the former outfit's second forty-five, 'Go Now', had been poised to knock Georgie Fame from Number One in Britain, while the latter were in the slow moment between 'He's In Town' and 'Poor Man's Son'. Yet by autumn 1966, both ensembles were sagging on the ropes.

The Berries were turning into a comedy act as evidenced by their spot on 1967's Royal Command Performance, and telegraphed by LPs in which 'The Laughing Policeman', 'I Know An Old Lady Who Swallowed A Fly', Benny Hill's 'Harvest Of Love' and so on nestled uncomfortably amongst sentimental ballads such as 'Ich Liebe Dich' and 'The Way You Look Tonight'; concessions to soul like The Dixie Cups' 'Iko Iko', and the Richard-Presley-Vincent-Lewis rockers hauled up from the Berries' years in Germany.

Meanwhile, the after-effects of 'Go Now' had enabled The Moody Blues to just about break even in the dance halls of northern Europe after drastically reducing engagement fees. First out was bass guitarist Clint Warwick "because he was the only one married with a kid," said Denny Laine. "For me, that was the beginning of the end. It changed the whole concept of the band. Because it levelled out with the Moodies – yet another tour of Germany, that sort of thing – it all got a little bit insecure."

With Laine's departure too, the group all but gave up. Nevertheless, they were to revive with a vengeance via a grandiose 1967 "concept" LP, *Days Of Future Passed*, and its single, 'Nights In White Satin'. Then it would be plain sailing as further albums breathed mystic chords into the hearts of millions. There were times, however, when excessive magniloquence resulted in unintended humour as "poetic" gems were declaimed in one ex-Krew Kat's vile Brummie accent over a thick orchestral melange.

Like The Moody Blues, Yes, that most pretentious of pomp-rock brand-leaders, stemmed from a British beat group that grew up in the Fatherland. With his elder brother Anthony, future Yes-man Jon Anderson was singer with The Warriors, an Accrington combo that moved in the same circles as Dave Dee And The Bostons in Hamburg where the younger Anderson, by his own admission, gleaned much from Dee's instinctive if indelicate interaction with the audience. Light years too from Yes's *Tales From Topographic Oceans*, was The Warriors' post-Germany single for Decca, 1964's 'You Came Along' with the Beatle-esque harmonies that also enlivened 'Don't Make Me Blue', The Warriors' contribution to *Just For You*, an all-styles-served-here conveyor-belt of pop ephemera B-feature on the ABC cinema chain, circa 1965.*

The mood of 1965 – the golden year of "protest" – was summed up more effectively in 'Wake Up My Mind', the maiden single by The Ugly's. "The name – and its curiosity value – was a big help in terms of getting us gigs," said lead vocalist Steve Gibbons. It also caught the eye of Alan Freeman, not the noted BBC radio presenter, but a Pye recording manager. He decided that The Ugly's were as likely to be the next Titans of Teen as anyone else. In their favour was a cache of their own songs such as 'Ugly Blues', later described by Steve as "a quirky little talking blues that formed a thread between The Ugly's and what I'm doing now". More instantly stunning was 'Wake Up My Mind' with

---

* The Warriors also contained Ian Wallace who was to drum for King Crimson, Alexis Korner, Alvin Lee and Bob Dylan amongst others

its adroit Gibbons lyric and intriguing changes of time signature.

If it elicited little response in Britain, airplay snowballed in Australasia, and 'Wake Up My Mind' was soon high in charts throughout the continent. A telegram bearing this news reached the group during a tour of village institutes in the West Country and Wales with The Hellions and The VIPs. "They should have sent us out there straightaway," shrugged Steve. "It did nothing for us financially as we'd signed such pitiful deals – something like a farthing off every record sold between all of us – but at least things were starting to happen."

The Ugly's were to be much admired for their weaving of quaint instrumentation into the fabric of 'Wake Up My Mind' and subsequent forty-fives. Riven with harpsichord, 'It's Alright' seemed bound to do at home what its predecessor had Down Under: "We were getting reports of it selling eight hundred copies a day," said Steve. "Colossal amounts then – but just on the point where it would have got into the charts, there was a strike and the distributors didn't get the single into the shops." Nevertheless, a petition – that included the signature of Gene Vincent – brought about a spot on *Ready Steady Go*.

Impetus was lost, however, with the follow-up, 'A Good Idea', which, with the candour of his fifth decade, Steve described as "atrocious. It had another gimmick – me on kazoo – and, because of the impact 'It's Alright' had made, we got on *Thank Your Lucky Stars*, but it was a mundane, nowhere song." Less deserved a flop was The Ugly's treatment of Kink komposer Ray Davies' nonchalant 'End Of The Season' when olde tyme whimsy was in vogue in 1966, typified by The New Vaudeville Band's 'Winchester Cathedral' and the revival of 'Goodbye Dolly Gray' that drew out the agony for the long-faded Mojos. In much the same bag, 'The Squire Blew His Horn' (with Gibbons blasting same) was The Ugly's' vinyl finale. "It was one of our novelty songs, a showstopper, but it certainly didn't transmit to record," admitted Steve. "You had to be there."

Steve Gibbons' time would come with a definitive rendition of Chuck Berry's 'Tulane', a 1977 single that shinned up to Number Twelve in the UK charts, a feat compounded by a showing in the album list for his in-concert *Caught In The Act*. Of all the British pop stalwarts that served time in Germany, Steve's tale encapsulated somehow the walking of that difficult line between stardom and the hand-to-mouth struggle that usually steered you back to a Proper Job.*

A blending of modest achievements and lingering hip sensibility guarantees that, regardless of passing fads, a loyal following will always pay to see you. An unexpected Top Thirty entry might precipitate a brief frenzy of media attention and a rise in booking fees before a foreseeable slide back to an interminable sense of marking time until another such peak comes again – if it ever does. There's always sufficient incentive to carry on jumping bandwagons ahead of most rivals, and, in the case of Steve Gibbons, during and after The Ugly's, infuse each with a true individuality.

More striking than The Ugly's were The Creation, derived from Kenny Lee And The Mark Four who'd lasted a roisterous autumn in Wilhelmshaven's Big Ben Club in 1964 – and a Liverpudlian bass player named Bob Garner who'd been at the Star-Club in The Lee Curtis All-Stars, and in a Zurich coffee bar backing Tony Sheridan. The following spring, The Creation were climaxing their act by splashing an action painting onto a canvas backdrop which was then set alight amid feedback lament from lead guitarist Eddie Phillips who pioneered the scraping of a violin bow across a fretboard on the group's brace of 1966 Top Fifty entries – and a hasty LP, *We Are Paintermen*, issued only in Scandinavia and Germany – where 'Painter Man', the second of the group's minor hits in Britain, had gone to Number One.

This – and allegations that their singles had been manoeuvred into the UK charts by their manager's under-the-bedclothes fixing – necessitated virtual exile in Germany for a year that included a Rolling Stones tour in which a native group, The Batmen, costumed accordingly, were among other supporting turns. Drummer Jack Jones also remembered a show at Munich's Circus Krone where "we set up our painting frame, but didn't know you needed a special licence with the fire brigade standing by. The next thing, everybody's spraying hoses to put the fire out, and the Gestapo arrive in leather coats, hats and dark glasses. They confiscated our passports."

All this was useful publicity ammunition, and a 1967 press release would describe The Creation – with some justification – as "Germany's third top touring group". However, somewhere along the *autobahns*, they ran out of ideas. With Garner shelving his bass in order to replace the decamped lead singer, they quit while they were ahead

---

* Like Noel Redding's as a Folkestone milkman during the interim between The Loving Kind's abject return from Germany and his glad acceptance of a post in The Jimi Hendrix Experience

commercially after farewell treks round Holland and Germany in 1968.

Three years earlier, The Fortunes had made Cliff Richard seem like Eddie Phillips jamming with Hendrix. Yet after a second Decca single, 'Caroline', was adopted as signature tune of the pirate radio station of the same name, it took just fifteen months for a hat-trick of Top Twenty strikes to begin with 'You've Got Your Troubles'. Next up were 'Here It Comes Again' and then 'This Golden Ring', also smothered with heavy-handed orchestration and characterised by an overdubbed vocal counterpoint near the big finish.

The Fortunes' middle-of-the-road Top Twenty bonanza in the mid 1960s excited nothing that was positive from me until May 1986 when I was keyboard player with Dave Berry And The Cruisers. After we'd played a variety show at an Amsterdam conference centre, I sought diversion in the complex's cabaret sanctum with its roulette wheels and dance floor. Waving the flag there were The Fortunes, and I was surprised to find myself glowing with patriotic pride as 'This Golden Ring' filled the front of the stage with smoochers. What was happening? There I was, tapping my feet to 'This Golden Ring' and everything else I'd despised – probably because it made more rock 'n' roll sense minus the massed strings that had soaked through the records. Beneath it all, I perceived a Midlands beat group made in Germany as much as The Krew Kats, Carl Wayne And The Vikings and The Rockin' Berries. If the good opinion of one such as I matters to them, then The Fortunes can die easy.

CHAPTER SEVENTEEN

Find My Way Back Home

"I had to make a lot of funny decisions about singing in German, and eventually I got into a mess with Polydor because I'd had enough of Germany after 1965. I wanted to play and record in America"

Tony Sheridan

The last straw might have been a booking in a club above an auto shop in Bremerhaven where a British group, emitting an almost palpable aura of self-loathing, took the stage before an audience of twelve. Small too was the agreed percentage of the gate, more and more promoters' preferred alternative these days. There was also a freak cold spell with heavy rain all day as well as something good on television and a strike by the local newspaper (thus precluding advertising). Having not taken the trouble to tune up properly, the musicians couldn't care less about the wavering bars of bum notes or Graham messing up the words to 'Love Potion Number Nine' or Ted, bless him, trying to make a show of it. Next day, it was discovered that all the new drummer's cymbals had been stolen.

That afternoon, Graham sent off for details and an application form for teacher training college. If they still thought kindly of the uncorrupted lad he once was, testimonials from the vicar and his old headmaster would return him to the fold by September.

Even The Beatles were expecting their time to be up soon. "It's been fun, but it won't last," John Lennon had insisted in the *New York Times*. "Anyway," he guffawed, "I'd hate to be an old Beatle." Be sensible. Could you imagine John spilling his metaphorical guts over 'Dizzy Miss Lizzy' at thirty; a middle-aged Dave Dee rupturing his throat during the bawled coda of 'Save Me' – or Ray Ennis nearing retirement but doin' the Hippy Hippy Shake with all of his might, not forgetting to scream "Waaaaaah!" into a microphone to signal the lead guitar break?

There was a *fin de siècle* feeling in the air whether it was Dave Sampson making despondent tracks back to England to commence a factory job in Walthamstow or the old bunkroom above the Top Ten being vacated for a reunion party after a performance at the Ernst Merke Halle on 26 June 1966 by The Beatles during the dinning weeks of their last and most public journey before downing tools as a working group.

Veiled in flesh, those now regarded as Local Boys Made Good were reappearing before their people like Moses from the clouded summit of Mount Sinai. On the bill too were Cliff Bennett and a Rebel Rousers that now included Roy Young – not yet casting covetous eyes on Cliff's position as front man – and a set that contained 'Got To Get You Into My Life', presented to Cliff in a dressing room one night by its composers, Paul McCartney on guitar and vocal, and John Lennon dah-dahing a horn section. That autumn, this James Brown pastiche was to be Bennett's biggest and final hit.

The entourage had completed dates in Munich and Essen before Hamburg where, just as the populace awoke, The Beatles arrived at the main station in a train usually reserved for royalty. Then they were whisked away in a fleet of glittering Mercedes – with *Polizei* outriders – to out-of-town seclusion in Tremsbuttel's Schloss Hotel. There wasn't a newspaper editor in Germany who wouldn't promise a king's ransom for an exclusive or a candid snapshot, but journalists – and anybody else – needed to spin an impossibly likely tale to gain admittance to a suite as impregnable as Fort Knox.

A knees-up at the Top Ten flat became impractical but a disguised Lennon and McCartney dared a nostalgic stroll along the Reeperbahn, and a few old faces such as Bert Kaempfert, Astrid Kirchherr and Lee Curtis were allowed past backstage security before showtime for selective reminiscences about the group's past that, through its fantastic outcome, had attained flashback grandeur.

In the queues outside, while none expected the waters of the Elbe to part, the show was on the scale of a World Cup Final, and they'd surely filter into the Ernst Merke lobby afterwards, having participated in the proverbial "something to tell your grandchildren about". Therefore, only a miracle could have rescued The Beatles' first "home game" since 1962 from anti-climax. After dishing out thirty minutes of stale, unheard music into the teeth of the screams, the four bolted pell-mell to the ticking-over back-alley limousines that would be speeding them back to Tremsbuttel even as the buzzing tribes shuffled out, blood pressure dropping, into the twilight.

Over in St Pauli, the bands played on. As the age of Aquarius dawned, British beat groups still lingered there: doughty anachronisms battling through the old 'Twist And Shout'-'Besame Mucho' warhorses, even as The Remo Four at the Star-Club and on *Smile!*, their 1967 Germany-only LP, crossed the frontiers between R&B and jazz. Not so adaptable, fellow Scousers Ian And The Zodiacs had headed back to England to expire quietly after turning down 'Even The Bad Times Are Good' which, picked up by The Tremeloes, made the Top Five.

Kingsize Taylor was getting tired of it too. Largely through the bad faith of the mobsters who ruled the venues where he'd finished up, he'd been left destitute and had had to apply for an assisted repatriation. As The Beatles jetted overhead, he heaved his guitars, amplifiers and suitcases into a second class compartment at Hamburg-Hauptbahnhof.

It wasn't that Kingsize had deteriorated as a rock 'n' roll entertainer; he'd become simply an old one, too out of touch with the business in London, and no more convinced, even momentarily, by anyone's buoyant optimism or big talk. Some like him would never concede that The Beatles – the only British unit of the old Hamburg school still able to take chart entries for granted – had been any better than them. Pop obeys no law of natural justice, does it?

How else could you explain why Paul Raven, rendered square by the group boom, was at the end of his tether as a *Ready Steady Go* programme assistant whose duties included working up an electric pre-transmission atmosphere for a majority of acts who were not his experienced equal as performers? Didn't it seem unfair that victory should belong to those with lookalike images and soundalike records while those of greater talent plodded from artistic maturity to business-as-usual repetition, just to maintain an endurable *modus vivendi* while the very names "Paul Raven", "Ian And The Zodiacs" or even "Gerry And The Pacemakers" became heavier millstones round their owners' necks?

A few clung on as renowned men-about-Hamburg, much-travelled – in West Germany anyway – worldly-wise and more than able to both keep down their drink and stand their rounds, but where else could they go? The let-me-hear-you-say-yeah routines were very behind the times, but it wasn't impossible to adjust to new ways, albeit without quite getting the point sometimes. When Roy Young ousted him as leader of what would be renamed "The Roy Young Band" in 1968, Cliff Bennett was to be linchpin of way-out Toe Fat – while The Fortunes strayed far from the orchestral slop that had made them with 1967's 'The Idol', classed as "psychedelia" when spun by certain "underground" disc-jockeys on European pop radio.

Back in the Black Country after their month in Dortmund, The In Betweens – now with Noddy Holder as lead singer and rhythm guitarist – had stuck their necks out by focusing on self-compositions of a "progressive" bent as well as items from the disparate but up-to-date likes of The Idle Race, Three Dog Night and The Mothers Of Invention. As "Slade", The In Betweens were to wrestle for dominance of the next decade's glam-rock craze with a gentleman they'd met in Germany.

Seven years before he became "Gary Glitter", Paul Raven's long spell in German clubs was to have a lasting and beneficial effect. "After the bleak time I'd been experiencing since leaving *Ready Steady Go*, it seemed too good an opportunity to miss." He was to be centre-stage with Boston International* after the time-honoured arduous train journey with all the gear to Hamburg at the height of its evening rush-hour. For three months in various clubs – notably a Kaiserkeller under new management – they earned their corn with fare that covered mostly soul and the Top Twenty; once in rotation with twenty-minute clips from ancient Elvis or James Dean movies. Next, it was on to Kiel's Starpalast – now with a skyscraper backcloth bought from the Hamburg Star-Club – where, as they may have been warned, Manfred Wotilla would appropriate their passports to keep them there.

While Boston International were wondering – like Johnnie Law And The M15 before them – how to escape from Wotilla's clutches, Tony

---

* Also known as The Boston International Show Band or just plain The Bostons (but nothing to do with Dave Dee, Dozy, Beaky, Mick And Tich)

Sheridan had left Germany for perhaps the last place you might expect to find him: "When I got through the Chuck Berry-Elvis thing and got more into black music with The Big Six, I didn't know where to go from there. The record company had made it pretty clear that we had to record something that was likely to sell. By 1967, they couldn't care less whether I was recording or not – so I decided to take off after seven years of it.

"I still hadn't been to America so I thought it might be good to answer a call from the US Forces, go to Vietnam for a couple of months and be appreciated by Americans there for playing their own music. I went out of the frying pan into another fire: Soho, St Pauli and then Vietnam – for sixteen months during the hottest period of the war."

Using the trio format with which he'd always felt most at ease, Tony took with him a German bass player and an Irish drummer – with Horst Fascher along to see to everyone's food, sleep and general health requirements. In a broader sense this entailed checking security, prising unwanted company out of dressing rooms and buttonholing promoters in venues from Saigon to the smallest makeshift village.

As a beehive can function for a while after losing its progenitorial queen, so groups continued to thrive in Hamburg without an equivalent of Sheridan, The Beatles, Dave Dee And The Bostons, Kingsize Taylor or any of the other detonators of earlier explosions. The record companies weren't coming round anymore either, especially as flower-power San Francisco was now as vital a pop Mecca as Hamburg was no more.

While no specific Beat or Sound from Germany had yet dominated the planet, homogenous acts taking their cues from North America – and Britain still – tended now to be more proficient than the Ted Herolds, Tommy Kents and Drafi Deutschers of old. If not exhibiting strong native characteristics, The Rattles were no longer the copyists who'd got those lush Scouse harmonies off to a gutteral "T". Much changed, they were as prominent in the domestic Top Twenty as any foreigner – notably with 'The Witch' in 1968, just as compulsory army service and other external factors plagued them almost to extinction.

However, bass guitarist Herbert Hilderbrandt proved a very professional tower of strength by taking a backseat as producer, composer and general *eminence grise* to a new Rattles enlisted in Italy and fronted by a pulchritudinous Israeli vocalist with the stage name "Edna". Remade with English lyrics, 'The Witch' not only flew into the UK Top Ten, but also gave The Rattles the distinction of being the first German group to enter the US Hot Hundred.

If the group was unable to secure a lasting place in overseas hearts, theirs was the most fruitful of all attempts by Germans who'd started by reinventing themselves as British beat groups. From the same root, The Lords – almost as popular as The Rattles at home – had diversified into a confusing if compelling mixture of styles whereby a set could flit from Lonnie Donegan's 'Have A Drink On Me' to 'Shakin' All Over' to a rocked-up 'Greensleeves' to 'Poison Ivy' – to a 'John Brown's Body' with *leitmotifs* from 'The Star-Spangled Banner' and Tchaikovsky's *1812* and a side-serving of taped bangs and gunshot whinnying – all underpinned by a perky, pseudo-reggae jerk. Mouldering in his grave? I expect Brown – like St Pauli – was spinning in it.

West Indian styles were more than a trace element in the music of The Equals, a racially-mixed bunch from north London who'd be remembered principally as the outfit in which 1970s star Eddy Grant cut his teeth. In 1965, The Equals had undertaken a long run of one-nighters on the continent where they developed into a sought-after concert turn. A presenter on Radio Hamburg liked the loose-limbed drive of 'Baby Come Back' better than the A-side of their second single. Other West German stations started programming it too, and 'Baby Come Back' leapt to the top in both Germany and the Netherlands, and their *Unequalled Equals* blockaded Europe's LP charts for months.

As The Equals became the next fresh sensation to ring changes in the week's new hit parade, recollections of Sheridan, Kingsize, Dave Sampson and the other old campaigners missing in action dimmed a degree more for those Kaiserkeller ravers of 1961, now married and turning thirty. It seemed so faraway now, an era that was coming to seem as bygone as that bracketed by Hitler's suicide and 'Rock Around The Clock'.

CHAPTER EIGHTEEN

Bye Bye Blues

"When The Beatles were talking about five sets a night, they weren't joking. We used to go on and off that stage like jacks in a box. It seemed to go on forever"

Ozzy Osbourne (Black Sabbath)

While the Summer of Love might not have gripped the imagination of young Germans as hard as it had their cousins in Amsterdam, London and San Francisco, hippies were becoming common enough, even in agrarian Bavaria, and psychedelia was represented in the Top Twenty in such as The Move's 'Night Of Fear', the BBC-banned 'My Friend Jack' from The Smoke, Traffic's pixified 'Hole In My Shoe' and, if you were blind to its irony, 'Zabadak!', pretty-but-nothing syllables strung together to carry a lush tropical island sound-painting by Dave Dee, Dozy, Beaky, Mick And Tich as they shifted further from 'Hold Tight!' towards the costume-drama epics that would touch a commercial zenith with 1968's whip-crack-away 'Legend Of Xanadu'.

In retrospect, the chasm between 'Zabadak!' and, say, Al Martino's syrupy 'Spanish Eyes' does not seem great – especially as Horst Jankowski covered both – but, if too mainstream to be psychedelic, the Dave Dee five could not be considered part of the counter-revolution of "decent music" either as it infiltrated continental territories far more than it did Great Britain, despite the islands' harbouring of risen anew suzerains of schmaltz like Harry Secombe and, for gawd's sake, Donald Peers plus newcomers such as Malcolm Roberts, John Rowles and, especially, Engelbert Humperdinck in its Top Twenty.

Like The Equals, Humperdinck had clicked in northern Europe a full year before his homeland caught on – and even when re-recorded in English, schmaltzy 'Merci Cherie', a Eurovision Song Contest winner for Udo Jurgens, had had the impact of a feather on concrete in Britain.

Though Bert Kaempfert had been guaranteed a fair hearing in the UK album list since 1965, the title track that set the ball rolling, 'Bye Bye Blues', was to be his only entry in the singles Top Fifty. Consumers were, nevertheless, assailed by stealth as 'Bye Bye Blues' and 'Strangers In The Night' joined 'Wonderland By Night' on the supermarket muzak bulletin. Moreover, Bert's bank account ballooned further when lyrics were grafted onto his 'Moonlight Over Naples', a 'Zabadak!'-like track on his *Magic Music Of Faraway Places* LP (the one before *Bye Bye Blues*) to become 'Spanish Eyes'.

Yet Kaempfert's triumphs by proxy or otherwise paled against those of Heintje, a *wunderkind* supposedly responsible for twenty per cent of Germany's total record sales in the late 1960s, following the discovery of this eleven-year-old soprano in 1967 by Ariola studio manager Adolf Klyngeld. Though Heintje's output was more the stuff of the sentimental elderly than his fellow adolescents, this Aled Jones of his day meant nothing in Britain but he was to swamp north and central European charts until his voice broke to a less appealing baritone.

Unless his records soundtracked the more perverse goings-on, the boy wonder was not heard in the red-light clubs where soul music and good old rock 'n' roll still held indefatigable sway, even as psychedelia came at last to the ports of Germany. Booked at the Star-Club one Saturday in 1968, Love Affair, for example, were still delving into 'Knock On Wood', 'Ride Your Pony' and the like to pad out a set built round 'Everlasting Love', 'Rainbow Valley' and other of the smashes that had placed them a cut above other derivative dance groups to be found everywhere.

If hitless, Boston International were peddling more proficient hand-clappin', foot-stompin' wares all over Germany, once supporting Bill Haley who'd now refined his art to a science. "He still had the same band and they were doing a tremendous act," said Paul Raven, himself no slouch on the boards now. "Paul was a great performer," affirmed Johnnie Law, "who never left the stage until he had the place jumping. A lot of people say he's not much of a singer, but he could put over some really moving soul ballads."

Raven's professional stature was such that he topped one town hall bill after watching from the wings as Jimi Hendrix, an overnight sensation in London, "did very badly, and was booed offstage. They had all come along to dance, but instead Hendrix played his guitar with his teeth, and his music was impossible to dance to. I just couldn't see how he had got the reputation he had." Apart from clottings of hipness in its bigger cities, Britain in general had been as ill-prepared for the Hendrix experience too. "We were headlining at a one-nighter on Southend pier at the height of the holiday season," recounted Tich Amey, "and Jimi closed the first half with 'Wild Thing' which included the whole works – squealing feedback and setting fire to his guitar – in front of a family audience ranging from grannies to babes-in-arms. The theatre didn't know what to make of it either as Jimi was such a quiet, polite bloke offstage."

When Hendrix returned to Germany for engagements that were less like a mixing of oil and water, he was better able to extort the pandemonium that also brought 1967's International Pop Music Festival at Monterey to its knees. Yet Jimi was not to be so untouchable an object of myth that Tich couldn't talk guitars with him when the pair went nightclubbing in Berlin – or Beaky and Dave Dee be afraid to jam with him – as they did after-hours in a Frankfurt auditorium – in spite of Hendrix's remark in *Melody Maker* that he was worried about "becoming the American version of Dave Dee".

Tich's Hendrix-esque fretboard touch-ups to 'Shame' on the back of 'Save Me', and on 'The Sun Goes Down' freak-out that likewise B-sided 'Zabadak!' might have epitomised the passing of the old order on record, but down in the Reeperbahn clubs and places like the Spectrum, a cynically opportunist new venue in Kiel, it was in the proffering of marijuana "joints" rather than pills as a gesture of free-spirited friendliness.

In the dance area, the mind-warping effects of the soon-to-be outlawed LSD possessed cavorting berserkers, shrouded by flickering strobes, ectoplasmic light projections and further audio-visual aids that simulated the chemically-induced glimpses of the eternal that were part-and-parcel of the psychedelic experience as nice-little-bands of progressive hue played on and on and on and on, evoking cheers not screams for an onstage allure hinged not so much on come-hither looks and tight trousers as virtuosity demonstrated in loud and interminable instrumental soloing; their teeth and eyelids clamped shut as if in pain.

Such diddle-iddle-iddling usually bore as much relation to the blowing, blowing, blowing of Acker Bilk's Paramount Jazz Band as dairy butter does to low-fat margarine, but the clientele were too stoned to mind or let it interrupt shouted chinwags or their popping off for negotiations with narcotics dealers in the toilets. "It used to drive us mad to think we were playing our guts out while all these guys were sitting around and chattering," snarled Bill Ward of Black Sabbath, "so we turned up the volume louder and louder until it was impossible to have a conversation."

Though a few youths on the dance floor continued to mime to fresh-air guitars, this ploy backfired when Black Sabbath became cynosure of an unnerving stare from what looked like a gigantic photograph of hundreds of silent and unresponsive Germans. "They just tried to be as cool as they possibly could," said vocalist Ozzy Osbourne. "We'd be belting away and, you know, like, nothing from them."

Yet Sabbath were enjoyed after a non-demonstrative fashion as Hamburg was now fair game to buy anything British labelled "heavy" or "blues". This meant that 'Besame Mucho' and any other of the old tearjerkers wouldn't wash anymore, and the new 'What'd I Say' was Willie Dixon's three-verse 'Spoonful' but cut, dried and dissected at triple-*forte* in imitation of Cream who filled almost one side of a 1968 album with it, and most of another with 'Toad', a truculent frenzy of cross-patterns and ringing silverware from drummer Ginger Baker. "We were not indulging ourselves so much as our audiences," grimaced the guitarist, ex-Yardbird Eric Clapton, "because that's what they wanted."

Black Sabbath likewise kept the customer satisfied. "We started doing longer solos," said their Tony Iommi. "It got so bad we ended up devoting entire sets to solos. We got Bill to do a drum solo which must have lasted half an hour. I used to do complete sets on my own on guitar. There was a time when we even managed to get Geezer Butler to do a whole set soloing on bass. I don't think anybody noticed to be honest."

Yet this 1968 season in Hamburg's Star-Club bestowed unto Sabbath's ensemble playing an apocalyptic brutality which, layered with Osbourne's straining attack, affected a bleak but atmospheric intensity. When it was time to go back to Birmingham, the four were sporting inverted crucifixes and like Satanic fetishist adornments, and delivering self-penned pieces – 'Hand Of Doom', 'Children Of The Grave', 'Behind The Walls Of Sleep' and so forth – indicative of Butler's fascination with Dennis Wheatley novels. "Most of the numbers are based on a certain riff," glowed Geezer with quiet pride. "We don't use a melody, just a raw type of riff."

From this surfaced the band's first album and consequent global renown as heavy metallurgists, though a bored Ozzy's later preoccupation with hard drugs, booze and crapulous debauchery would be among internal frictions that would culminate in his departure from the group in the late 1970s. Yet Johnnie Law would remember Osbourne as "full of life, laughing and joking the whole time. The rest were quieter guys but very friendly. At the time, a lot of the groups from Britain – particularly London – were coming on real cool, and we started thinking that there was something wrong with us – because we always wanted a good laugh. Well, we decided to start being cool also, and that we weren't even going to speak to the next group that comes – and who was the first guy to come in? Ozzy Osbourne!"

Sabbath were rebooked by the Star-Club for four more residencies that would monitor both a rapid breaking of the house attendance record and their unwitting teasing of intemperate fanaticism from elements in an otherwise passive audience. Some children of the grave would insert their heads into yawning speaker bins to receive the full mega-decibel blast of Butler's bass. Neither can evidence be refuted that it was in the Star-Club too that the brain-damaging practice of "headbanging" was born.

Less to do with Sabbath than the post-flower-power drift of the times were those clad in garb even more androgynously startling than that of the Duchess of the Roxy, and the behaviour of a fellow, nondescript apart from an immaculate Al Capone-esque white suit, who strode into the club when Sabbath were on, for no other purpose than to perform a seemingly impulsive handstand, and walk out again, leaving the contents of his pockets littered on the floor. A man's gotta do what a man's gotta do, but if this was an Art Statement, the only Art Reply he got for his act of mild lunacy was no-one appearing to take the slightest notice.

After Black Sabbath's manager, Jim Simpson, arranged a two-month stint at the Star-Club for The Ace Kefford Stand – with ex-Sorcerer Cozy Powell on drums – in late 1968, its leader would be tickled by the memory of one weekend "when Spooky Tooth were topping the bill. We did our set, and, for some reason, all the kids started laying down handkerchiefs for Dave Ball, our guitarist, to stand on like he was God. I was doing all the screaming and jumping about, and the audience was going mad. Spooky Tooth finished their first number and didn't get one clap."

Kefford's previous group, The Move had first impinged upon national consciousness with a stage show that involved Carl Wayne charging onstage with a chopper to hack up effigies of political icons before turning his attention to imploding televisions. For Ace, the legacy of this was the blackballing of the Stand by British promoters: "A lot of venues wouldn't have us because of The Move being obnoxious, telling them to fuck off, and leaving stages with big holes where the axes had chopped 'em up.

"The Stand was a covers band really – Led Zeppelin's 'Communication Breakdown', Steppenwolf's 'Born To Be Wild', 'Spoonful', that sort of stuff. We only had to do four three-quarter hour spots as opposed to seven to ten hours in the days of The Vikings. The Stand became a good group. Cozy used to do a solo. I can't imagine what he's like now, but he was incredible then." Following the drug-addled Kefford's disbandment of the Stand, Powell fell on his feet in The Jeff Beck Group in 1971.

Three years earlier, another Hamburg bit-part player, bass guitarist Alex Young of The Bobby Patrick Big Six, had had his fifteen minutes as "George Alexander" in Grapefruit, who almost made the UK Top Twenty with 1968's 'C'mon Marianne' when associated with – but not actually signed to – The Beatles' Apple Corps, a company devoted to a diversity of maverick scientific and artistic ventures. However, its only money-spinner was its record label; even the Zapple subsidiary whose output would be dismissed with commendable honesty as "a load of rubbish" by George Harrison.

For all Apple's quixotic antics and the marijuana-smoking music they were making these days, The Beatles were probably the same as they always were to those who remembered five teenage Liverpudlians with eyes on stalks arriving to make their nervous debut at the Indra. Raising a derisive laugh too had been this "transcendental meditation" lark that they'd cottoned onto in 1967: that wouldn't have cut much ice down the Herbertstrasse, would it?

Then there was the behaviour of Lennon whose pranks were infinitely more bewildering than that of the chap who did a handstand before Black Sabbath. They could be dated from his teaming-up with Yoko Ono, a Japanese-American who was to Art what Screaming Lord Sutch was to politics. A John Lennon that no-one had known before was annihilating all that remained of cosy illusions about The Beatles through penis display, Bed-Ins, sending acorns to world figures, "Bagism" and turning his life generally into a ludicrous and open book in order to say things most people didn't want to hear.

"It doesn't give me any pleasure," wrote his estranged songwriting partner in a press release that prefaced Messrs Harrison, Lennon, McCartney and Starkey's formal disassociation as a business enterprise after an age of shilly-shallying between the colour-supplement Art that culminated with the valedictory *Abbey Road*, and ineffectual endeavours to get back to their unvarnished genesis through the desecrated elegance of the *Let It Be* sessions – with guest organist Billy Preston. He'd kept in touch since he and The Beatles had met in 1962, but his contributions to both their new songs and the jamming of rock 'n' roll classics half-remembered from the Star-Club could not lift the self-interested depression that was accelerating the four's bitter freedom from each other.

The movie to which the *Let It Be* LP was yoked documented the subtleties of the harangues and grievances that fanned the flames of The Beatles' funeral pyre, but you couldn't help wondering if those who watched it up to the closing credits would have been as fascinated if it'd been Dave Dee, Dozy, Beaky, Mick And Tich studiously avoiding open confrontation, running through old numbers and risking grief as soon as they tried anything fresh.

It wasn't until the summer of 1969 that they had their last hit, 'Snake In The Grass'. Had they not then split in two, it is conceivable that the Salisbury outfit might have revived as they had after 'Touch Me Touch Me'. As it was, Dave followed the "quality" route *à la* Bern Elliott, while the rest as "DBMT" were in a state of indecision about whether to cut themselves off from their 'Hold Tight!'-'Zabadak!' past or use it to get work whilst developing a hitherto unprecedented musical introspection akin to that of Crosby, Stills, Nash And Young, prize exhibits at the Woodstock Music And Arts Fair in August 1969, viewed from a distance of years as the crowning glory of hippy culture.

As 'Bend It' at Number One in Texas had been the zenith of Dave Dee *et al*'s record success in the States, DBMT concentrated on the possible by probing the European student market, even though its greatcoated males – whose parents made them get their hair cut when they came home for the holidays – had disliked 'Zabadak!' on principle, and enjoyed hostel room discussions over a reefer about how "interesting" this or that band, "nice little" or otherwise, had been in the university's Great Hall on Saturday night, delivering artistic insights that were not immediately accessible. There was, you see, a vast gap now between "rock" – which only the finest minds could appreciate – and vulgar "pop".

As "Balls", Steve Gibbons with Denny Laine and Trevor Burton, once of The Move, caught a mood of turn-of the-decade rock with a style based on acoustic guitars and pastoral lyricism. This was tested in two Midlands colleges where cool oozed as profusely as it had during Black Sabbath's Star-Club period. "It was very much goldfish-bowl time," noticed Gibbons, "with all the audience sitting cross-legged. The first gig went down like a lead balloon, but the second was an absolute storm." But soon must come the hour when fades the fairest flower, and so it was that Steve "eventually told Tony Secunda, our manager, that it wasn't going anywhere, and that I had family responsibilities whereas Denny and Trevor were free agents".

Making more headway in the campuses – particularly in northern Europe – bands such as Taste, Ten Years After, Free and Stan Webb's Chicken Shack were making hay from a second wave of mass interest in electric blues as interpreted – frequently in the most ham-fisted fashion – by white Britons and a lot of the North American outfits that had started to work the bigger clubs in Germany and Holland. The "blues boom", however, had little effect on Traffic, now down to three lanes, and who, like DBMT and Balls, were less gut-wrenching than intense in their low volume restraint.

As Traffic were connected genealogically to Midlands beat groups, so Man were to those in South Wales like The Corncrackers, The Bystanders and Smokeless Zone. Like other British bands now tilting at the colleges, Man were big in Germany as shown by recurrent appearances on the now incongruously-titled *Beat Club*. Yet the Land of Song's foremost "progressive" ensemble found the going rough at home where most undergraduates wasting their grants on albums couldn't recall listening consciously to any track by a combo that would provoke the *Melody*

Maker headline: MAN: HEROES IN EUROPE, IGNORED AT HOME.

Man* and Traffic's realisation of musical moods through open-ended improvisations was a large part of the independently-nurtured and less stylised *modus operandi* of Faust, Amon Duul, Can and other nascent "kraut-rock" groups smouldering into form from long-haired "collectives" in which individuals could pursue projects tangential to the central structure's *conceptual continuity*. Yeah, well...Amon Duul, for instance, had assumed shape in 1968 from a pool of entertainers associated with an "alternative" commune in Munich as evinced in lyrics (in German and English) that dwelt on the New Left radicalism that was motivating former flower children to follow the crowd to the tub-thumping university sit-ins and, with Vietnam the common denominator, genuinely violent protest marches, demonstrations and moratoriums.

In September 1969, Paul Raven had been active in this after a self-concerned manner following the occupation of two empty mansions in the heart of London by a multitude of homeless hippies. Soon the block was encircled by an attendant sea of journalists, TV cameras and assorted riff-raff watching the fun as police were marshalled for an eviction. Ever the opportunist, Raven had gained entry one afternoon and, from a balcony, was leading an *ad hoc* choir consisting of the squatters and the crowds outside in 'We're All Living In One Place' – topical lyrics to the tune of 'Amazing Grace' – which was to be released as a single by Rubber Bucket, namely Paul in yet another guise.

'Give Peace A Chance' it was not, but Raven was a desperate man by then, having been forced back to England after work in Germany dried up to such an extent that he'd taken up a post in Kiel as the Spectrum's resident disc-jockey. Nothing, however, could stop Paul's ante-Merseybeat contemporary, Dave Sampson singing, and, sure enough, by the later 1960s, he'd been fronting a local outfit, The Leroys, in the Lorne Arms, a huge local pub. Though the proceedings closed generally with forty minutes of classic rock, Dave – sporting shoulder-length hair and a trendy beard – was now changed almost beyond recognition from the 'Sweet Dreams' hitmaker and Hamburg club rabble-rouser-in-chief as he coped with up to four hundred customers a night and a repertoire drawn from the likes of Santana, Joe Cocker, Creedence Clearwater Revival and Redbone.

---

* The sunshine and showers of the outfit's career are chronicled by its singing guitarist, Deke Leonard in *The Legend Of Man, A Rock 'N' Roll Band* (Northdown Publishing, 1996) which made me laugh out loud more often than I felt sick to the stomach – which I was about some of Deke's anecdotes about life on the road *sur le continent*

While Dave's two conspicuous years at the Lorne Arms enabled him to chuck in his factory job, The Pretty Things kept Straightsville at arm's length by feeding off one-nighters on Europe's "underground" circuit where they brushed up against the likes of Tyrannosaurus Rex, The Social Deviants, The Edgar Broughton Band, Eire Apparent and Hawkwind. Indeed, a guitarist from the Broughton bunch had replaced Dick Taylor who had quit the treadmill of the road to be, amongst other things, console midwife to Hawkwind's first album.

When further hardship and bitter disappointment induced the Things to take a brief sabbatical in 1971, EMI gave Wally Allen a full-time post as a staff producer just as Atlantic had Adrian Barber after he'd left the Star-Club on the invitation of a post-Twist Joey Dee to redesign the sound system to the Peppermint Lounge. Three of Dee's ex-sidemen had joined The Young Rascals who, along with the Velvet Underground, The Allman Brothers Band and, later, Aerosmith, were to benefit from Barber's skills in the recording studio after Atlantic's successful headhunting of him.

As a result, Adrian in the United States was not a practical consideration when Johnny Gustafson thought aloud about a suggested regrouping of The Big Three. Raring-to-go reformation, however, was contrary to the sense of impending hangover in the late 1960s as more old heroes and non-heroes went down. Noel Redding, for example, had played his final concert for Hendrix – who was fated to die in September 1970, soon after an appearance on Denmark's Isle of Fehmarn at a so-called "Love And Peace Festival" where discomfited snarls signified a murderous mood as onlookers grappled for both a good view and shelter from the heavy rain and unseasonably freezing temperatures.

More dismal was the situation for such as The Swinging Blue Jeans, Wayne Fontana and The Nashville Teens, displayed as curios from the recent past in an outer darkness of dance halls in Belgium, Finland and Germany. Fontana was to join other old cronies on a "British Invasion Reunion" tour of North America on which The Searchers gave Neil Young what he merited in a long, long work-out of his 'Southern Man' diatribe as if to show that even if they'd never been in a sit-in or played a Love And Peace Festival, The Searchers were still hip. Nevertheless, they – like most of the other participants – then fell back on the European civic halls and social clubs that had become their lot since the bubble burst.

CHAPTER NINETEEN

Hello Hello I'm Back Again

"Leslie and I had had enough. We felt that there was more to life than playing in Germany, so we jumped on a Lufthansa jet and came home"

Maggie Bell (Stone The Crows)

Just as some English history primers start with the battle of Hastings, so you could argue that that the date that divided the Dark Ages from the mediaeval period of British beat's Hamburg era was sometime in April 1962 during the Top Ten season with Tony Sheridan, The Jaybirds, Rory Storm And The Hurricanes and a Beatles still wearing leathers and Brylcreem, yet to make a record, and with Pete on drums and Stuart on bass. Alternatively, you might stick to the same location but with Dave Dee And The Bostons presiding over an assortment of passing groups – or else make it the Star-Club in 1964 and a wider regional cross-section of acts, ie The Nashville Teens, Spencer Davis Group, VIPs, Shades Five and The Hellions, just before there was some kind of future, one way or another, for any of them.

You can be as divergent in picking when its twilight began to descend: the "glorious sunset mistaken for a dawn", as Debussy described *Das Rheingold*. Was it Dave Dee, Dozy, Beaky, Mick And Tich's triumphant debut at the Star-Club, The Beatles' Ernst Merke Halle bash or the final edition of *Beat Club* in 1971? Perhaps it was as late as spring 1973 when Traffic and Spooky Tooth, tired and hungry after a show at the Musikhalle, discovered that, instead of reserving tables in a quiet restaurant, the promoter had laid on a loud disco with flashing lights and junk champagne so that exorbitant admission charges could be levied on autograph hunters and groupies desirous to meet the stars.

Did the Hamburg scene peter out just as it had petered in? Maybe there was no confirming full-stop whatsoever – because, in the 1970s, it was still considered a worthwhile exercise for new groups from Britain to win their spurs in Hamburg as it was for middle-aged brethren to fit in a date there for reasons other than for old time's sake. Most outfits that had remained intact since their 1960s heyday now roamed the Earth in a nostalgia netherworld in which current chart status has no meaning, regaling anyone willing to listen with endless anecdotes about what John Lennon said when he first met Frank Allen at the Star-Club in 1962.*

Those who hadn't stayed the course had returned to another kind of anonymity, but whether they remained inside or outside showbusiness, real and imagined horrors about this unmarried mother or that outraged Mr Big still induced certain ex-beat group players to renege on their past and start at shadows. Some had good cause. Plain fact is that a Nashville Teen was to answer the door on two separate occasions to a different German teenager, both claiming an irregular kinship – while, supported by Dick Taylor's comment that "he has a capacity to upset people that's unparalleled", there was hearsay that fellow Pretty Thing Viv Prince had a Mafia-like contract out on him.

Conversely, the biters were bit if there is truth in allegations about a musician of hulking build keeping a low profile as a suburban shopkeeper ever since fleeing back to England in the mid-1960s, following an incident that had the *Polizei* searching him out to "help with enquiries" after two German gangsters were found battered to death.

Everyone has skeletons in the cupboard, but against the slim catalogue of those who offended German "godfathers", committed felonies or brought unwanted babies into the world, there were far more who preferred to sever links with pop for reasons other than troubled consciences. Now something-in-the-City, another ex-Pretty Thing, Brian Pendleton thought it wisest to stonewall a Things trainspotter who accosted him in a London megastore. Howie Newcomb, former guitarist with The Casuals, had nothing to hide but his sometime membership of a group too when he was spotted

* "Ah yes. It's Frank, isn't it? I've talked to other people in the club and it seems that, next to Cliff [Bennett], you're the most popular member of the band. I don't know why. Your harmonies are fucking ridiculous"

managing an electrical goods emporium in Greater Manchester. Likewise, pub landlord Mick Wilson wearied of pulling pints whilst recounting for inquisitive customers how crazed females had stormed the stage at the Circus Krone when he was with Dave Dee's lot. When Dozy, Beaky and Tich plus the new Mick invested their earnings in a Marbella club, Wilson, no longer *mine host*, sank his into a driving school in Salisbury.

The pipe between the teeth, the clipped beard and the brown leather elbows on the tweed jacket epitomised the complete adjustment to respectability by a fellow we shall call Grenville, nicknamed "Griz" when lead guitarist in a outfit that also worked at the Top Ten in 1964. A primary school teacher twelve years later, he doodles on the assembly hall's upright piano during the lunch hour when not marking exercise books in the staff room. His income is supplemented by teaching guitar at home and, on other evenings, running "rhythm and improvisation" workshops at the nearby adult education centre. Both participants and listeners seem to enjoy the sessions in a knowing, nodding sort of way – well, at least no-one dozes off.

By chance, Gretel, a lady Grenville had known in Hamburg, arrives as guest speaker at the centre's final German lesson of the term. Recognising his voice, she puts her head round the door of the music class. She's fuller of face, her hair is clenched in a tight bun, her make-up is unpancaked, but the bold eyes and soft *"Guten abend, Griz"* confirms that it's her all right, and throughout the resonance of the particularly *avant-garde* cluster of notes from Grenville's guitar, he and Gretel are back at the Top Ten. She sees not a balding thirty-year-old with a pregnant wife but a curly-headed teenage boy as beautiful as a girl, letting his then-easy smile rest on the front row – and then specifically on her for a split-second that lasted a thousand years. He feels the arc-lights beating on his head as he tries not to appear too transfixed by her brazen endeavours to grab his attention.

Back in the present, they strike up an awkward conversation over coffee and biscuits in the refectory after their respective tutorials. Yet beyond the crow's feet and like ravages of early middle-age, he can still discern the pocket Venus with the urchin-cut that magnified the raw drama of her panda eyeshadow and high Prussian cheekbones – and nothing a curt Grenville ("Please don't call me 'Griz'. I don't want it to get around") says or does then can diminish him in Gretel's eyes. She senses that he wants to but can't invite her back into his life once more. He wants to but can't rewind to 1964 when everything was possible.

The same thoughts may have crossed Dave Sampson's mind when behind the counter in a record shop. Who could blame him if they recurred even when he commenced a well-paid spell up north in bow-tied cabaret? It was all rather lacklustre after the Top Ten and even the Lorne Arms, but still he took the stage as "Lee Nelson" with pick-up outfits that could be as small as an organ-drums duo.

Around the same time, there was a more substantial attempt at rebirth as an entertainer by Spencer Davis who, smothering thoughts of studying comparative philology in Berlin, reformed his Group – minus the Winwood brothers – to reach back over the years with two LPs and attendant forty-fives before falling apart – as did Johnny Gustafson's 1970s version of The Big Three with Brian Griffiths and Spencer's drummer, Nigel Olsson.

The Pretty Things' comeback, however, wasn't as transient. With a seemingly perpetual turnover of new recruits, Phil May, John Povey and Skip Allen rallied with 1973's *Freeway Madness* (produced by a pseudonymous Wally Allen) and a maiden tour of North America that reminded them at times of Hamburg in the sense that bad boys attracted bad girls. "In one tumbleweed town," elucidated May, "we played in a club connected to this strip joint. The birds would come and watch us in their negligées, and then we'd come and watch them. We shared the top floor of this hotel with them too." During the same jaunt, the late Nancy Spungen, future girlfriend of Sid Vicious, the most unstable Sex Pistol, invited the Things over for an open-minded afternoon by her parents' swimming pool.

Professionally, the ensemble's relentless touring paid off with two albums in the lower reaches of the *Billboard* chart – and they were often a Surprise Hit at this or that outdoor festival in Europe. Distressing details why aren't relevant here, but this small-scale winning streak didn't endure, and the group became "like a body that had been fatally wounded but kept walking, not knowing how critical the wound was," lamented Phil. "It screwed me up, and I went to live in Paris."

Tony Sheridan used the same verb to describe his state after Vietnam: "My mind was completely screwed up. I decided to shake off my past –

which included dropping my British passport and changing my nationality to Irish because I didn't want to be part of what the British were doing in Northern Ireland. I went to London, Hamburg again, Hanover – and Munich where I hooked up with Abi Ofarim who had made a lot of money with 'Cinderella Rockefella'* and so forth, and was looking for people to produce. He and I never got that far – though I liked him and appreciated his talent. He had a lot of success in Germany with singalong things with an artist called Peter Petrel with whom I lived in Hanover with our women and kids for a couple of years."

The leader of Tony's old backing Six, Bobby Patrick had been back in Germany too, working the US air bases as leader of Power. With him were brother Bill, Les Harvey – and Maggie Bell, a hard-faced contralto of gutbucket persuasion, who polarised mess dance areas where unofficial segregation – negroes on one side, caucasians on the other – still persisted. "I just opened my mouth and sang Aretha Franklin's 'Respect'," averred Maggie, "and for the rest of the time, we only played to black guys."

After she and Harvey became an "item", they flew back to Glasgow to form Stone The Crows with Bell as a sort of Hibernian Janis Joplin but without the onstage histrionics. The group had completed a US tour supporting Mad Dogs And Englishmen and had plugged a forty-five titled after this vast retinue (headed in theory by Joe Cocker) on *Top Of The Pops*, when Les Harvey stepped forward to make an introductory announcement one night in Swansea. He touched the microphone and, because the wiring of the PA system had been tampered with by persons unknown – probably youths loafing about and grinning mischievously during the soundcheck – Les absorbed more than enough high voltage to kill him.

Big brother Alex's days were numbered too, but before he suffered his fatal heart attack in Zeebrugen, Belgium on 4 February 1982 – the last date of a European tour – he had languished in Glasgow, trying to reconstitute the Soul Band as a local ballroom's resident combo. Personnel included Maggie Bell – until she was replaced by Isobel Bond, back from a long stay in Hamburg – and the other members of what would become Power after the place was turned into a roller rink.

Alex and Isobel then sought independent fortunes in London; she in two flop singles that preluded her emigration to Canada – and he as

---

* Ofarim and his singing wife Esther had been forever on television variety shows throughout Europe and had recorded *Noch Einen Tanz* and other albums in different languages before scoring a million-seller with 'Cinderella Rockefella' in 1968

guitarist in the West End production of the *Hair* musical. Following some abortive projects of his own, he went home, and the country at large forgot his existence until fame came late for Alex Harvey.

He was reincarnated as bombastic front man of The Sensational Alex Harvey Band, mid-1970s hitmakers – notably with 1975's exhumation of Tom Jones' 'Delilah' (that lent the social club staple an understated but appropriately homicidal mood), and albums peppered with much the same type of eclectic and unlikely covers that had punctuated the Soul Band's hours on the boards at the Top Ten.

Though Alex himself might have disputed it, his new group were seen by many as latecomers in the glam-rock stakes for its use of cheap theatrics and the lead guitarist's wearing of catsuit and clown greasepaint as a foil to Harvey's not entirely assumed role as street-wise hard case in his perpetual jeans and broad-striped rugby shirt.

Perhaps Dave Dee, Dozy, Beaky, Mick II And Tich might have had more latter-day luck had they emphasised the glam elements they'd always had when they resumed their recording career together with 1974's 'She's A Lady' – a ballad that was more Dave Dee than DBMT. Each separate faction had notched up but one minor European hit apiece before coming to realise that audiences couldn't or wouldn't disconnect either with the previous collective incarnation that, for all its casually strewn mistakes, had committed to tape instinctively the smashes that the reconstituted quintet couldn't get to save their lives now.

The Searchers would encounter a similar basic difficulty when signed to the hip US Sire label in 1979 for two albums that were well-received by the critics. One of the spin-off singles, 'Hearts In Their Eyes', almost charted, but at a showcase in London's Nashville Rooms, listeners found the juxtaposition of the remembered classics and the unfamiliar new numbers unsettling. Some dingbat shouted, "Where's Chris Curtis?" during the set, and afterwards another asked Mike Pender how the new boy was settling in – meaning no successor to Curtis but Frank Allen, a Searcher for nigh on a quarter of a century.

The true benefit of this episode was that the group appeared on European television again for the first time in years – as did The Barron Knights who had proved that, if not as cool as The Searchers, they weren't the has-beens once imagined either after they bounced back with a British TV series, and 1977's 'Live In Trouble', their first UK Top Twenty strike for over a decade. These developments began a run of British hits – in the album list too – that saw them into the 1980s and pushed up fees in the citadels of "quality" entertainment where their aural caricatures and wallyish brand of comedy had always been in demand.

No-one had known which way they were supposed to take Paul Raven when he was thrown up near the top of both the UK and North American charts with 'Rock 'N' Roll Part 2', a call-and-response chant with a quasi-military beat. Of much the same soccer stadium stamp were 'Hello Hello I'm Back Again', 'I'm The Leader Of The Gang', the slower 'I Love You Love Me Love' and other massive trans-Europe sellers that would ensconce Glitter-Raven in his trademark silvery suit on the very throne of glam-rock. Nevertheless, this elevation had been far from certain when, with the successor to 'Rock 'N' Roll Part 2' yet to be issued, he was reunited with Bill Haley in the artists enclosure at a 1972 rock 'n' roll revival extravaganza in London – "and the first words Bill said were, 'Well, you Made It after all!'"

Haley was riding another re-emergence of olde tyme rock 'n' roll after it had fermented fit to burst through the efforts of Crazy Cavan And His Rhythm Rockers, Shakin' Stevens And The Sunsets and others who had been boiling it up in the biker clubs of Britain, Germany, France and the Netherlands – a truer "underground" than any Students Union dance – since the late 1960s. Fusing classic rock with glam, Wayne Bickerton and Tony Waddington, formerly the "Lennon-McCartney" of one of Pete Best's post-Beatle combos, created a new group round singer Alan Williams – the chap who'd been in The Medium in Munich – after 'Sugar Baby Love' was rejected by existing acts. *The* hit song in Europe in 1974, this cauldron of insane falsetto, shooby-doo-wahs and spoken bridge passage gave the white-capped Rubettes a flying start as European hit parade contenders and concert attractions, particularly in France where they were touted in the press as *"les nouveaux Beatles"*.

For all his silver threads, Tony Sheridan may have been well-placed to board the glam-rock bandwagon. After all, Paul Raven had got away with a weight problem, and Alex Harvey had taken full-page advertisements in the music press to announce his fortieth birthday. Even Shane Fenton was disinterred and back in the Top Twenty as "Alvin Stardust" after a decade in a song-and-dance act. Yet, as it had been during Beatlemania, Tony bided his time in Hamburg. Nowadays, he was leading a divided existence artistically: "I was trying to leave my past behind by playing completely different music and writing new songs – biographical James Taylor stuff with no band, just me and an acoustic guitar. Of course, a couple of weeks later, I'd be back with a band, raving like mad and doing rock 'n' roll again. Both things were parallel.

"I was still playing clubs. By now, St Pauli was unimportant, and I got into the scene in Hamburg that started in the early 1970s in an after-hours club in Eppendorf called Onkel Pö. The concept there was to present music that was either different or hadn't happened in Germany. It was a showcase for record companies who were looking for something other than bierkeller drinking music and rock 'n' roll the way it had developed in Germany.

"Jazz people from the States were coming there. Al Jarreau's career got off the runway there there when the German press acclaimed him as the best singer in the world. You heard trad in Onkel Pö too – and skiffle because there was a beginning of a revival of it in Germany around that time. It drew intellectuals just like it had in Britain in the 1950s."

The commercial manifestation of the new interest in skiffle was 'In The Summertime', the anthem of 1970's wet summer, by Mungo Jerry. The same raggedly carefree *joie de vivre* was heard too in McGuinness-Flint, Medicine Head and Lindisfarne. Ironically, what they all supplied was as much drinking music as that of an oompah band in that it was best appreciated in the singalong, beery atmosphere of licensed premises where there was laughter, gaiety – and dancing, despite the players being seated, rent-party fashion, and the absence of a drummer; foot-stamping and a pot-pourri of home-made percussion devices maintaining a basic pulse in a repertoire that encompassed jug-band, rockabilly, blues and folk.

At Onkel Pö's, the academics within the audience tempered revelry with deliberation. As you'd expect too from these younger siblings of the Exis of old, their scholarly natures dictated researching beneath skiffle's chewing gum-flavoured veneer to its mostly North American bedrock. Responding to the demand, Radio Hamburg contracted Tony Sheridan to present three hours of the stuff every week, and the Philips record label roped in Alexis Korner to assist in the preparation of a series of album releases of vintage Chicago blues.

Even older than Alex Harvey, Korner had, nevertheless, just become a pop star; his smoky growl to the fore on early 1970s hits by The Collective Consciousness Society – CCS – big band whose 'Whole Lotta Love' became the theme tune to *Top Of The Pops*. When CCS proved too cumbersome and expensive to take on the road, smaller outfits backed Alexis when he attended to a European itinerary that took him most of all to Germany. In December 1971, Hamburg had hosted a "Tribute To Alexis" concert to mark his quarter-century in the music business – with the *Abendblatt* publishing a special poster-cum-supplement annotating his life story.

Korner was to remain a huge attraction in the Fatherland whilst being reduced to voiceovers in ITV commercials back home. Indeed, the popularity of blues in general lingered in Germany long after the late 1960s "boom" had subsided. Fleetwood Mac had been even more of a "new Beatles" there than The Rubettes were to be in France until leader Peter Green left shortly after a visit to an LSD-nourished commune in Munich. "Peter was never the same after that," said drummer Mick Fleetwood – and neither were the group who became wholesomely Americanised and far removed from the rough-and-ready blues quartet they'd been when formed by Green in 1967.

As a barometer of the original Fleetwood Mac's impact, the void had to be filled by many others who, if on the periphery in Britain, enjoyed a renaissance in Germany. Chicken Shack, Savoy Brown, Stone The Crows and Streetwalkers were four that arrested decline through standing-room-only tours over the North Sea. After bowing out with a concert album in late 1977, Streetwalkers survived in spirit via grizzled lead singer Roger Chapman's subsequent stage performances and solo albums that were anchored too in black stylings, albeit sieved through Leicester-bred Chapman's nanny-goat vibrato, a trademark that was still filling German stadiums in the 1990s even though he may have lost his shirt had he attempted the same in Britain.

Twenty years earlier, concert-goers of more "ethnic" taste had had occasion to be grateful to Jim Simpson's Big Bear conglomerate in Birmingham. Through its agency, American Blues Legends revues came so often to Europe that a zealot in, say, Hamburg or Dusseldorf would see more of the genre's Mississippi and Chicago practitioners in person than his counterpart in Detroit or Laramie had ever done – for many a blues grandee had reached the evening of his life without once performing professionally on his native soil. A lot of them had had to take time off work to trudge round Europe, acoustic guitar in hand, as did Lightnin' Slim from his Michigan metal foundry and Chicago barman Big John Wrencher.

If the likes of Wrencher, Slim, Snooky Pryor, Good Rockin' Charles, Dr Ross ("The Harmonica Boss") and Hi-Hat Harris weren't as immortal or venerable as Howlin' Wolf or Muddy Waters, at least they were more disposed towards crossing the Atlantic to be shown respect by a hitherto-unrealised audience of white teenagers. Perhaps the oddest public expression of their overseas surfacing in the 1970s was both a *Birmingham Evening Post* "Pop Special" and the music section of several West German newspapers printing full-colour pin-ups of the wizened troupe of Big Bear's American Blues Legends 1973 package – which included heart-throbs like Homesick James, Washboard Willie and Boogie-Woogie Red. You might laugh, but two years later, sexagenarian Country Joe Pleasants managed a European chart entry with one of his Big Bear singles. Instead of some befuddled dotard moaning to his six-string, Country Joe was a jive-talkin' showman, more Lee Dorsey than Sleepy John Estes, declaiming his blues with, as he put it, "a modern feeling". He had an album to plug after all – not a reissue either, but one freshly minted under Big Bear's auspices in England.

With little time to rehearse, star and pick-up group would frequently entertain with mutually familiar standards of the 'Dust My Broom'-'Sweet Home Chicago' variety. Black skin pigmentation and advanced age weren't necessary qualifications to go down well at Uncle Pö's as demonstrated by well-received entertainments by thirty-year-old Johnny Mars and King Biscuit Boy, a white Canadian. Nevertheless, pseudo-hip purists, tainted by an inverted colour prejudice, would blame musical errors on the band rather than the jet-lagged *kindischer Gries* fronting them. He was the genuine article, wasn't he? What did the white *Dummkopfs* accompanying him know about blues? Yet one such Onkel Pö audience would swerve from sufferance to delighted acclamation when the boys in the band were introduced near the finish. It turned out that they were personnel from Fairport Convention, then at a commercial zenith in Germany.

Big Bear reached a different kind of summit in Europe when it became convenient to open an office in Cologne, so intense was the firm's workload, especially in Germany. Hired to back many of Big Bear's US imports, Pete York, drummer with both the old and new Spencer Davis Group, moved to Munich to commute more easily to where the work was.

To the same end, another old face from the 1960s, Jack Bruce, was living in Germany at the time too. Since the disbandment of Cream, this singing bass guitarist had inclined towards a form of jazz-rock that – particularly in his hand on 1972's *Escalator Over The Hill* album with Carla Bley – had strayed towards the borders of kraut-rock that, from the late 1960s explorations, was now exuding a more universal if icily urban appeal mostly via state-of-the-art musical machinery keeping pace with detached singing in English and outbursts of Art terrorism.

Leading the way, Tangerine Dream, Faust, Neu!, Can, Kraftwerk, Guru Guru and Amon Duul II each amassed an extensive booking schedule on being promoted in a similar manner to Hawkwind and The Third Ear Band. As much hippy communes as groups, their lengthy works included little that could be edited down tartly enough for singles. Nevertheless, kraut-rock albums in general sold steadily if unremarkably in the wake of regular tours of Europe that embraced Britain as much as any other country.

Teeming with interlocking links, segues and *leitmotifs* and all that, "works" – which meant not having to come up with hit forty-fives anyway – were very much the order of the day in the mid 1970s. With *Tubular Bells* setting the standard in 1973, Hawkwind, Yes and any number of kraut-rockers had a go. As many worlds away from 'Hold Tight!' as Jon Anderson was from The Warriors, Dave Dee sang on one by Jean Musy, a bearded Frenchman whose overlooked *Few And Far Between* was perhaps the least overblown of them all, certainly less so than 1976's *Go* by Stomu Yamash'ta, the Japanese percussion virtuoso in whom Chris Blackwell had perceived rock icon potential. Another Blackwell client, Steve Winwood was chief among vocalists required to pick the bones of meaning from its metaphysical libretto.

On returning to England in 1974, ostensibly to continue his radio broadcasts at the BBC, Tony Sheridan became the central figure in a "work" of sorts: "Paul Murphy had produced me with The Big Six in

Hamburg when the German producers had had enough of us. He was one of the few people who still said, 'Sheridan, we've got to do something to get you where you deserve to be.' We did an LP with Pye that was never released. I wrote all the songs, and we performed it live with the Royal Liverpool Philharmonic in the city's Philharmonic Hall as the first concert of the season on 5 September 1975. I'd worked on the arrangements with the orchestra's principal bass player. Half the audience was composed of the Liverpool rock 'n' rollers from Hamburg. The whole concert was recorded by the BBC, and there must be copies of the tape all over the world – but otherwise it was forgotten."

To be precise, it was almost forgotten – because Buk, Murphy's independent label, put out 'Lonely' from the session in 1975, but by then anything from Tony Sheridan was expected to make as much impression on the public as a tract from the Flat Earth Society unless it had him rockin' and rollin' all over the place like he used to with the long-disbanded Beatles – whose EMI singles were to be re-released on the same spring day in 1976. Perusing the consequent UK Top Forty, a *Time* correspondent was moved to enquire rhetorically, "Has a successor to The Beatles finally been found? Not at all – it is The Beatles themselves."

This campaign was bracketed by the respective issues of 1975's regressive and non-original *Rock 'N' Roll* by John Lennon, and 1977's *The Beatles Live At The Star-Club In Hamburg, Germany; 1962*. The contents of both can be summarised visually by Jurgen Vollmer's 1961 photo on the *Rock 'N' Roll* sleeve, depicting a youthful Lennon in a Hamburg doorway with the caption: "You should have been there."

Recorded by Kingsize Taylor on a domestic machine during The Beatles' last residency in Hamburg, the Star-Club offerings were documentary rather than recreational, but there was sufficient of them for a tardy 1979 supplement to the double-album that had been made available, courtesy of Paul Murphy's Lingasong company, after the doctoring of their atrocious sound quality.*

However, *The Beatles Live At The Star-Club* was considered "their finest record" by Billy Childish, a leading light during the first stirrings in the later 1970s of a Medway Towns group scene of agreeably retrogressive bent and as self-contained in its quieter way as

---

* During the same season in 1962, Atila, a US record company, had made a better job of immortalising Johnny And The Hurricanes on tape, but did not bother with any of the British acts on the same bill

Merseybeat. Verily, a twenty-track mono LP by one of Childish's outfits, The Milkshakes, would contain nothing but 'Money', 'Sweet Little Sixteen', 'Some Other Guy', 'The Hippy Hippy Shake' and other items that hadn't been played in the region's jive hives since the days of Bern Elliott And The Fenmen until the advent of pub-rock.

Like punk after it, pub-rock was supposed by definition to preclude stardom, but certain of its groups were to storm Top Forties throughout Europe – notably Dr Feelgood whose *Stupidity* (titled after Kingsize Taylor's near-hit from 1964) topped the British album chart in autumn 1976. *Don't Munchen It*, recorded "live" in Munich by the late Johnny Kidd's reformed Pirates; the turntable fuss made throughout Europe over a reissue of Vince Taylor's 'Brand New Cadillac', and Tony Sheridan being signed to a German label "to do all the old stuff again", (eg a "live" at the Sporthalle in Berlin) were three lesser symptoms of a reaction against pop's ante-punk slow moment with its "works", twee singer-songwriters, "laid-back" tedium, "adult-orientated" rock and smug superstars (and attendant "supersidemen"), forever in America.

The "street level" allure of pub-rock was one umbrella under which pop's neglected teenage audience sheltered. Another was disco, then sashaying towards *Saturday Night Fever* and smaller apogées such as a 'Zabadak!' for the dance floor by The Saragossa Band, a studio entity that took it high up the German Top Ten in 1979. That more and more hitmakers had no physical form beyond the range of television cameras was reflected in clubs that, rather than groups, were now inclined to book disc-jockeys and maybe dance troupes or acts that mimed or sang to tapes – like West Germany's Silver Convention, a white female vocal group assembled to market a series of releases directed at Euro-disco.

They struck hard at home in 1975 with 'Fly Robin Fly' – all jittery rhythm, two-line lyric and string synthesiser overlay – though this would seem small-time after it shot to Number One in the States and won a Grammy as Best Rhythm-and-Blues Instrumental Performance. While the going was good, two further smashes were each supplemented by an album as the girls battled on for another year which was highlighted by a meticulously choreographed 'Telegram' for their country in 1977's Eurovision Song Contest.

More intriguing if not so bankable was tall, blonde jet-setter Amanda Lear with a voice like a Dietrich coming round from the anaesthetic after a tonsillectomy. She'd been launched as a White Disco Queen amid publicity that cast unfounded doubts about her gender.

It was as trendy then for Udo Lindenberg, now the Fatherland's very own David Bowie, to record the standard 'Lover Man (Where Can You Be)' with no lyrical alterations to expose further what he called his "flexible" sexuality and the campness of multi-media presentations featuring wrestlers, trampolinists and similar non-musical support acts. Lindenberg was also forthcoming about New Left political views via his membership of Germany's Green party and its peace movement, and in compositions such as 'Father You Should Have Killed Hitler' and 'They Don't Need Another Führer' that expressed concern about a very real revival of Nazism.

Whilst keeping the wolf from the door with "all the old stuff", Tony Sheridan was less conspicuously committed than Lindenberg as a dweller in "a left-wing commune back on the edge of Hamburg. I was getting into Gestalt, group therapy and green politics. It was during the Baader-Meinhoff period. Student rebellion was in the air again."

One of the side-effects of such unrest was that rock festivals in Germany became flashpoints for riots motivated by the belief that music should be free. That was all very well, but how were its providers to keep themselves alive? No less than any other hippy-derived movement quailing as punk gathered strength, kraut-rock was starting to feel the pinch. Guru Guru were one outfit that narrowed its goals to the domestic circuit before quietly disbanding – and, despite working up some interest in North America, other pre-eminent kraut-rockers were so close to break-even point financially that there was little margin for them to risk following it up by uprooting from Germany.

Yet though kraut-rock had, supposedly, lost impetus, Kraftwerk were suddenly at Number One in Britain in 1982 with 'The Model' – which, like The Equals' 'Baby Come Back', had started life as a B-side. The group that appeared on *Top Of The Pops* were not, however, hirsute and motley like Faust or Can, but looking as dapper and devoid of humanity as shop-window mannequins. Moreover, Kraftwerk's ace face could have been a favourite nephew of Anton Diffring, the late actor who always plays a Luger-packing Nazi officer in old war films. Their music too had taken kraut-rock to its logical conclusion, characterised as it was by push-button synthesizer programming, understated vocal discipline and Euro-disco rhythms of water-torture exactitude.

This was okay by me – though I never acquired any Kraftwerk records until they turned up in car boot sales. However, The Human League bought them new, and David Bowie and Iggy Pop had hung around with Kraftwerk when they were resident in Berlin circa 1978 for the recordings at a complex near the Wall of the albums *Low*, *The Idiot* and *Heroes*. The influence of kraut-rock was felt most on *Low*, dominated as it was by mordant instrumental mood music and sketchy pop songs framing a drawn-curtain menace made all the more wracked by impassive lead vocals floating effortlessly over treated sound layered by musicians from Bowie's touring band plus notable guests like Brian Eno – and, summoned from Hamburg, Roy Young who proved an unexpectedly adaptable pianist.

Before fragmenting, his Roy Young Band had had mixed fortunes. Club residencies in Beirut, the Bahamas and back in Europe had cast them in a mould that had that faintly sickening word "funky" dripping from the pens of scribes extolling them in the early 1970s. This, however, had not been enough to get people to buy The Roy Young Band's two albums in vast quantities, although the horn section – that included Howie Casey – was employed in 1973 on Roger Daltrey of The Who's first solo LP in 1973, thus affirming the respect felt in rock circles for anyone with a Roy Young session on his *curriculum vitae*.

The Fortunes were as buoyed by hard-bought experience, but, unlike Young, their steady consistency was translated as "squareness" by youths in headbands whose desperate diversions included headbanging, streaking and the imbibing of cheap spirits. Leaving aside the hard core of fans disenfranchised by post-Woodstock rock, whether the group's new releases charted or not depended almost entirely upon commercial suitability.

They had got off the ground again after signing to Capitol, EMI's North American outlet. Then had come a climb to Number Fifteen in *Billboard*'s Hot Hundred with 'Here Comes That Rainy Day Feeling Again'. The single sold well in Europe too but it wasn't until autumn 1971 that The Fortunes had regained a hold there, peaking in the British Top Twenty at Number Six with 'Freedom Come Freedom Go'. That this hadn't been a fluke was demonstrated when they did it again in early 1972 with 'Storm In A Teacup'.

Thanks to this second coming, the group were back on television again. The bulge would still be apparent in the later 1970s when, if he ever thought about The Fortunes, a punk intellectual may have translated their singing the praises of a fizzy drink in an ITV advertisement as Warhol-esque nihilism, and aligned their tuxedos and chunky coiffeur with the formal garb and tidy quiff of Bryan Ferry, one of few older pop idols to be rated by the Blank Generation.

What couldn't be tolerated even remotely was the scenario of grubby "joints" being passed among crouched greatcoats in the mud-splattered company of a decreasing minority of tired girlfriends longing for a toilet. Half a mile away in the spotlight's glare on a massive stage open to the sky, matchstick figures with guitars, a stack of keyboards and drum kits with two kick-basses cavort and pull faces, oblivious to megawatt distortion moaning in the wind.

That outmoded "heavy" band up there could have been Ritchie Blackmore's Rainbow. On leaving Deep Purple for ten years in 1975, the guitarist's projected solo album had evolved into a group effort during its recording in a Munich studio. Product that followed revealed the adoption of a more commercial approach as shown by hit singles that gilded huge album sales throughout the 1970s, and the enlistment of musicians of the calibre of Cozy Powell, direct from UK Top Twenty success as a Sandy Nelson of the 1970s.

The inspired amateurism of rising acts as diverse as The Damned and Television may have sounded a death knell on outfits of similar ilk to Blackmore's, but Germany would remain especially amenable to Rainbow until its dissolution when Ritchie reunited with his Deep Purple cronies. A final album, *Difficult To Cure*, contained a Rainbow approximation of Beethoven's *Ninth*. This may, perhaps, be seen as an apotheosis of all the kitsch and unconscious humour inherent in pop's time-honoured habit of rocking up the classics as epitomised in the 1960s by Sounds Incorporated's robust 'Wilhelm Tell (Twist)' and Ritchie's own penchant for like instrumentals before and during his time in Hamburg. Certainly, his succinct if free interpretation of the German composer's symphony on *Difficult To Cure* was how anyone who hadn't heard much of Ritchie since he was an Outlaw may have imagined him sounding after twenty years of advancing fame, technology and budget.

Because Blackmore and other fretboard heroes picked mostly Gibsons or Fenders, the Rickenbacker had declined in popularity by its inventor's death in 1976. Another factor was its ear-catching synonymity with the 1960s. Nonetheless, during the high summer of punk, a vintage model was seen in the hands of Paul Weller of The Jam and musicians in his artistic debt – and after when The Jam surfaced as founding fathers of a consequent and fleeting relaunch of Mod.

When this spottier, punier *nouveau* Mod caught on in Britain, Germany was still coping with punk – with Hamburg's Markthalle a leading venue. Indeed, Hamburg's role in punk's prehistory had been acknowledged vaguely in a review in the now-defunct UK pop paper *Sounds* of *The Beatles Live At The Star-Club*. It had noted the contemporary implications of the back cover photo of 1960s teenagers congregating beneath the club's attributive neon sign, *Treffpunkt Der Jugend* ("youth rendezvous") before concluding waspishly that in 1962 "The Beatles couldn't play either".

Maybe a more shadowy circle was completed in 1979 by The Pop Rivets, among the last Britons to play at the Star-Club before its relocation to the Grossneumarkt. An auction of bits of the now rotting stage filled one interval between sets lasting up to three hours each by The Buttocks – German punk rockers – and The Rivets who embraced the Hamburg set-works that would survive the outfit's metamorphosis into The Milkshakes. In the highest tradition of both punk and the wilder British beat groups, Chatham's finest "liked insulting the audience," said Billy Childish. "We learnt some rudimentary swearing at the audience in German, and added German-sounding bits to our speech – and occasionally Greek (*sic*) too as in 'Bo-us Diddley-us' and 'Chuck-us Berry-us'.

"We added 'Himmel!' and 'Mein Gott!' to everything. We used to do a bit of goose-stepping, occasionally wear Hitler moustaches, and we used to do 'When The Saints Go Marching In' with the climax being 'Eng-land 1945! Eng-land 1966!' [World Cup]. We also did 'Who Do You Think You Are Kidding, Mr Hitler?'. The only people who got annoyed about it were American GIs."

Everything was the same from The Rivets being badgered about the *carnet* before even boarding the ferry to Zebrugge to the *gratis* beer provided by the club.

Everything was different too. "We came out of punk rock, and our only drug was alcohol," stressed Billy Childish. "We didn't get pushed stuff, we weren't interested in stuff, we weren't looking for stuff." The *Polizei*, however, were. They were also more rigorous in dealing with under-age music-lovers than their counterparts in the free-and-easy 1960s. Thirty young punks were rounded up during one Pop Rivets recital, memorable also for the switching-off of the power and the hail of now-illegal weaponry and sachets of cannabis onto the floor from the pockets of "Gas guns? Dope? What? Us?" onlookers afraid of *Polizei* who no longer let the city's vice areas police themselves. So it was that the only violence that impinged upon The Rivets' stay in Hamburg was at an engagement supporting the full-on punk assault of Killing Joke that re-ignited an on-going feud between skinheads and punks.

Back in 1981 as The Milkshakes, Billy and his boys worked new clubs like the Chicago and what now stood on the site of the old Star-Club: the Salambo, an erotic cinema run by a gentleman nicknamed "the Sex Pope". Part of the payment for those booked for the pop nights held every Sunday was free tickets to weekday sex shows, and accommodation shared with mostly native acts like Abwarts, Einsturzende Neubaten, Christiane F, X-Mal Deutschland and a new wave of kraut-rockers who were not as admiringly deferential towards British visitors as their recent predecessors had been. "A couple of them were secretly fans of ours," estimated Childish, "but they had to be careful because they were meant to be German and austere."

Crucially, another perk of the job had vanished too. Pulling birds was no longer the pushover it had been. That only one Rivet-Milkshake actually got off with a girl during the not-insufficient time available when either group was there may have been the truest indication of the passing of the age.

further diversions at these extravaganzas were archive films, flea markets of memorabilia, and sets by mop-topped quartets with big-nosed drummers, moon-faced bass players, dour lead guitarists and fellows holding Rickenbackers high up the chest like Tony Sheridan.

At get-togethers that paid like homage to the 1960s, there are more direct reminders of all that younger devotées have missed. Resident at La Belle Otero in Cannes, stout John Tebb still slips in the smashes he'd had when singer with The Casuals. With no hits of his own to blast open memory banks, Lee Curtis was piling into those of Elvis Presley when working the same St Pauli venue that had contained The Blues Band, Chicken Shack *et al* in 1991.

For the same reason, Johnnie Law – or John Latimer Law as he prefers to be known nowadays – had an open choice of repertoire too. In it, he chose commendably to insert items unfamiliar to a pop audience, notably the self-penned songs and arrangements of banner-waving Scottish anthems like 'Skye Boat Song' and 'Scot's Wha Hae'. These were to be the highlights of *Beat The Drum*, a remarkable 1993 album that adds weight to the theory that pop is a lottery. Perhaps in another dimension, Law is cruising by limousine to the Hollywood Bowl during the US leg of his sell-out global tour while Rod Stewart is commencing his second leather-trousered stint before a small but appreciative audience in some Freiheit club. Cemented in place in Hamburg like a brick in a wall, Rod has been long used to the notion that a dark corner of this particular foreign field will be forever Scotland.

Johnnie had been there so long that it was an odd Dom beer festival that didn't have him as part of the musical entertainment. It was also quite in order for him to portray "rock 'n' roll from the Star-Club" in *Hamburg Special Days*, a cultural delegation to Japan in 1989 – "but I think it rubbed a lot of people on the City Chambers up the wrong way, because I heard a few whispers like, 'What is a Scottish singer doing representing Hamburg?' Sometimes I wish I'd never left home, but what keeps me going is that if I had done, I don't think I would be singing now. Possibly I would, but not in the same way."

The MI5's drummer, George Gibb was still in Hamburg too – as an RCA promotion manager, and it was through him, that his old colleague came to support The Eurythmics at a promotional party in an auditorium named after its postal address, Grosse Freiheit 36. The following night, Law and his backing combo – still called The Tremors – unwound on the small stage of the Beer Shop in combination with Ritchie Blackmore and the rest of the reborn Deep Purple. Afterwards, there were the inevitable *steins* that kicked off the retrospection that had the chap who hadn't been around Hamburg in the old days dragging on his cigarette and giggling politely at the stories told about places he'd never been, people he hadn't known.

For something to say, one of the entourage asked Johnnie what type of music he and The Tremors played. "I started humming and hawing, as we say in Scotland," said Johnnie, "not knowing what to say – and do you know what Ritchie said? He said that we played unpretentious, very good rock 'n' roll. 'Well,' I said, 'That was very nice, Ritchie. That'll do for me.'"

When the building that had once housed the old Star-Club was torn down finally in April 1986, it had been fitting that a shot of John Law And The Tremors on the ruins of the stage had been printed in the next day's *Morgenpost*. A few years before, a fire had set the wheels of demolition paperwork in motion while the staircases fell in and, bit by bit, the walls crumpled. "When we were over there in about 1984," said Tich Amey, "an old boy in his sixties who used to drive some of the bands around, went over to the site. He bent down and picked up a charred photograph, and it was of Dave Dee, Dozy, Beaky, Mick And Tich." If it had been a scene from a horror film, you'd have heard the ranting abandon of 'What'd I Say' as a spooky drift as if from a seaside conch, and seen a spectral Manfred Weissleder wailing and rattling chains to the beat.

Cancer had carried off Manfred in 1980. Gone too was Peter Eckhorn – though the third prong of the triumvirate, Bruno Koschmider, now in his eighties, is still in the club business, his main concern being a place called the Alodria. His Kaiserkeller has regained its original title, and a Top Ten is still standing – as a disco just like the Aquator, the Grunspan and all the rest of the newer dance halls. Other once-prestigious St Pauli clubs are characterised by the padded wallpaper peeling off, here and there; the dust on the heavy drape curtains; the depressed forbearance of the staff – all the tell-tale signs of having known better days when the groups were falling over themselves to work there.

Now they only bothered with festivals and places like the Markthalle or the hangar-like Fabrik which boasted a reading room and record library. It was here in genteel Altona that Dave Dee, Dozy, Beaky, Mick And Tich had been filmed in concert in December 1984. They had started again a few months earlier at the Markthalle, an unusual choice as punk and heavy metal were the sounds heard most often there. Nevertheless, the group seemed as delighted as the capacity audience that both their 'Hold Tight!' bashes and the 'Xanadu' period epics were so rabidly remembered.

Apart from Dee with his executive post in a major record company, the lads had had a lean time of it since 'She's My Lady'. Tich, for example, had been driven to thrum bass for The Troggs on a German tour in the early 1980s, provoking shouted requests for the likes of 'Touch Me Touch Me' and 'Zabadak!'.* This bore out Rainer Haas's argument that the old firm could make easy money – even if, as Tich discovered, "We were getting paid one amount, and Dave was getting paid another." Moreover, it wasn't uncommon for Dozy, Beaky, Mick And Tich to hold the stage for the first twenty minutes or so before their leader made a Grand Entrance, albeit after an overture of facetious comments from the others.

Dave was now a pop singer to be loved more as a favourite uncle than demon lover. Though the group stirred 'Whole Lotta Shakin'', 'Hippy Hippy Shake' and 'Kansas City' into the brew, not even the most susceptible onlooker could pretend that this is what it must have been like down the Top Ten in 1963. Over a generation later, she's among Rockers, Mods and hippies, now in their forties and rotten with money. They are dressed in the "smart casuals" expected on "Sounds Of The Sixties" evenings held not only in the dinner-and-dance clubs on dry land but also on board steamers like the Peter Pan, pottering between Germany and Sweden.

If they have the stomach and wallet for it, they punish pricey liquor and guzzle selections from a menu's six starters, eight main courses and seven desserts. Discreetly, a sunken orchestra sight-reads as showtime creeps closer. In the wings, a buffoon of a compère is polishing up his introduction: "Without further ado, ladies and gentlemen, I'd like to bring on some greeeaaat entertainers I know you're all going to enjoy. Well, my great-grandmother was very fond of them..."

Yet Dave Dee, Dozy, Beaky, Mick And Tich were resilient enough to continue firing pot-shots at the charts with such as an excavation of 'Do Wah Diddy Diddy', complete with aberrant state-of-the-art drum machine, and grafting a blues-boogie rhythm onto 'Here We Go', the soccer match doggerel that lives only in its melody from Offenbach.

---

* A longterm mania had taken hold in Germany with regard to 'Zabadak!'. In the late 1980s alone, a best-selling all-purpose "party" album would be titled *Za-Za-Zabadak!*, and Dave Dee recorded his second 'Zabadak!' with German comedy duo, Klaus And Klaus

'Here We Go' did not feature Dave Dee as he and the others had begun recording and performing separately once again in the late 1980s. Only available in Germany, 'Scirocco', a 1989 single attributed to "Dave Dee And Marmalade", merged aspects of 'Zabadak!' and 'The Lion Sleeps Tonight'. Then followed a long vinyl silence from Dee until a fresh assault on the market in 1996 with a new album produced by Sandy Newman, mainstay of Marmalade – with whom Dee is, to all intents and purposes, "featured singer" these days.

Awaiting release is a Dave Dee version of 'Don't Look Back In Anger' from Oasis who, in common with Pulp, The Bluetones, Supergrass and other "Britpop" rivals, are regarded by tidy-minded (or lazy) journalists as a modern equivalent of whatever 1960s outfit they could be heard echoing, however superficially, on any given record. These assertions are buoyed by the frequency with which, say, a Creation riff, a Phil May mannerism or a Beatles cover arises in Britpop's canon.

Oasis also kept a 1970s group's name before the public via an overhaul of 'Cum On Feel The Noize' – which had crashed straight in at Number One in Britain for Slade in 1973. However, with the passing of glam-rock, Slade's career had assumed an erratic course, and, by 1990, the group had lost half its number – crucially, chief show-off Noddy Holder – and was all but extinct.

"The obvious idea hadn't occurred at that time," said Dave Hill, "until, out of the blue, Len Tuckey, Suzi Quatro's ex-husband and guitarist, rang me and suggested using both the band's name and Don Powell as there was a lot of work going in Germany and elsewhere – about which I knew nothing. Four years on, Slade II has played to more than a million people. That's probably more than we did during our heyday – because I've been to East Germany, Russia, the Ukraine, Czechoslovakia and other places where the old Slade never worked."

That was how Dozy, Beaky, Mick And Tich kept afloat too – for in West Germany, "Rainer had Dave Dee And Marmalade," sighed Tich, "and didn't need us. It was a bit sad, but then a promoter from the east side rang up and offered us a lot of work in new territory."

Tony Sheridan was to venture further than that from the old sphere of work when "a guy from the States knocked on the door one day. He'd been sent over to look for me to promote the 'My Bonnie' session tapes that somebody in California had bought for a lot of money. So I emerged out of my 'healing period' and went over. I didn't want to come back to Germany ever again. It was my first time in America, and I was flabbergasted at waking up one morning in the mountains of California among deserts and Indian reservations.

"Anyway, the people who'd bought the tapes found out they'd been stolen from the archives in Hamburg, and couldn't be marketed. So they thought of doing something with Tony Sheridan and Elvis Presley's old band – Ronnit Tutt, James Burton, Glen D Hardin, very competent (and expensive) musicians.

"This seemed a good idea when I first heard it, but the production team were real dilettantes who, just like the Germans, were not able to see that Tony Sheridan was no longer the rock 'n' roller he was, and was capable of doing a whole lot of other things. They had lots of money, but no feeling or creativity. They wanted me to suggest some items that I'd done with The Beatles. We finished up doing one side of Chuck Berry and Little Richard badly, and one side of country – hence the album's title, *Worlds Apart* – that included one of my own songs, 'Looking Back', an autobiographical ballad.

"Also, the musicians basically played that stagnated sort of rock 'n' roll they'd done with Elvis in Las Vegas. They all wore these diamond-encrusted 'TCB' [Taking Care of Business] badges that he'd given them. Ideally, I should have gone to New Orleans, Texas or somewhere and done it with JJ Cale, Ry Cooder or someone like that. However, I visited Klaus Voorman in his place in Los Angeles. He was disillusioned with the American music business as well, and I suggested that we ought to get hold of a drummer and do something together.* All that came out of that was that he played bass on one track of *Worlds Apart* – which was sold through a video we did expressly for TV, and pushed as a semi-Beatles album with the Elvis Presley band. It wasn't in the shops."

Dispiriting though the Los Angeles sessions had been in their squeaky-clean nonchalance, Tony had been thought, nevertheless, worthy of the trouble and cost, even though it was essentially The Beatles who'd made it all possible. However, back in Johnnie Law and Rod Stewart's parallel universe, misfortune, managerial incompetence, administrative chicanery and "musical differences" had yanked apart this none-too-successful 1960s beat group in the late 1960s. All the same, a

* "My impression was that, at the time, he needed something to take his attention away from his marital situation," added Tony Sheridan. Within a couple of years, Voorman would be living in Hamburg again. The decades in the close company of every grade of pop star stimulated demand for his services in the recording studio. Before he "realised that production wasn't my thing", Klaus had proved very competent. This was demonstrated in 1982 when his 'Da Da Da' by Germany's own Trio climbed charts all over Europe

reconciled Pete Best, George Harrison and Paul McCartney united once more in 1988 for pub engagements round Merseyside. After a while, this became so lucrative that Best jacked in his detested day job as an stock controller at a tractor factory but McCartney clung to his as part-time presenter on Radio Merseyside, and Harrison to his calling as a curate across the river in Birkenhead.

John Lennon, now a slightly batty sculptor, is asked to rejoin but he must decline, he says, because his wife – a Japanese performance artist he'd met at a 1967 "happening" at the Bluecoat gallery – won't let him. He feels wistful about his Beatle past sometimes but had pretended to be embarrassed when the group were among the subjects of a "Where Are They Now?"-type series in a national tabloid. As his marriage deteriorates, he starts boozing heavily with Gretel, Grenville's Top Ten fräulein now teaching German at John's old school, as mother confessor and confidante on the next bar stool.

No longer putting up an intellectual front, Lennon in his cups begins rambling on with misplaced pride about The Beatles' meagre achievements. On one such maudlin evening, he brings along his photo album ("us with Tony Sheridan", "me, Paul and George with Ringo Starr at the Top Ten. Ringo was in Cream later on, you know..." *ad nauseum*). Gretel cannot allow herself to believe that suddenly she finds both the reminiscences and John's pictures mind-stultifyingly boring.

In real life too, long-dormant rock 'n' rollers peered out from the most unexpected people like the Hamburg housewife who came to check out The Milkshakes at the mouldering Star-Club, and introduced herself afterwards as a former Liverbird. Back in England, Colin Milander, now retired after attaining high rank in the police force, was sounded out about blowing the dust off his guitar and joining his old mates from The Jets at the 100 Club Skiffle Party.

Also resident in Southampton, ex-Lonely One Chris Warman left his frozen seafood business to look after itself in 1988 so that he could indulge a supreme caprice. He was going to beat his drums again – just like he had in Frankfurt – on a self-financed revival of 'Out Of Time', Chris Farlowe's 1966 chart-topper. He hired me as musical director and procurer of my sometime employer Dave Berry as vocalist. I had also been involved inescapably in Berry's previous release, 1986's *Hostage To The Beat*. Publicity leverage from this *cause célèbre* of an LP was allied to the marketing skills that Chris Warman had learned since hanging up his rock 'n' roll shoes, but 'Out Of Time', Dave Berry's last single to date, could not be sold to the public in great quantities.

Warman's attempts to interest record labels of more import than Flagstaff, the Hampshire firm that pressed up a thousand copies, had taken him back to Hamburg and the memories it kindled. To Chris, the city had had "a certain buzz – which is still the same today. The vice area, however, is now more seedy and more dangerous." It was indubitably less open-minded about human frailty and temptations of the flesh as it had been before its brothels were put under government licence, turning their employees into what could be described technically as civil servants with all the attendant by-the-book correctitude. "Today, it's a real island of sin," said Tony Sheridan, "void of even the sea-faring element."

Appearing at the Fabrik with Marmalade in 1990, Dave Dee made a crack about the Herbertstrasse when confronted with a lady so carried away by it all that she'd trespassed onto the boards to show the audience her knickers. Down on the Street Of Windows itself, girls had always done things like that to break the ice for potential clients, but in Dick Taylor's estimation, "It wasn't quite the visible meat market that it is today, but the metal gates are still there, and it's still *verboten* for under eighteens and women not sitting in windows. In fact, the thing that really strikes me about the Reeperbahn area – and, as far as we were concerned, that was really the whole of the Hamburg area – is that it is so nearly the same now as it was then."

For one such as Dick who isn't a consumer of St Pauli's fiscal sex or drugs more perilously available than ever, the district might have seemed the same outwardly. Ten minutes' dawdle away from the Grosse Freiheit, the Seamen's Mission still serves steak, chips and peas, and, in another direction, there's a contradiction of familiar mystery when the relocated Star-Club rears up like a Woolworth's in Manhattan.

If gone from the disreputable hotbed of the Reeperbahn, the main Star-Club – with a façade just like the old one – remains a monument for sightseers to tick off a mental list that also includes the Top Ten, the Kaiserkeller and lesser golgothas now that Hamburg, like Liverpool, has fallen back on its cradling of The Beatles.* To go with the plaques and guided tours, there are souvenir shops and the statue of John Lennon, who was shot dead on a New York pavement in December 1980. In parenthesis,

---

* Nevertheless, Hamburg city council ordered a puzzling shutdown on the playing of tracks from The Beatles' *Anthology 3* in its shopping malls or any public places

Bert Kaempfert suffered a fatal coronary when on holiday in Spain a few months earlier. The statue was unveiled by Horst Fascher, still an eminence at the Star-Club, whose affinity with the slain Beatle's birthplace had been strengthened by an espousal to the daughter of Faron of Flamingos fame, and, perhaps, the launching of their son into life with the name "Rory". Horst was conquering the desolation of the baby's cot death, but hell's magnet pulled him down again when, less than a year later, a daughter by his next wife died from a heart condition despite surgery by specialists brought from New York to London by Paul McCartney.

Ringo and George hadn't let Horst down either when they ambled on at the opening of the new Star-Club in 1978 to shake hands with the headlining Tony Sheridan, one whom they and other Hamburg veterans couldn't help but visualise in some fixed attitude with his old Gibson SG, doing what he'd done way back when. For those who'd lost touch with Tony, rumours had abounded about what had happened to him. The most far-fetched was that he'd been killed in Vietnam. A legend had taken shape, but few could cite precise sources of information until the "wilderness years" ended with his return to Hamburg. "I lived in the States for about a year," he explained. "Then I was making records in Scandinavia where I was very pleased with the situation because I was encouraged to do my own stuff. Why hadn't that happened in LA? At times, I felt a little bitter about it. Having said all that, I am very grateful for everything I've experienced in life – and especially for being a musician – and perhaps an innovator too."

After his prodigal's return, it was noticed that Tony was still wild up there at the companionable Star-Club spectaculars like a Rock 'N' Roll Revival Jubilee which brought together St Pauli pioneers from almost every trackway of its pop yesteryears: Kingsize Taylor, Cliff Bennett, Tony Ashton of The Remo Four, Chris Andrews, the "Johnny" in Johnny And The Hurricanes, the "Fats" from Fats And The Cats, and Ric Lee of The Jaybirds (and then Ten Years After), you name 'em. Of them all, it was the ageing Elvis of the Reeperbahn who recreated the most magic. For both those there from the beginning and Grossneumarkt latecomers, Tony Sheridan was everything they hoped he'd be. Rocking as hard as ever he did, he brushed aside the millennia that had passed since 1960 like so many matchsticks.

INDEX

Coutts, Donnie 176
Crazy Horse 216
Cream 90, 98, 128, 190, 214, 230, 246, 263, 280
Creation, The 232, 235
Crouch, Nicky 206
Curtis, Chris 76, 127, 152, 199, 223, 258
Curtis, Lee 102, 192, 194-195, 200, 210, 225-226, 235, 238, 275
Curtis, Lee And The All-Stars 210

Dave Dee, Dozy, Beaky, Mick And Tich 15, 169, 203, 224, 226, 228-230, 240, 243, 249, 253, 271, 273, 276-277
Davies, Trevor 17
Dee, Dave 13-14, 17, 27, 39, 72, 78, 85, 88-89, 102, 104, 106, 112, 133, 137, 160-161, 164, 168-169, 171, 175, 176, 180, 203-204, 224, 226, 228-230, 233, 238, 240-241, 243, 245, 249, 253, 255, 258, 263, 271, 273, 276-278, 281
Dee, Joey 150, 172, 177, 190-191, 252
Dee-Jays, The 14
Deep Purple 223-224, 268, 276
Diddley, Bo 35, 148, 218
Dietrich, Marlene 45, 153
Dominettes, The 87, 173, 201
Domino, Fats 35, 115, 145, 155, 182, 231
Donegan, Lonnie 28-29, 54, 59, 242
Dowlands, The 207
Dozy 13, 15, 89, 110, 112, 160, 167, 169, 176, 203, 224, 226, 228-230, 240, 243, 249, 253, 255, 258, 271, 273, 276-278
Drifters, The 205, 208, 231
Drummond, Ian 17
Duchess, the 128, 247

Eager, Vince 33, 54
Eckhorn, Peter 60, 69, 82, 85-86, 102, 105, 112, 179, 183, 193, 276
Elliott, Bern And The Fenmen 38, 101, 175, 203, 225, 265
Ellis, Plum 210
Ennis, Ray 125, 156, 240
Episode Six 173-174
Epstein, Brian 147, 188, 191, 205, 210, 213-214
Equals, The 50, 242, 244, 266
Escorts, The 214
Everly Brothers, The 28, 30, 34, 84, 101, 182, 202
Exis 140-145, 258, 274

Fabrik 276, 281
Faith, Adam 28, 64, 123-124, 141, 195, 207
Fame, Georgie 14, 42, 232
Farlowe, Chris 101-102, 163, 272, 280
Faron's Flamingos 65, 80, 87, 107
Fascher, Horst 23, 26, 48-49, 61-63, 72, 113-114, 166, 198, 200, 241, 243, 274, 282
Fats And The Cats 49, 63, 282
Faust 251, 263, 266
Fendermen, The 215
Fenn, Carl 102, 200
Fisher, Matthew 223
Five O'Clock Club 212
Fleetwood Mac 261
Flintstones, The 99, 102
Fontana, Wayne 17, 39, 173, 252
Ford, Tennessee Ernie 37, 49
Fortunes, The 153-154, 163, 236, 238, 267-278
Four Kings, The 229
Francis, Paul 222
Freddie And The Dreamers 89, 161, 204, 209
Freight Train 30
Funny Crow 216
Fury, Billy 36-37, 42, 124

Gallagher, Rory 214

Garner, Bob 235
Garrity, Freddie 17
Georgie And The International Monarchs 66, 135
Georgie And The Monarchs 185, 187, 204
Gerry And The Pacemakers 68, 103, 152, 158, 174, 199, 201, 209, 240
Gibb, George 106, 275
Gibbons, Steve 17, 87, 233-235, 248, 272
Glitter, Gary 240
Good, Jack 30-31, 42
Gordon, Dave And The Rebel Guys 229
Governors, The 207
Graduates, The 101, 115
Grant, Eddy 242
Grapefruit 248
Greco, Juliette 140
Green, Peter 261
Griffiths, Brian 107, 256
Gustafson, Johnny 84, 205-206, 214, 252, 256
Gyre and Gimble 30

100 Club 274, 280
Haas, Rainer 273, 277
Hagen, Nina 271
Haley, Bill 28, 31, 46, 71, 192, 217, 244, 259
Hardy, Rick 17, 187, 274
Harris, Jet 153, 195
Harris, Rolf 222
Harrison, George 73, 92, 117, 126, 129, 147, 183, 189, 191, 197, 227, 248, 280
Harry, Bill 202
Harvey, Alex 31, 35, 39, 54, 82, 88, 102-103, 116, 152, 158, 166, 172, 177, 182, 193, 201, 207-208, 258-259, 261
Harvey, Les 257
Harvey, Tony 42
Hawkshaw, Alan 192
Heintje 244
Hellions, The 87, 167, 218, 231, 234, 253
Hendrix, Jimi 54, 214, 228,

235, 245
Henroid, Henry 111, 116, 201
Herman's Hermits 74, 229
Hi-Lites, The 98, 207
High Society 223
Hilderbrandt, Herbert 241
Hill, Dave 101, 174, 278
Hines, Iain 54-57, 58, 63, 98, 102, 111
Holder, Noddy 101, 238, 278
Hollies, The 214
Holly, Buddy 28-30, 34, 177, 215
Honeycombs, The 124, 176, 229
Hopkins, Nicky 105
Howland, Chris 50, 188
Howlin' Wolf 206, 217, 262
Hutchinson, Johnny 116, 214

Ian And The Zodiacs 107, 194, 207, 225, 239-240
Impact 15, 29, 40, 44, 65, 158, 172, 215, 234, 244, 261, 272
In Betweens, The 74, 101, 174, 240
Indra 67-689, 82, 248
Iommi, Tony 154, 246

Jacaranda 67-69
Jackson, Tony 17, 76, 109, 121, 197-198, 222-223, 274
Jagger, Mick 216, 218
Jankowski, Horst 26, 48, 243
Jaybirds, The 102, 175, 188, 203, 214, 253, 282
Jenkins, Barry 101
Jets, The (the Swansea group) 221
Jets, The 16, 39, 45, 54-64, 67-70, 105, 122, 135-136, 186, 188, 219, 221, 280
Jones, Davy 97-98, 183
Jones, Jack 235

Kaempfert, Berthold 48-49, 156, 187-188, 190-192, 212, 238, 244, 282
Kaiserkeller 14, 50-51, 54,

56-58, 60-63, 67-69, 71, 88, 92, 98, 103, 105, 110, 117, 164, 223, 227, 240, 242, 273, 276, 281
Kefford, Ace 65, 82, 85-86, 135, 138, 160, 232, 247
Kemp, Gibson 106-107, 190, 214
Kidd, Johnny And The Pirates 36, 40-41, 128, 144, 158, 180, 208, 265
Kinks, The 14, 217, 225
Kirchherr, Astrid 106, 144-146, 238
Klub Kon-Tiki 173
Korner, Alexis 25, 189, 212, 218, 233, 260
Koschmider, Bruno 50, 54, 57, 67, 71, 110, 117, 276
Kovacs, Ron 189
Kraftwerk 263, 266-267
Krew Kats, The 74, 170, 201, 232, 236

Laine, Denny 17, 66, 74, 202, 232-233, 250
Law, Johnnie 15, 39-40, 72-74, 78, 82, 84, 97-98, 100, 102, 104, 106, 112, 118, 120, 132, 148, 150, 168, 180, 183, 196, 214-215, 220, 227, 240, 244, 247, 275, 279
Law, Johnnie And The MI5 72-74, 78, 104, 180
Leander, Mike 115
Lee, Albert 101, 104, 170, 224
Lee, Alvin 102, 233
Lee, Dave 100
Lee, Kenny And The Mark Four 235
Lennon, John 69-70, 92, 95-96, 104, 115-116, 135, 147, 159, 167, 170, 181, 190-191, 197, 199, 205, 213, 237-238, 248-249, 254, 264, 280-281
Les Cyclones 202
Les Sunlights 202
Lewis, Jerry Lee 30-31, 34, 55, 159, 182-183, 223
Limpinski, Ollie 56-58
Lindenberg, Udo 26, 266,

272
Little, Carlo 41, 224
Little Richard 24, 30, 97, 148, 155, 159, 175, 179-181, 217, 231, 279
Liverbirds, The 87, 107, 194
Loch, Siegfried 196
Lodge, John 74
Lords, The 228, 242
Love Affair 200, 244
Loving Kind, The 214, 235

MacKay, Ron 76, 136
Magics, The 49
Mandrake Root 224
Manley, Colin 74, 97, 108, 132, 147, 159
Mann, Manfred 182, 214, 217, 272
Markthalle 25, 269, 276-277
Marsden, Gerry 16, 70, 94, 115, 142, 156, 159, 181, 200, 272, 274
Marvelettes, The 35, 153, 194
Marvin, Hank 30, 33
Mason, Dave 167, 220
May, Phil 17, 40, 86, 101, 122, 148, 225, 256, 278
McCartney, Paul 35, 82, 92, 104, 117, 146, 149, 159-160, 164, 182, 190, 199, 204, 238, 249, 280, 282
McNally, John 76, 126, 152, 198
Medium, The 222, 259
Merseybeat 103, 154, 172, 199-202, 204, 206-207, 211, 217, 227, 265, 274
Merseybeats, The 206, 210, 214
Milander, Colin 55, 63, 106, 131, 190, 280
Milkshakes, The 265, 269-270, 280
Mingay, Roger 223
Mojos, The 126, 200, 206, 234
Moody Blues, The 74, 202, 232-233
Morrison, Van 67, 156, 163, 185, 187, 217

ALSO AVAILABLE FROM
SANCTUARY MUSIC LIBRARY

MIND OVER MATTER – THE IMAGES OF PINK FLOYD
£30.00/$39.95   by Storm Thorgerson   1-86074-206-8

DEATH DISCS – AN ACCOUNT OF FATALITY IN THE POPULAR SONG
£14.99/$19.95   by Alan Clayson   1-86074-195-9

LIVE & KICKING
£12.99/$19.95   by Mark Cunningham with Andy Wood   1-86074-217-3

BORN UNDER THE SIGN OF JAZZ
£14.99/$22.50   by Randi Hultin   1-86074-194-0

SERGE GAINSBOURG – VIEW FROM THE EXTERIOR
£12.99/$19.95   by Alan Clayson   1-86074-222-X

LONELY TEARDROPS – THE JACKIE WILSON STORY
£14.99/$19.95   by Tony Douglas   1-86074-214-9

LET THEM ALL TALK – ELVIS COSTELLO
£12.99/$19.95   by Brian Hinton   1-86074-197-7

JONI MITCHELL – BOTH SIDES NOW
£12.99/$19.95   by Brian Hinton   1-86074-160-6

GEORGE GERSHWIN – HIS LIFE & MUSIC
£9.99/$14.95   by Ean Wood   1-86074-174-6

THE QUIET ONE – A LIFE OF GEORGE HARRISON
£9.99/$14.95   by Alan Clayson   1-86074-184-3

RINGO STARR – STRAIGHT MAN OR JOKER?
£9.99/$14.95   by Alan Clayson   1-86074-189-4

CELTIC CROSSROADS – THE ART OF VAN MORRISON
£9.99/$14.95   by Brian Hinton   1-86074-169-X

SEVENTEEN WATTS? THE FIRST 20 YEARS OF BRITISH ROCK GUITAR, THE MUSICIANS AND THEIR STORIES
£19.99/$34.95   by Mo Foster   1-86074-182-7

PETER GREEN – FOUNDER OF FLEETWOOD MAC
£9.99/$14.95   by Martin Celmins   1-898141-13-4

THE KINKS – WELL RESPECTED MEN
£9.99/$14.95   by Neville Marten & Jeffrey Hudson   1-86074-135-5

HAPPY BOYS HAPPY – THE SMALL FACES, FACES & HUMBLE PIE
£9.99/$14.95   by Uli Twelker & Roland Schmitt   1-86074-197-5

For more information on titles from Sanctuary Publishing Limited, please contact Sanctuary Publishing Limited, 82 Bishops Bridge Road, London W2 6BB Tel: +44 (0) 171 243 0640 Fax: +44 (0) 171 243 0470. To order a title direct, please contact our distributors: (UK only) Macmillan Distribution Limited Tel: 01256 302659. (US & Canada) Music Sales Corporation Tel: 1 800 431 7187. (Australia & New Zealand) Bookwise International Tel: 08268 8222.